"Todd Billings has done it again. In the clear and heartfelt prose we have come to expect, he presents a constructive theological project in the 'catholic-Reformed tradition.' Here he calls the church to renewal through deep engagement with the Lord's Supper as the 'true icon' of the good news of Jesus Christ, the form of the gospel that we can taste and see. Take this book and savor it. It will do you good."

— MARTHA MOORE-KEISH
*Columbia Theological Seminary*

"In this richly devotional volume, Todd Billings commends the Lord's Supper as a source of nourishment for God's people, an essential practice not just for the church's remembrance of Christ but also for its sanctification. Billings's work displays the wide learning, sound judgment, and social conscience that readers have come to expect from his writings. This book represents 'Reformed catholicity' at its very best."

— GREGORY W. LEE
*Wheaton College*

"Regular Eucharist reminds us what we are prone to forget: Matter matters. Billings clearly (and ecumenically) understands this enchanted world where God is showing up everywhere, particularly in the Eucharist. Readers of this significant work will walk away with an invitation to experience greater (re)formation through the sacramental imagination—an imagination demanding that we literally *taste and see* that God is, in fact, good."

— AJ SHERRILL
*Mars Hill Bible Church, Grandville, Michigan*

"This book will help you remember more gratefully, commune more alertly, and hope more resolutely when you come to the table to receive freely that great gospel promise—the gifts of God for the people of God."

— MICHAEL ALLEN
*Reformed Theological Seminary, Orlando*

"Todd Billings is one of our leading interpreters of John Calvin. He has given us here a superb study of eucharistic theology in the Reformed tradition. A call to think deeply about what it means to encounter Jesus Christ in Word and sacrament."

— TIMOTHY GEORGE
*Beeson D*

# Remembrance, Communion, and Hope

*Rediscovering the Gospel at the Lord's Table*

J. Todd Billings

WILLIAM B. EERDMANS PUBLISHING COMPANY
GRAND RAPIDS, MICHIGAN

Wm. B. Eerdmans Publishing Co.
2140 Oak Industrial Drive N.E., Grand Rapids, Michigan 49505
www.eerdmans.com

27  26  25  24  23  22  21  20  19  18          1  2  3  4  5  6  7  8  9  10

ISBN  978-0-8028-6233-4

**Library of Congress Cataloging-in-Publication Data**

Names: Billings, J. Todd, author.
Title: Remembrance, communion, and hope : rediscovering the Gospel at the
    Lord's Table / J. Todd Billings.
Description: Grand Rapids : Eerdmans Publishing Co., 2018. |
    Includes bibliographical references and index.
Identifiers: LCCN 2017039680 | ISBN 9780802862334 (pbk. : alk. paper)
Subjects: LCSH: Lord's Supper. | Mystical union.
Classification: LCC BV825.3.B55 2018 | DDC 264/.36—dc23
    LC record available at https://lccn.loc.gov/2017039680

*To Tim,*
*Colleague, Mentor, and Brother in Christ*

# Contents

CONTENTS

# Foreword

In June 2017 I traveled to Italy for two weeks with my wife, Patricia, and three close friends. Our itinerary included three days and two nights in Siena. Wandering the narrow streets of Siena late one afternoon, I happened upon a small art studio that displayed several icons in the front window. It was immediately apparent that this was no tourist shop selling cheap souvenirs. Intrigued, I stepped inside. The artist was working in solitary silence on a large altarpiece featuring Mary, the Mother of God. As the Orthodox say, she was "writing" the icon. When I entered, she lay down her brush, smiled, and welcomed me into her studio. We spent half an hour trying to converse about icons, she in Italian, I in English. We succeeded modestly in making ourselves clear, though our gestures were clearer than our words. The icon was beautiful—not as a Michelangelo painting is beautiful but only as an icon can be. It was mystically beautiful—otherworldly, mysterious, and mesmerizing. I found myself staring at the icon; before long I realized that the icon was staring at me, too, as if saying, "Your world is too small!"

Icons occupy a liminal space between two worlds. One is the fallen world where we live and where the subject of the icon played a specific and important role in her earthly life. The other is the heavenly world where God reigns as Lord and where the subject of the icon now lives, having died and undergone glorious transformation. The subject thus stands at a threshold. She stares into our world, the world of fallen creation, but lives in another world, the world of renewed creation. It is not surprising that iconographers cite the story of the Transfiguration as a pivotal narrative for their own artistic labor. It describes the quintessential liminal place.

Protestants do not "write" icons, nor do we exhibit the icons of saints in our churches. Iconography is part of a strange world to most Protestants, however intriguing and even appealing. But we are not as bereft and ignorant as we might at first think. We have the larger concept of the sacrament of the Lord's Supper, the bread and wine of which serve as window, symbol, and instrument of God's gracious work in the lives of believers. They are sign and seal of the gospel, of justification, sanctification, and union with God through Christ.

Todd Billings has chosen to use the unfamiliar word—*icon*—as a dominant motif in his insightful and accessible book on the Lord's Supper. He aims to reclaim the Lord's Supper as an icon of the gospel and as the means by which believers can be renewed in faith. He argues that this sacrament is essential for such renewal, a renewal that we in the West so desperately need.

I have met Todd Billings only once, though we have talked several times on the phone. The occasion of that one encounter was unforgettable. If anything, it too was a kind of liminal experience. I was visiting Grand Rapids at the time to speak at Calvin College. A mutual friend, Tim Brown, president of Western Theological Seminary in Holland, Michigan, invited Todd and me to meet with some thirty guests (pastors, professors, students) over dinner to carry on a conversation about suffering. Both Todd and I have written books about suffering that emerged out of personal experiences of loss. Our mutual friend thought an open conversation would be useful for all involved—including, of course, the two of us. That evening was a rare gift to me. During dinner I sat across from Todd, which allowed us to get acquainted. Then we stood before the guests and began to reflect both personally and theologically about suffering. It was indescribably rich. The room felt light, as if we were afloat in grace, but heavy, too, because we were bearing the weight of questions we could not answer, of people whose burdens we could not bear, of terrors we could not avoid or escape.

On this rare evening I learned that Todd is more than an astute theologian, though he is certainly that. He is a deeply Christian man whose faith has been forged in the fires of affliction and deepened in library, classroom, church, friendship, prayer, and reflection. He is committed to the task of doing theology for the sake of the church and her growth in the gospel. He believes, as this book makes clear, that the Lord's Supper can be an agent and catalyst for renewal, provided we rediscover and retrieve its biblical and historical significance. The purpose of this book is to serve as a guide and resource in that process.

The Lord's Supper has suffered significant erosion in the American church, as Billings points out. Our "functional theology" of the sacrament, as he puts it, falls far short of the official theology that we espouse. It is thin, superficial, and myopic, sometimes overly rationalistic, sometimes overly emotive, sometimes overly individualistic, but rarely whole and healthy. It has been stripped of the depths that can be found in the Bible (e.g., John 6); in many theological traditions, including the Reformed (Billings' own); and in the use of various historical practices (e.g., Holy Fairs). Moreover, popular "cultural liturgies," a term first coined by Jamie Smith, compete with and often eclipse Christian liturgy and sacrament, including, of course, the Lord's Supper. It is clear that we have much work to do.

I can bear witness to this in my own experience. I have visited churches in which the pastor invited people to the table without as much as mentioning the words of institution, and congregants served themselves the sacrament as if the communion elements were appetizers. I have observed people glancing impatiently at their watches when it became apparent to them that the Lord's Supper was going to lengthen the time of worship beyond the magical one-hour mark, as if observing the sacrament was like adding a fifth movement to a symphony that should have ended with four. I have listened to doctrinal interpretations of the Lord's Supper that gave the impression that the meaning of the sacrament is in the thinking, not the receiving, as if knowing the properties of a medicine can serve as a substitute for actually taking it. Clearly, the Lord's Supper has suffered diminution, though there are signs here and there of attempts to reclaim the sacrament as central to the life of the church.

Todd Billings has written a book to help us rediscover the theological depth and spiritual significance of this sacred meal. He strikes a balance that is rare in theological writing, at least in my experience. His book is informed but not dense. It is consciously Reformed but not exclusive and argumentative. It is generous but not obsequious and spineless. It is theological but not inattentive to pastoral and practical concerns. It is anchored in the great tradition of historic orthodoxy but not oblivious to and dismissive of modern cultural trends.

Billings is calling us back to old truths and practices, to the richness of the Lord's Supper as the church understood and experienced it before church divisions confined us to camps and modern movements—think Enlightenment and popular revivalism here—drained it of mystery and complexity. The old arguments—the *family* arguments—that surfaced during the age of Christendom, when Christianity was the only game in town, must make room for and take on new and bigger problems, such as raw secularity, that are now too obvious to ignore. The age of Christendom is ending. Our work as theologians must adapt accordingly.

Christians might still disagree about how to interpret and administer the Lord's Supper, even beginning with what to call it! But we must never forget the desperate cry of an unbelieving world, of people in crisis who lack spiritual resources, of a culture that assumes it has outgrown its need for Christianity without realizing how much it has benefited from Christianity. We need theologians who are writing good theology with these new circumstances in mind, and good theology always speaks not only *from* the Bible and history but also *to* the world. We need writers who can speak cogently and clearly to people who find Christianity increasingly alien and yet who need it now more than ever before. Billings is emerging as one such voice.

This book is not for everyone. No book is, however popular and appealing. But this book is for many. When reading it, I imagined the kind of people who would find it valuable and useful. Trained theologians should (and will) read it because it is a rich resource, having both breadth and depth. Billings lives in the world of theology; he moves in that world like a skilled tennis player effortlessly covers the entire court. Pastors should read it because it bridges the gap between formal theology and the life of the church. Billings explains the Lord's Supper as a life-giving practice, not simply as an abstract idea. And ordinary church people should read it because they—in truth, *we*—want and need renewal. Our faith feels thin and flat. In the face of secularity it feels increasingly obsolete. But it is not the faith itself that is obsolete. It is our tired and anemic understanding and experience of it. Christians once dominated the field of play, but such is no longer the case. Many Christians are sensing that there is more to faith, and that they need more from it, too. Strangely, the sacrament of the Lord's Supper is often left out of the conversation. Billings makes a good case to reintroduce and reclaim it.

Why do I think this book worth reading? Three reasons come to mind.

First, it conveys a human quality. Billings writes as a person to persons—life to life, not just brain to brain. He recognizes the role that human longings play in the spiritual life. He celebrates the power of the senses: "O taste and see that the Lord is good!"; "Unless you eat my flesh and drink my blood. . . ." He uses historical examples—Holy Fairs, for instance—to show that even Reformed Christians were not always as cerebral as they seem to be now but once reveled in their senses and displayed emotion at the Lord's table. He uses congregational case studies to underscore the importance of lived experience in the Lord's Supper. In short, Billings writes as a real human being, even though this book is highly theological.

Second, this book is biblically and historically informed. Billings is comfortable citing and expositing Scripture. He explores 1 Corinthians 5 and 6 as background to 1 Corinthians 10 and 11. He takes on the highly complex discourse of John 6. Then again, he can turn on a dime to investigate the various Reformed views of the Lord's Supper and how these differ not only with each other but also with other traditions, such as Roman Catholic. He believes in robust engagement, not bland ecumenism. Affirming Reformed "distinctives," he addresses other traditions from that formidable tradition, but does so respectfully and humbly. If anything, his interaction with other Christian traditions serves to enlighten and deepen our understanding of the Reformed heritage itself, much like travel to other countries enables one to rediscover the uniqueness and goodness of one's own country.

In the end, this book is a celebration of the gospel itself, the whole gospel that has the power to make us whole people. This book is profoundly, winsomely, enthusiastically Christ-centered. It is Jesus Christ who is at the center of the Lord's Supper; he is sacrifice and priest, victim and victor, suffering servant and Lord of all.

Finally, Billings locates both understanding and experience of the Lord's Supper in a larger landscape of meaning, especially the Trinity, which enlarges our view of the sacrament itself. According to Billings, the church has become functionally non-Trinitarian. A recent study showed that only a handful of worship songs published in the last twenty-five years make any reference to the Trinity. They honor the Father, adore the Son, and glory in the Spirit, as if they were separate gods; but they do not exalt God *as* triune, as Father, Son, and Holy Spirit. Billings grounds the Lord's Supper in a Trinitarian understanding—and experience—of God.

He also situates the Lord's Supper in the larger biblical narrative. It is a feast of remembrance, communion, and hope. Thus we *remember* not simply Christ's sacrifice on the cross but the entire biblical story, which we both recall and inhabit in the sacrament. We *commune* with the triune God and with his people, not only here but also everywhere, not only now but also throughout history. We *live in hope*, the hope of a renewed creation, which Christ's ascension to the Father, his exaltation as Lord, and his sending of the Holy Spirit anticipate and promise.

The biblical story announces that God has acted in Christ and through the power of the Holy Spirit to rescue and repair broken humanity and broken creation. The Lord's Supper is an icon of the gospel. Billings invites us to take our place at the table, feast with God's people, and embrace God's gift of grace, and so receive nourishment until we finally take a seat at the banqueting table of the Kingdom and there celebrate what God has done to make all things right and whole and well.

I will never approach the table again as I once did, as hurried and distracted and superficial. This lovely and challenging book is the reason why. Read it. Taste and see that the Lord is good.

GERALD L. SITTSER

# Acknowledgments

After revising my dissertation on Calvin's theology of union with Christ into a book,[1] I developed the conviction that I should write a constructive account of how the Lord's Supper can move congregations into a deeper, more multi-faceted understanding of the gospel. There was just one problem. I needed to learn a lot before I could write the book. I had to learn from many pastors and scholars, congregations and individual laypeople, students and mentors. Ten years ago I set upon this project, and I am grateful to many as it has reached its completion.

First, I am grateful to the Association of Theological Schools for award-ing me a Lilly Theological Scholars Grant (2007–2008) to take the first major steps in this project. I was able to dig much more deeply into sacramental theology and start to find my footing in the territory with a few articles and a book chapter in *Union with Christ: Reframing Theology and Ministry for the Church* (Baker Academic, 2011).

John Witvliet provided invaluable support and advice, joining with James K. A. Smith to gather a group of scholars in West Michigan to give in-put on the project. Over the last decade, John has patiently addressed nu-merous questions about sources and scholarship in sacramental theology, and Jamie has continued to support the project both through encouragement and through the inspiration of his scholarship. In addition, the Meeter Center, the Hope College–Western Seminary Theology Seminar, and the International Reformed Theological Institute have provided forums for valuable feedback on the project.

---

1. *Calvin, Participation, and the Gift: The Activity of Believers in Union with Christ* (Oxford: Oxford University Press, 2008).

In 2012, I had a vision of where the book needed to go, and I was energized. In August, I was editing a chapter draft as I waited on my doctor in a patient room. To my surprise, the doctor delivered news that shattered my productive streak on the book: incurable cancer. In the midst of cancer treatment, I moved my reflections toward providence and lament, leading to *Rejoicing in Lament* (Brazos, 2015).

In due time, friends, colleagues, and students who had read portions of this book on the Lord's Supper convinced me to return to it, even though side effects from chemotherapy left my energy in short supply. I'm grateful for their persistence, especially Andy McCoy at Hope College, for making the case to me that I needed to push through the fatigue and physical pain to finish this book as an offering to the church. I needed his exhortation.

I'm grateful for input on various parts of this project from a fine collection of scholars and pastors, including Michael Allen, Jared Ayers, Eric and Miriam Barnes, Andy Bossardet, Jon Brown, Jim Brownson, Ann Conklin, Chris DeVos, Jonathan Gabhart, Kent Fry, Megan Hodgin, Kristen Johnson, Brian Keepers, Dustyn Keepers, David Komline, Suzanne McDonald, Ronald Rienstra, Steven Rodriguez, Sue Rozeboom, Jennifer Ryden, Brandon and Stephanie Smith, Tanner Smith, Marijke Strong, and Josh Van Leeuwen. I received invaluable insight from Han-luen Kantzer-Komline on my use of Augustine in the project. Christopher Dorn and Alistair Roberts gave helpful input to various chapters from their scholarship in liturgical studies.

I am also immensely grateful for the students whose wisdom and meticulous work helped to bring this project to fruition. Over the course of the last decade, many have contributed their insights on the Lord's Supper in class, or given feedback on a particular chapter draft. I cannot name them all. But a special thanks to Katlyn DeVries, Audrey Edewaard, Ross Hoekstra, Emily Holehan, Katy Johnson, Alberto La Rosa, Nathan Longfield, Mark Mares, Andrew Mead, Anna Radcliffe, and Stephen Shaffer.

Numerous congregations provided insight for concrete examples throughout the book. But I'm particularly thankful to First United Presbyterian Church in Cambridge, Massachusetts, and First Reformed Church in Holland, Michigan, for providing some of the material in the congregational snapshots in chapters 5 and 7. Thanks as well to Rev. Barrett Lee and the congregation of North Presbyterian in Kalamazoo, Michigan, for welcoming my family and me to worship, which then provided material for the congregational snapshot in chapter 6.

Eerdmans Publishing displayed confidence in this project from its outset, and I'm grateful for their patience as the project underwent various delays, and then multiple stages of development. Thanks to Alexander Bukovietski, Jon Pott, and Michael Thomson for their encouragement each step of the way.

This book is dedicated to my colleague and mentor, Timothy L. Brown, who is currently president of Western Theological Seminary in Holland, Michigan. When Tim moved from the pastorate to teaching at the seminary, he suggested that the seminary adopt a weekly celebration of communion in chapel. The seminary did so, and the practice has helped to cultivate a Christ-focused, Scripture-soaked renewal among students, faculty, and staff. For Tim, the gospel and the Supper belong together. That is not his abstract theory, but his embodied practice. Tim memorizes and dwells in Scripture; he eats the words, proclaims the Word, and offers the Word for nourishment in the bread and the cup. Because Tim has entered into a drama that is much bigger than his own vision or personality—the triune drama of God's action—his ministry has edified many. I am blessed to count myself among them.

# Abbreviations

| | |
|---|---|
| *BC* | *Book of Confessions: Study Edition.* Louisville: Geneva Press, 1996 |
| *CO* | *Calvini opera quae supersunt omnia.* Corpus Reformatorum. Edited by W. Baum et al. 59 vols. Braunschweig, 1863 |
| *CC* | *Calvin's Commentaries.* Edited by D. W. Torrance and T. F. Torrance. 12 vols. Grand Rapids: Eerdmans, 1960–1972 |
| CTS | *Calvin's Commentaries.* Translated by Calvin Translation Society. Edited by John King. 22 vols. 1845–1856. Reprint, Grand Rapids: Baker, 1981 |
| *Institutes* | John Calvin. *Institutes of the Christian Religion.* 1559. Edited by J. T. McNeill. Translated by F. L. Battles. 2 vols. Philadelphia: Westminster, 1960 |
| *Our Faith* | *Our Faith: Ecumenical Creeds, Reformed Confessions, and Other Resources.* Faith Alive Christian Resources, Christian Reformed Church in North America, and Reformed Church in America. Grand Rapids: Faith Alive Christian Resources, 2013 |
| *WJE* | *Works of Jonathan Edwards.* Vols. 1–26. New Haven: Yale University Press, 1957–2008 |

# A Wager

This book presents readers with a wager: that a renewed theology and practice of the Lord's Supper can be an instrument for congregations to develop
a deeper, more multifaceted sense of the gospel itself. The fundamental reason for this is not anthropological but theological: the Supper is God's own
instrument for conforming believers to the image of Christ. The Supper is a
God-given icon—displaying the Word in signs and actions in the assembled
community—an icon that draws us into a divine drama by the power of the
Spirit.[1] In this icon, we do not simply reflect from a distance but we enter in,
living into our new identities as adopted children of the Father and tasting
fellowship with Christ and others in the covenant community.

In pursuing this goal, this book is necessarily a synthetic and constructive
work. It engages sacramental theology and soteriology, church ministry and
history, and biblical exegesis and doctrinal clarification. While it is an inter-
disciplinary endeavor, I enter into it with my own expertise in systematic and
historical theology, and a genuine love for the church and for congregational
ministry. In terms of my theological identity, I seek to be both "Reformed"
and "catholic" in a way that reflects other works and projects.[2] For this work,

---

1. I am grateful for and indebted to Kevin Vanhoozer's work on the Trinitarian "drama"
of divine and human action, even as I develop the metaphor in my own directions in this work.
See Kevin J. Vanhoozer, *The Drama of Doctrine: A Canonical-Linguistic Approach to Christian
Doctrine* (Louisville: Westminster John Knox, 2005).

2. Numerous works seeking to inhabit the Reformed tradition in a catholic way have
emerged in the last few decades, including works by Michael Allen, George Hunsinger,
James K. A. Smith, Scott Swain, Kevin Vanhoozer, and many others. For an account of my particular vision for recovering a Reformed identity in a catholic way, see J. Todd Billings, "Afterword:
Rediscovering the Catholic-Reformed Tradition for Today; A Biblical, Christ-Centered Vision

my Reformed and catholic identity brings certain opportunities and limitations. In terms of opportunities, a broadly Reformed sacramental tradition on
the Supper can find a home in a broad range of ecclesial communities—from
Anglican to Baptist, from Presbyterian to nondenominational charismatic. I
hope that readers from this wide spectrum of ecclesial locations, and beyond,
will take up my "wager."

And yet, working within the Reformed tradition has certain limitations
as well. The Reformed tradition, unlike Eastern Orthodox, Roman Catholic,
and Lutheran traditions, has generally not required fixed liturgical forms. For
most who self-identify with the Reformed tradition, fixed liturgical forms have
been an option rather than a requirement. As a result, the liturgies for the
Lord's Supper have not been "a privileged norm for doctrine."[3] Some liturgical
scholars see this as a deficit.[4] And it is not easily remedied. While there is a
beauty to the work of Orthodox authors like Alexander Schmemann that reflects upon the life "that stems from the liturgical experience of the Orthodox
Church," that would not be possible for a broad Reformed tradition.[5] There is
simply not a set of liturgical texts that the Reformed tradition could consult as
a shared authority that extends as broadly as its confessional reach.

Thus, while I am very grateful for the burgeoning work in Reformed
liturgical studies in the last few decades, I have chosen to engage their insights
from within a fairly "traditional" Reformed theological method: drawing upon
Scripture as the primary and final authority, with confessions and the larger
theological tradition as secondary authorities. I cite liturgical forms from time
to time, but I do not assume that readers worship in congregations that use
these forms or a written liturgy. However, this does not mean that this book is
inattentive to the concrete experience of worship. If we desire congregational
transformation, it is not enough to simply give biblical exegesis and doctrinal
commentary on the traditional topics of sacramental theology. The congregation needs to enter into the triune drama of God's action through the Spirit's
power. We need to take an honest look at the functional theologies within
our congregations, even as they contrast with the official "stated" theologies.
We need our imaginations kindled, our affections engaged, and our symbolic

---

for Church Renewal," in *Reformed Catholicity: The Promise of Retrieval for Theology and Biblical
Interpretation*, by Michael Allen and Scott R. Swain (Grand Rapids: Baker Academic, 2015).

3. See Christopher Dorn, *The Lord's Supper in the Reformed Church in America: Tradition
in Transformation* (New York: Peter Lang, 2007), 94.

4. For an overview of these criticisms, see Dorn, *The Lord's Supper*, 100–121.

5. Alexander Schmemann, *For the Life of the World: Sacraments and Orthodoxy*, 2nd rev.
and enlarged ed. (Crestwood, NY: St. Vladimir's Seminary Press, 1973), 7.

worlds disrupted by the triune God's work. With a concrete, congregational context in mind, I explore these issues in chapters 1–2, and this cluster of concerns runs through the whole book, especially in the congregational snapshots of chapters 5–7.

In addition to theological reasons for prioritizing Scripture and confessional traditions (rather than fixed liturgies), I draw upon these sources because of the particular ecclesial audience of this book. I want to invite Baptists, Pentecostals, and nondenominational Christians to rediscover the Lord's Supper as an instrument for growing more deeply into the gospel, not just Anglicans and disciplined Presbyterians who make careful use of their written liturgies. While there is value to the "Canterbury trail" and the move of evangelicals to more "high church" traditions with fixed liturgical forms, that is not the only way to embrace the ecumenical unity of the church or a renewed theology and practice of the Lord's Supper.[6] The Reformed theological tradition can be fertile soil for a wide variety of worship traditions to flourish. Indeed, when prominent Baptist Charles Spurgeon (1834–1892) sought to deepen his tradition's theology of the Lord's Supper, he did not go to Rome or Canterbury, but to theology reminiscent of Calvin. "We firmly believe in the real presence of Christ which is spiritual, and yet certain."[7] Spurgeon never came to agree with Calvin on baptism; he did not become a Presbyterian. But following Calvin's overall approach to the Lord's Supper became the way for this prominent Baptist preacher to inhabit deeper catholic waters.

In the end, I hope this work can join the larger chorus of work from liturgical theologians, biblical scholars, pastors, and others who seek to renew the theology and practice of the Lord's Supper in the church today. Specifically, I hope in this book to both listen to and join in singing the melody that holds together the Supper with the drama of God's gospel in Jesus: union with Christ. This is the song of adoption by the Father through the Spirit—of incorporation into the Son as sons and daughters. The song travels the road of dying and rising with Christ, a feast that renews our hunger for the one who is life—a remembering and hoping in fellowship with Christ and his people. It is my hope that the Spirit may use this song, even my imperfect rendition of it, to enliven God's people to "taste and see that the LORD is good" (Ps. 34:8).[8]

6. See Robert E. Webber and Lester Ruth, *Evangelicals on the Canterbury Trail: Why Evangelicals Are Attracted to the Liturgical Church*, rev. ed. (New York: Morehouse, 2013).

7. Ch. H. Spurgeon, "Mysterious Visits," in *Till He Come* (London: Passmore and Alabaster, 1894), 17.

8. Unless otherwise indicated, all quotations from the Bible in this book come from the New International Version (2011).

# PART 1

❧

# Functional Theologies and Desiring the Word

The wager presented in the introduction makes an assumption that can be contested: that a renewed theology and practice of the Supper would actually make a difference in the individual and corporate life of the worshiping congregation. Does this suggest that we simply need to adopt the right theological ideas and then put them into practice? In light of this wager, some readers might expect me to begin with doctrinal topics such as how Christ is present at the Supper, and the character of eucharistic fellowship.[1] Once a right understanding of these issues is in place, congregations can "implement" them, putting right theology into practice, and thus seeing transformation in their life together and witness to the world.

We will come to these traditional doctrinal topics in due time. But first, we need to examine the *functional theologies* of the communities that gather in worship. If we do not, then I fear we are likely to embrace idolatries that resist the radical work that the Spirit does through Word and sacrament. If we give our lives over to cultural practices that serve gods other than King Jesus, then we refuse to till the soil for the gospel Word to bear fruit. In the

---

1. This book will refer to the celebration of the Lord's Supper with various terms. My preferred term is the biblical phrase the "Lord's Supper" (1 Cor. 11:20), because of the way it prioritizes the sovereign presence and gift of the Lord at the Supper. The terms "Eucharist" and "eucharistic" can be valuable as well, highlighting the significance of "thanksgiving" at the Supper. As Brian Gerrish points out in describing Calvin's view, "the meal is a gift from God, but—like every gift—it is also an invitation to give thanks" (B. A. Gerrish, *Grace and Gratitude: The Eucharistic Theology of John Calvin* [Minneapolis: Fortress, 1993], 19). Other valuable terms include "the Lord's table" (1 Cor. 10:21); and "Holy Communion," or just "communion," referring to the fellowship with Christ and one another at the meal (1 Cor. 10:16–17).

two chapters of part 1, I unpack the significance of functional theologies for congregational ministry in the late modern West. Then I present a constructive theological vision for how humans as affective creatures are drawn into a Trinitarian drama, finding delight in Christ and their embodied, communal identity in him. This vision underlies the theological and pastoral vision in the rest of the book.

CHAPTER 1

◯∿

# Salvation, the Supper,
# and the Drama of the Triune God

Celebrating the Lord's Supper can change our lives. As a site for the triune God's action, it affects not only our stated theologies but also the whole life of Christians and Christian communities. This chapter begins by unpacking the notion of "functional theologies" that guide—often in a hidden way—the theologies expressed by our lives, even when they contrast with our "stated theologies." We will see how this is particularly true for the relation of the gospel to the Supper. Then we will move to a brief biblical-theological exposition that is foundational for the rest of this book: the way in which humans were created to long for and delight in God's Word in Christ, mediated by the Spirit, as adopted children of the Father.

## Functional Theologies and Symbolic Worlds

What is your theology of "salvation"? The question is subtler than it may seem. If we are speaking in terms of functional theologies, the answer is not necessarily the same as what one would mark on a multiple-choice quiz in a Sunday school class. If we are going to be honest about where we are on the path of discipleship and where we need to go, we need to approach this question in a broader way.

Yet, as I am speaking of it here, "salvation" is not a specifically Christian—or even religious—concept. Functionally speaking, agnostics and atheists have just as much of a theology of salvation as Christians or Buddhists. How does a person or a culture define "healing" as opposed to "sickness"? What is happiness? What is success? Why is one way of speaking, acting, and living "good" while another is "bad"? While most of this book will speak of the gospel, the good news of Jesus Christ received in the Word of God, our initial inquiry needs to examine the concrete, lived side of the equation: the patterns of a person's action display their functional theology of salvation.

Thus, questions about salvation are not abstract, theoretical questions for debate among academics. They are concrete, existential questions that are answered by one's life. In response to questions such as these about salvation, many in today's Western culture will quickly take refuge in subjectivist responses to these questions: "No one knows," "It depends upon the person's circumstances," and so on. But these are not truly responses. Anyone who *acts* in the world has a functional conception of what the "good" is, what the purpose of life is, and what constitutes healing as opposed to sickness. Action in the world is unavoidable, as even passivity is a form of action. So also, action always has implications for one's sense of how the world is and how it should be. Everyone has a functional theology of salvation.

Even atheist philosophers like Friedrich Nietzsche have a theology of salvation. In several books, preeminently *Thus Spoke Zarathustra*, Nietzsche analyzes acts of pity: coming close to those who suffer, to empathize with them or comfort them, or ameliorate their suffering in some way. What do these actions of pity say about the way the world is and how it should be? According to Zarathustra—a figure who would not accept the categories of "good" and "evil" in any remotely Christian sense—there *is* such a thing as a sin. Acts of pity are a sin. Why? Because "pity is obtrusive" to sufferers. "Whether it be a god's pity or man's—pity offends the sense of shame. And to be unwilling to help can be nobler than that virtue which jumps to help."[1] Ultimately, acts of pity are a "sin" for Zarathustra because the very acts of compassion for the sufferer imply that the present suffering should not exist. But if we do not accept a primal world of peace (Eden) or a final redemption free of suffering (the new Jerusalem), then our action should not indicate that suffering "should not exist." Suffering always was, is, and will be for Zarathustra. Rather than act in pity toward those who suffer, we should "pass by" the suffering, thus not exposing sufferers to pity.[2] To pity is to *protest* against the present state of the world. But if "salvation" is to *affirm* the state of the world as it is (with all its suffering), as Nietzsche thinks, then "passing by" the sufferer is an action that enacts that theology of salvation.

Yet, to discern theologies of salvation one must analyze much more than

---

1. Friedrich Nietzsche, *Thus Spoke Zarathustra*, in *The Portable Nietzsche*, trans. Walter Kaufmann (New York: Penguin Books, 1977), 377.
2. Nietzsche, *Thus Spoke Zarathustra*, 388.

the actions of individuals or even groups. We need to take stock of the cultural rituals, symbols, and signs that shape who we are as people. It is often noted that Westerners live in an individualistic, consumerist culture. While true to a degree, that observation should not lead us to conclude that we actually wield great, conscious power in defining our "identity," sense of "good," and view of the world. We live in a society that gives us the *illusion* of the consumer's choices being central. In fact, our lives are being shaped in many ways by the world of symbols, rituals, and signs that hover around and within us.[3]

Think for a moment about the red and white insignia for Coca-Cola. In terms of trade and consumption, Coca-Cola is not even ranked among the top twenty-five transnational companies, and yet that insignia is one of the most widely recognized symbols on planet earth.[4] Coca-Cola is not just one of many cheaply produced sugary drinks. Through advertising, Coca-Cola connects its product to rituals of American life. When successful athletes promote Coca-Cola after a hard workout, the product is associated with strength, strategy, and the ritual of having a refreshing drink after an athletic event. When an advertisement shows Coca-Cola at a holiday celebration, the drink is associated with the beauty of the partakers, the joy of conviviality, and the ritual of providing Coca-Cola at parties and other celebrations. If you drink Coke, you are entering into the story and drama of celebrations like this one. The symbol and ritual are powerful, and they reinforce one another, creating a symbolic world that we inhabit, existentially confirmed and reinforced by ritual.

Indeed, the symbol of Coke can lead us to participate in a narrative, a story, even if we are not consciously thinking about the red and white insignia. For many, the automatic response to the question of what beverage to drink at a restaurant or a friend's house is "a Coke." Coke becomes nearly synonymous with "a drink," "a beverage." To ask for water might be a slight or an insult to the host or the restaurant server—it says this occasion is not worth the energy or expense of "a Coke." Coke is not just a symbol. It generates a ritual, a "cultural liturgy" that shapes the habits (and the bodies) of those who participate in this symbolic world.[5]

3. For more on the power of globalization to shape our sense of the good life, see Rebecca Todd Peters, *In Search of the Good Life: The Ethics of Globalization* (New York: Bloomsbury Academic, 2006).

4. For a sociological account of the symbol of Coca-Cola, see Carole Counihan, ed., *Food in the USA: A Reader* (New York: Routledge, 2013), and Marieke de Mooij, *Consumer Behavior and Culture: Consequences for Global Marketing and Advertising*, 2nd ed. (Thousand Oaks, CA: SAGE Publications, 2010).

5. See James K. A. Smith for the notion of secular "liturgies" and their formative

But what if one resists inhabiting this symbolic world? This task is much more difficult than it may at first seem. If one resists drinking Coca-Cola or eating at McDonald's or other chains, one is entering into another ritual—that of avoidance *because* of the red and white symbol of Coke or the McDonald's golden arches. Ironically, this can reinforce the power of these symbols: an "anticonsumerist" advocacy group risks being defined *by its enemy*, by its fixation upon the corporate forces it seeks to resist. The person who is constantly retweeting negative articles about his or her least favorite multinational corporation is *preoccupied* with that multinational corporation. The power of corporate symbolism lies not in forcing persons to act in a single way, but in creating a symbolic world that makes one see Coke as something other than a cheaply produced soft drink and McDonald's as something other than a place for burgers. The corporate symbols are bigger, more powerful than that. They generate cultural rituals and liturgies that form our desires and our habits.[6] Even the ritual of resistance does not call into question the power of these symbols. Rather, it recognizes their power in a different way than drinking a Coke or eating a Big Mac would recognize it.

Symbolic worlds and their ritual counterparts are ubiquitous, and globalization extends the reach of a Western, consumerist version of this around the earth. For Christians and non-Christians alike, these symbols and rituals help to shape our sense of "salvation": where the "good" and "beautiful" are found, what it means to be "healed" from sickness, "free" from restriction, etc. It happens through advertising where redemption is frequently associated with wealth, beauty, sexual satisfaction, and so on. But symbols and rituals have a much wider power than that.

The power of symbol and ritual extends to the gathering of the church as well. Unintentional symbols and rituals are just as powerful as intentional ones. If you are handing a gospel tract to someone, what symbolic value does that tract have? What does it say about salvation, about what Christianity itself is? What does that altar call at the end of every service of Sunday worship symbolize? It does not matter that the Christians giving tracts and issuing altar calls might be allergic to the language of symbol and ritual. Both actions involve symbols and rituals with unmistakable power—that is, after all, why they are used. Each act has an implicit theology and functional theology of salvation. Presumably, both acts say that God is very concerned that individuals (of rea-

---

power. Smith, *Desiring the Kingdom: Worship, Worldview, and Cultural Formation* (Grand Rapids: Baker Academic, 2009), 85–88.

6. I am indebted to the analysis of Smith here in *Desiring the Kingdom*.

soning age and capacity) make a decision for God—whether for salvation, or recommitment to God. They communicate that the rational human will is at the center of God's concern. There is much that these approaches do not bring into focus as well (God's initiative in salvation, a biblical salvation-history, whether God has a purpose for infants and the mentally impaired, etc.). What is obscured from focus is just as important as what is brought to center stage by these symbols and actions.

In a similar way, imagine a congregation that has a rich symbolic action—such as a weekly celebration of the Lord's Supper—but is uncomfortable with the notion of Jesus as Savior. Jesus is named in services, but members get very nervous talking about him outside of the service, for fear that non-Christians might find the mention of Jesus offensive. In this case, what is the broader significance of their worship service? It cannot be limited to a reflection upon the signs and actions of the Supper. A broader web of cultural symbols and rituals is in play. Their functional theology is decisively formed by a broader cultural liturgy of what Mark Searle calls "religious privatism": that "My religious beliefs are my own business and no one else's."[7] Rather than the person of Jesus having cosmic significance, he is reduced to a character in "my religious beliefs," which do not have implications for anyone else. This cultural strategy for coping with "religious pluralism" has a profound impact upon the character and significance of the worship itself.[8]

At this point, one may wonder: *Is there no escape?* If cultural forces show such power over our functional theologies, is it futile to resist them? And if symbol and rituals are truly inescapable, what are we to do? On one level, it is important to recognize that our culture will inevitably shape us in certain ways; we are shaped by the symbolic world and rituals that we inhabit. Yet, as Christians, we should not leave it there. We are called not to be "conformed to this world," but to be "transformed by the renewing of [our] minds" (Rom. 12:2 NRSV). We can and should have different lives—and different functional theologies of salvation—than those sharing the same culture around us. But how can this happen?

As long as one's symbolic world is shaped simply by the dominant culture, resistance alone will not be enough. Indeed, resistance to our symbolic "enemies" may reinforce the culture's symbolic power. Thus, another means

---

7. Mark Searle, "Private Religion, Individualistic Society, and Common Worship," in *Vision: The Scholarly Contributions of Mark Searle to Liturgical Renewal*, ed. Anne Y. Koester and Barbara Searle (Collegeville, MN: Liturgical Press, 2004), 187.

8. See Searle, "Private Religion," 187–88.

of living counterculturally is needed. To do this, one needs to display habits and practices shaped by a different symbolic world. For example, while I was language learning in a village in Uganda, the Ugandans repeatedly called me *ambogo*, a "big" man. Often this would be connected with physical gestures about being "big." As an American, I was somewhat hurt by this. I was not greatly overweight—why were they picking on me? I gradually came to see that my physical size had a profound symbolic value for them that completely eluded the power of the American symbolic world. For an American, heaviness was a symbol for ill health, laziness, and shame. For the Ugandans, a heavy body was a symbol of an important person. Only those who were desperately poor were thin, making thinness an undesirable state. But if one had enough leisure to carry a few extra pounds, this was testimony to the person's success and prosperity. The Ugandans escaped the symbolic power of an American "overweight" or "thin" body by taking another angle—an angle from their own distinct symbolic world.

### Tasting God's New World

The church is filled with symbols and rituals that can shape our identity, moving us into a narrative that is bigger than we could conjure up ourselves. In the gathering of a people, prayer and praise, proclamation of the Word, the washing with and feeding upon the Word in baptism and the Supper, we taste God's new world. We will always be "of" the world. Yet, as our imaginations are fired with God's new world, the symbolic world of consumer culture around us begins to look strange. Specifically, as we feed upon our new, gospel-defined identity in preaching and the Lord's Supper, a different symbolic narrative comes into view: what we previously thought was "freedom" is bondage, what we thought was "healing" is sickness. In light of Christ's reign, "freedom" is not mainly about the absence of constriction but is about the positive harmony with God and neighbor that the Spirit enables. "Healing" is not restoration so we can go our own way, but is a redirection of our misdirected desires toward loving God and our neighbor. It is not sufficient to simply say no to the shaping symbolic culture, such as a consumer culture. A fuller way of resistance is to enter into *a different world of symbols and rituals*, shaped by the Spirit, participating in Christ's reign. The Lord's Supper, as a foretaste of the wedding banquet of the Lamb and his bride, gives us a taste of God's new world.

Although symbols such as the cross and Christian language like "redemption" and "salvation" can seem almost ubiquitous in Western culture, they are often utilized for purposes that are foreign to those shown to us in God's new world, in Scripture. Often they become domesticated, torn from their context in divine revelation to suit our own ends.[9] In a context like this, we need to practice two complementary skills: first, we need to analyze our functional theologies, being attentive to the cultural idols that may be blocking our vision from encountering God's Word coming to us; second, we need to cultivate a positive sense of how we should seek to inhabit God's Word more fully. Scripture opens up a reality to us that we did not invent; by God's Spirit, it places us in a drama in which we are not in control. Slowly and gradually, we come to understand "redemption" and "salvation" as realities much deeper than we had first recognized. Precisely by being honest about our tendency for idolatry, we recognize the flavorful taste of the Word when we encounter it.

To be honest about our communal idolatries—for the purpose of deepening our God-given identity in Christ—we need to examine our theology and practice on the ground level. Thankfully, God doesn't wait until we have "perfected" our theology before he moves in his people. Yet, our functional theologies, displayed in our shared practices, often point to ways in which we are resisting the Spirit's ongoing transformation.[10]

Thus, we face the question: How do congregations in the West today actually experience the Lord's Supper? Drawing upon some fictional "types," I seek to show some common patterns of worship in the late modern West, especially among evangelical and nondenominational Protestants. In what follows, I consider a couple of Sunday worship examples—with "T" standing for traditional and "C" for contemporary "worship styles."[11]

---

9. Vincent Miller, in *Consuming Religion*, describes this commodification of religious terms and symbols as "pastiche" or "bricolage" in the "endless adoption and juxtaposition of styles and diverse symbols" where words and meanings are "sundered from the contexts that give them meaning." Vincent J. Miller, *Consuming Religion: Christian Faith and Practice in a Consumer Culture* (New York: Bloomsbury Academic, 2005), 154.

10. See chapters 1 and 4 of J. Todd Billings, *The Word of God for the People of God: An Entryway to the Theological Interpretation of Scripture* (Grand Rapids: Eerdmans, 2010).

11. I use scare quotes here because the common labels are problematic: all worship services reflect and exhibit traditions—even if the "tradition" is an heir of "spontaneity" in prayer and worship leading. Even the most charismatic worship service has normative patterns, giving the participants cues for what to expect and how to act with their bodies, voices, and attention throughout.

## Snapshots: Sunday Morning at T Church and C Church

As the congregation at T church arrives at the sanctuary for Sunday worship, a few parishioners recall that last Sunday it was announced that communion would be celebrated this week. For most of those gathered, this leads them to think about their own need for repentance; for others, it has not led to much "spiritual preparation" besides their usual wearing of Sunday-appropriate clothes. It does lead some to expect the service to go about ten to twelve minutes longer than usual. Scanning the bulletin, these members look to make sure that the pastor has not overloaded the service so it will end up going on for ninety minutes.

As the people find their pews, they face the front of the sanctuary with a pulpit on one side of a raised platform, and on the other side, an empty table with "Do This in Remembrance of Me" inscribed on the front. After a call to worship, a hymn of praise is sung, a psalm is read responsively, and another hymn is sung. Following this, in the pastoral prayer—after a moment for confession—the first mention is made of celebrating the Lord's Supper. At this point, others in the congregation come to expect the longer service, and some start to look forward to a time of silent reflection that they associate with the Supper. Scripture passages are read, and a sermon is preached that ends with a brief reference to the saving power of the cross of Christ, and the pastor gestures to the empty table.

Next, the invitation to the table is given, and the elders bring forward shiny trays containing small juice cups on one side and tiny white bread wafers on the other. The pastor prays a prayer of thanksgiving and gives the words of institution, climaxing with emphasis on "do this in remembrance of me." The organ starts to play very softly as the elders distribute the plates to the congregation to pass down the rows. After the bread is distributed, the congregation eats the wafers simultaneously, and then goes back into a private mode of reflection with the organ as background. Most of the congregation has their eyes closed, in a time of focused reflection on the cross, perhaps replaying the scenes from a movie of the crucifixion in their minds. They give thanks for forgiveness of their sins through this cross, though they do not deserve forgiveness. They thank God that they can enter heaven.

After parishioners drink from the small cups in response to the pastor's instruction, a short psalm of thanksgiving is read, and a final hymn of thanksgiving is sung. At this point, some members are filled with gratitude for the good news of forgiveness in Christ. Others check their watches—how long are we over the normal time? Eleven minutes—better than last time. The hymn finishes, and the congregation is dismissed with a benediction.

As the congregation at C church gathers for the service, some notice that the communion table has been placed in the center with a loaf of bread and a bunch of grapes on top. The worship band is playing music with a rousing beat; some congregants greet each other with an occasional jovial high five, feeding on the rock-concert-like energy. Most just find a seat in one of the side-by-side chairs and observe the musicians on the stage in the front, while some sing the words being projected onto a screen above them.

An enthusiastic worship leader in blue jeans greets those gathered, and says a short prayer before the worship band strikes up another rousing song. The congregation gets to their feet and sings the words from the screen in front—occasionally looking over at the guitarist, occasionally noticing the communion table, occasionally raising their hands in praise. After three lively songs of praise, the worship leader transitions to a slower ballad-like song. With this, the congregation sings about their love for Jesus and their desire to follow in his way. As the room becomes quiet, the pastor approaches the stage, reads a Scripture passage, and delivers a sermon complete with relevant practical applications. Then, with a few references to the way in which human traditions have muddled the simple ways of discipleship, the pastor moves to the table and gives the words of institution. "If you are a disciple of Christ, come to this table—and remember his sacrifice," the pastor says.

Some worship leaders are given part of the loaf and a cup, and they move to stations to distribute the elements. Some in the congregation walk to a station right away, while others remain where they are, closing their eyes while the praise band plays a song in the background. Eventually, all interrupt their personal moment of remembering the cross to receive the bread and the cup, and to look at one another while walking from the station. Some notice the words of the song from the praise band—about the weight of our sin, the sacrifice of Christ's cross, and entry into heaven. Some are led to think about their own sin, to confess personal sins. Others think about their conversion experience and relive it for a few moments in their heads. Others thank God that they are going to heaven. Others' minds wander. After this, the pastor returns to the front and dismisses the congregation with God's blessing.

These fictional "snapshots" may not fit every congregation exactly, but they evoke various dimensions of common worship experiences in the modern West around the Lord's Supper. Even if neither of the above "matches" your congregational experience, hopefully the snapshot gives some sense of how Sunday worship and the Lord's Supper are often viewed on a functional level. Some aspects of the functional theology represent deep wells of nourishment, and other aspects are missed opportunities. While the above snapshots were written in a way that highlights some of the deficiencies, this is not meant to undermine the aspects that are both faithful to the integrity of the Supper and significant for the congregation in the example. A new pastor would not do well to come in and give a scathing critique of a practice without recognizing what the congregation is doing well. In both congregations, the Supper does important work; in it, many reflect upon Christ's cross and meditate on the significance of forgiveness of sins. Those are central biblical truths that are essential to the gospel of Jesus Christ. These practices focus the attention of worshipers on this indispensable aspect of the gospel. They provide a moment of quiet in a culture of hurry, which is no small accomplishment. And even though there is an individual focus in both practices of the Supper, there is still a communal dimension to the celebration that is meaningful for the congregations.

On the other hand, the celebrations depicted above could become much more broadly biblical, much more centered in the multifaceted gospel of Jesus Christ. The congregations in these snapshots suffer from a myopic and incomplete vision. Late modern idols cast their shadows long, obscuring a more expansive view of the Supper and life in Christ. As such, the snapshots display characteristics of the near-sighted vision experienced in many congregations today.

In informal surveys among the seminary students I teach who serve in congregations that employ both "traditional" and "contemporary" worship styles in both self-identified "evangelical" and "mainline" churches, the primary meaning that they identify for the Lord's Supper is "remembrance of the cross." For many, it is also a Supper of repentance, as well as offering a personal, silent moment to think about their personal relationship with Christ. Students from a Lutheran or Episcopal/Anglican tradition tend to give different responses such as that the Lord's Supper is a partaking of the body and blood of Christ or an eschatological banquet. But for most students from Reformed, nondenominational evangelical and other evangelical congregations, "remembrance of the cross" is by far the most common response. This response also fits with the more formal survey work that Martha Moore-Keish has done among mainline Presbyterian Church (USA) congregations: "To the question 'What is the meaning of the Lord's Supper for you?' the most popular overall response was 'reminds us of the Last Supper of Jesus and his death.'"[12]

In this context, my seminary students sometimes assume that sacramental renewal would be generated simply by leading the congregation to "right

---

12. Martha L. Moore-Keish, *Do This in Remembrance of Me: A Ritual Approach to Reformed Eucharistic Theology* (Grand Rapids: Eerdmans, 2008), 124.

thinking" about the Supper. Thus, they plan a series of adult education classes on the confessions or the doctrinal statements of their tradition on the sacraments, thinking that will solve the problem. *The eucharistic prayer means this, the words of institution mean that, the bread signifies this, the cup signifies that.* Once this has happened, it is just up to the will of the congregation to implement sacramental renewal.

On the one hand, church catechesis is in urgent need of renewal in the modern Western church; whether one is Reformed or Roman Catholic, Lutheran or nondenominational, there is a vital need for congregational doctrinal instruction today. But those who believe that bare doctrinal instruction will automatically lead to a gospel-centered sacramental renewal are sadly mistaken.

The Lord's Supper is more than a mental act of meaning making. It is an embodied practice in community, engaging all our senses in the context of worship. The two examples above contain numerous cues about what celebrating the Supper means to the two congregations. There are indications from the preparation (or lack thereof), from the music (does it evoke private reflection or communal celebration?), from the physical setting of the sanctuary, from the elements themselves and how they are distributed. Many of these practical dimensions of both "traditional" and "contemporary" worship lead to what Moore-Keish discerns as a key functional theology of the Supper for participants: the Supper as "individual devotion" where participants "focus inward" and upon "the real 'meaning' of communion rather than the outward 'doing.'"[13] This emphasis fits quite well with the practice of connecting the Supper almost exclusively with the last supper of Christ and his cross. With the way that the Lord's Supper is celebrated in both "traditional" and "contemporary" evangelical contexts of worship, "remembrance" carries the day. There is value to this emphasis, as noted above, but apart from other themes such as nourishment by Christ and hope for his return, it tends to lead to a reduced, one-sided vision of the Supper.

The fact is that in many congregations in the modern West, participants do not *desire* a more frequent and full celebration of the Lord's Supper. If "remembrance" is the primary or exclusive meaning of the Supper, then one is likely to face the congregational objection: if we celebrate more often, it will lose its significance. An underlying issue, however, is whether they can fit remembrance into a broader framework—one in which they are hungry for Christ and need to be nourished by Christ via the Spirit. This involves remembrance of the cross through communion in his presence and hope for

13. Moore-Keish, *Do This in Remembrance*, 134–35.

his return. Congregations need both to see and to taste the power of the Lord's Supper anew in worship for this to take place. Teaching and catechesis can fill a very important role in this process, but we are affective creatures, and congregations need to develop a hunger and a desire for the table.

## Icon of the Gospel

In my view, the most important move in kindling a sense of a congregation's hunger for Christ and the multifaceted character of the gospel is to champion the connection mentioned above: the Lord's Supper as an "icon" of the gospel. John Calvin expresses the groundwork for this notion powerfully when he says that a sacrament "represents God's promises as painted in a picture and sets them before our sight, portrayed graphically in the manner of icons."[14] John Witvliet notes that some seventeenth-century Reformed theologians considered the Lord's Supper, in particular, to be the "only true icon" of Christ.[15] This "icon" is not two-dimensional, but a sign-action involving the whole congregation, a sign-action of the covenant people of God. This crucial sign-action is a place to encounter Jesus Christ and the good news of the gospel in him. Thus, the sign-action of the Supper and the meaning of salvation in Christ have a rough parallel, even though the Supper is not viewed as the *means* for receiving salvation.

For Calvin, the deep connection between the good news of the gospel and the sacraments of baptism and the Lord's Supper is this: at the center of both is union with Christ by the Spirit. In broad terms, union with Christ by the Spirit involves acquittal of the sinner for the sake of Christ (justification) and the fruit of new life by the Spirit (sanctification). Both of these are received in union with Christ through the gift of faith. Calvin calls this a "double grace": "Christ was given to us by God's generosity, to be grasped and possessed by us in faith. By partaking of him, we principally receive a double grace: namely, that being reconciled to God through Christ's blamelessness, we may have in heaven instead of a Judge a gracious Father; and secondly, that sanctified by Christ's spirit we may cultivate blamelessness and purity of life."[16]

---

14. Calvin, *Institutes* 4.14.6, translation from John D. Witvliet, *Worship Seeking Understanding: Windows into Christian Practice* (Grand Rapids: Baker Academic, 2003), 140. While Battles translates the final term as "images," Witvliet is right to translate this as "icons," since Calvin departs from his Latin in order to use the Greek term here, *eikonikos*.

15. Witvliet, *Worship Seeking Understanding*, 139-41.

16. Calvin, *Institutes* 3.11.1.

Calvin believes that the double grace of union with Christ, in the "newness of life and free reconciliation" that "are conferred on us by Christ," is itself the "sum of the gospel."[17] This sum of the gospel is not an abstraction. The double grace of union with Christ is received in the preached Word together with the sacraments, for "the sacraments bring the clearest promises" for embodied, material creatures like ourselves.[18] Held together with the Word preached, the sacramental Word of the Supper is a communal, embodied, participatory sign-action that draws believers more deeply into the covenantal fellowship in Christ.

## Functional Theologies and Becoming Hungry Again

Even if they were not formed by Calvin's notion, my informal surveys of students indicate a rough correspondence between the answers to two questions posed to their congregations: "What is the meaning of the Lord's Supper?" and, "What is the meaning of salvation?" In many churches, the answer to the former is "remembrance of the cross." The answer to the latter is nearly always "forgiveness of sins." When the answer to one question differs, there is usually a correspondence in the answer to the second.

Why this parallel between the functional theologies of the Lord's Supper and salvation? In general, these congregations do not see a "causal" connection between the Lord's Supper and salvation. Rather, on the level of functional theology, there is a sense that the Lord's Supper should point to what is most significant about the message of salvation. If salvation is consistently defined only in terms of the forgiveness of sins, then "remembrance" is likely to be the primary—if not only—congregational mode for experiencing the Lord's Supper.

While remembrance and the forgiveness of sins are absolutely vital biblical themes about salvation and the Lord's Supper, many congregations have blind spots to the themes that the final two chapters of this book will explore—the present communion of Christ and the anticipation of the eschatological banquet in both the Supper and salvation. To recover from this anemic vision,

17. Calvin, *Institutes* 3.3.1. While Calvin's phraseology of the "double grace" in union with Christ is somewhat distinctive, this basic formulation has considerable continuity with contemporaries such as Vermigli and later sixteenth- and seventeenth-century Reformed theologians and confessions. See J. Todd Billings, "John Calvin's Theology of Union with Christ, and Its Early Retrieval," in *Calvin's Theology and Its Reception: Disputes, Developments, and New Possibilities,* ed. J. Todd Billings and I. John Hesselink (Louisville: Westminster John Knox, 2012).

18. Calvin, *Institutes* 4.14.5.

we need biblical exegesis and a theological vision, but we also need to enter into this in a way that helps to make us hungry for Christ's presence, engages our longing for ongoing nourishment by God's Word, and reorients our desires. If all we do is assign abstract "meanings" to the liturgy and the elements, we have not faced the real challenge: to help congregations glimpse a more compelling vision of the gospel than "maintenance" of belief in God so that one receives the forgiveness of sins as a ticket to heaven. Congregations need to not only glimpse this good news, but also taste and know of it. This good news is that the triune God has united us to Christ and his people by his Spirit. This reality is one that Christians should soak in, rejoice in, act in, in both the church and the world. Renewal of a congregation's theology of salvation and the sacraments requires much more than tweaking and improving their mental map. It involves walking with them into the strange new world of God's Word—one that redirects our deepest longings. Let us turn now to the fundamental biblical and theological character of this larger vision that the book will expand upon in later chapters, this larger world opened up by God's Word.

### More Than an Abstraction: Delighting in God's Word

The triune God is free—the Lord of creation and redemption can bring transformation however he chooses. But again and again, through the Old Testament and the New, God chooses his Word as the instrument of transformation by the Spirit. Yet this Word is not an abstraction. When the psalmists show us the proper posture toward God's Word, they do not simply speak of the Word giving a "correct theology," and that "correct theology" leading to transformation. They long for God's Word; they feed upon and ache for the Word. God chooses to transform his people as his people hear and taste God's Word by the Spirit, longing and aching for God's Word, finding their nourishment upon God's Word in a parched land. The Word is not just an abstraction for cognition in the prayer of Psalm 119:20:

> My soul is consumed with longing
>   for your laws at all times.

Rather, God's Word (and law in Ps. 119) is the heart's greatest desire—a consuming passion that never leaves us alone. Indeed, as Christians confess, Jesus Christ himself is the eternal Word, the fulfillment of God's good law; we are right to worship him, and the path to him is the path of God's word in Scripture.

Does the psalmist ache for God's Word out of a great sense of duty? Again, if it is "duty" on an abstract, merely cognitive level, the answer must be negative. The psalmist longs to "see wonderful things in your law" (Ps. 119:18), to "meditate on your precepts" (v. 15), for God's Word brings "delight" when obeyed, for

> I rejoice in following your statutes
>> as one rejoices in great riches. (v. 14)

While the psalmist speaks God's laws with his lips, it is the human heart—as the center of human identity—that must be caught up in this love for God's ways.

> I seek you with all my heart;
>> do not let me stray from your commands. (v. 10)

Knowing God's Word, God's law, and God's way takes more than cognition.

In commenting upon this passage, John Calvin hints toward the disposition that such an approach to God's Word requires. "Our true safeguard, then, lies not in a slender knowledge of his law, or in a careless perusal of it, but in hiding it deeply in our hearts. Here we are reminded, that however men may be convinced of their own wisdom, they are yet destitute of all right judgment, except as far as they have God as their teacher."[19] To truly come to God as our teacher requires a sense of the destitution of life on our own, life lived from our own resources. Thus, we love God's Word as something that is outside of ourselves, even as we have God's Spirit dwelling in us. We "hide" God's Word in our hearts (Ps. 119:11) not to bury it away, but as an act of feeding upon and delighting in the Word that leads us in God's way through the indwelling Spirit.

A core instinct in Christian worship is that we need to do more than think about God's Word; we need to hide it in our hearts. Enlivened by the Spirit, we soak in God's Word, delighting in it, attending to it, redirecting our deepest desires and affections in and through it. Whether we memorize Scripture passages, or use a prayer book incorporating numerous Scripture passages, or meditate on Scripture in some other way, we are all seeking to move from the head to the heart, from the open level of analytic consciousness to the deeper level of hiddenness. Because when it comes to hiding God's Word in our heart, "the hidden things will go to work on us."[20] Hearing and responding

---

19. Ps. 119:11, CTS.
20. My thanks to Katy Sundararajan for expressing this insight so eloquently.

to God's Word is not mainly about spontaneously having the right thoughts and feelings in a key, dramatic moment; it is a Spirit-enabled delight in God's Word that is so deep that we hide it, we hide it deep so that the Spirit does work through the Word in us, going beyond what we could do by our conscious effort.

In a dramatic moment in the *Confessions*, Augustine speaks of his anguish, the restlessness of his heart, that emerges from living on his own strength: "Terrified by my sins and the dead weight of my misery, I had turned my problems over in my mind and was half determined to seek refuge in the desert. But you forbade me to do this and gave me strength by saying, 'Christ died for us all, so that being alive should no longer mean living with our own life but with his life who died for us' [2 Cor. 5:15]."[21] Augustine then brings to mind Psalm 119:18, showing how this passage was working on him, showing that ultimately we live in such a way that we seek refuge in ourselves *or* in the Lord and his Word.

> Lord, I cast all my troubles on you and from now on "I shall contemplate the wonders of your law" [Ps. 119:18]. You know how weak I am and how inadequate is my knowledge: teach me and heal my frailty. Your only Son, "in whom the whole treasury of wisdom and knowledge is stored up," has redeemed me with his blood. "Save me from the scorn of my enemies" [Ps. 119:122], for the price of my redemption is always in my thoughts. I eat it and drink it and minister it to others; and as one of the poor I long to be filled with it, to be one of those who "eat and have their fill." And "those who look for the Lord will cry out in praise of him."[22]

For Augustine, we are created as desiring creatures, and he can pray, "You made us for yourself and our hearts find no peace until they rest in you."[23] But in his use of Psalm 119:18 here, the central movement is from one direction of desire to another—from taking refuge in that which is not God, to taking delight and pleasure in the Lord and his Word.

Augustine speaks of eating and drinking and ministering to others the Word of God. The written Word of the Bible discloses the Son, Jesus Christ, the eternal Word. Augustine eats and drinks and serves this Word, and yet

---

21. Augustine, *Confessions* 10.43, trans. R. S. Pine-Coffin, New Impression ed. (1961), 251.
22. Augustine, *Confessions* 10.43, pp. 251–52.
23. Augustine, *Confessions* 1.1, p. 21.

he is not satiated. He is as "one of the poor" who longs to be filled. With the psalmist in Psalm 119:20, his "soul is consumed with longing for your [God's] laws at all times." When Christians meditate, delight, and feed on God's Word, it should not lead to satiation now, but to a deeper hunger for God and his presence. In Gregory of Nyssa's meditation on another psalm, he expresses the insight well: "To those who have tasted and seen by experience 'that the Lord is sweet' [Ps. 34:8], this taste becomes a kind of invitation to further enjoyment. And thus the one who is rising toward God constantly experiences this continual incitement toward further progress."[24] In the words of the Westminster Shorter Catechism, the chief end and thus the creational purpose of human beings is "to glorify God and to enjoy him forever."[25] We were created to glorify and enjoy God, and so, knowing the Word of God means much more than developing and refining certain abstract ideas (although ideas are nonetheless important). At its core, knowing God involves reorienting the loves at the center of our identity and entering into a new reality created by God and his Word.

## Knowing God in and through the Trinity

Ultimately, this portrait of knowing God requires a Trinitarian account of how the Spirit incorporates human beings into the sent Word, Jesus Christ, as children of the Father. In this Trinitarian account, knowledge is not about the narrator in our head performing analytic feats of wonder that lead to an increase in the knowledge of God. Our conscious mind is important, and growing in knowledge of the triune God has profound effects on our conscious thinking, but we are immersed into the reality of the triune God, which is much larger and deeper than we can comprehend. My point is not simply that we are finite, and thus cannot comprehend God on the level of God. (Although this is true! For this, the distinction between archetypal and ectypal theology is crucial.)[26] The point here is that even when we know God, it is a knowing that involves our whole person—body and soul—and is much deeper than any

24. *From Glory to Glory: Texts from Gregory of Nyssa's Mystical Writings*, ed. Jean Danielou and Herbert Musurillo (New York: Charles Scribner's Sons, 1962), 213.

25. Westminster Shorter Catechism, question and answer 1, *BC* 229.

26. Archetypal theology is God's perfect knowledge of himself, while ectypal theology is relational knowledge of God for humanity, accommodated to the limited capacities of creatures. I explore the usefulness of these categories in J. Todd Billings, *Union with Christ: Reframing Theology and Ministry for the Church* (Grand Rapids: Baker Academic, 2011), 83–89.

mental map that we can establish. It is a Spirit-enabled knowing—a feeding upon the Word that is inseparable from the embodied actions of corporate and individual worship, confession, intercessory prayer, kneeling, raising our hands in worship, and much more.

Consider Paul's prayer (3:14–19) and doxology (3:20–21) in this passage from Ephesians:

> For this reason I kneel before the Father, from whom every family in heaven and on earth derives its name. I pray that out of his glorious riches he may strengthen you with power through his Spirit in your inner being, so that Christ may dwell in your hearts through faith. And I pray that you, being rooted and established in love, may have power, together with all the Lord's holy people, to grasp how wide and long and high and deep is the love of Christ, and to know this love that surpasses knowledge—that you may be filled to the measure of all the fullness of God. Now to him who is able to do immeasurably more than all we ask or imagine, according to his power that is at work within us, to him be glory in the church and in Christ Jesus throughout all generations, for ever and ever! Amen. (Eph. 3:14–21)

Paul introduces his prayer by bending his knees (κάμπτω τὰ γόνατά μου) to the Father—praying for the believers to be strengthened "through his Spirit in your inner being, so that Christ may dwell in your hearts through faith." In this word picture, believers, "together with all the Lord's holy people," kneel at the throne of God the Father, as the deep inner being of believers is strengthened—as Christ dwells in them through faith. In this way, Paul is not using the Trinity as an abstract idea. The Trinity is the context for Christian identity—an embodied identity *enacted* through prayer. And the Christian identity imaged is very telling.

Paul's prayer is that through the Spirit, Christ would dwell in their hearts—thus, the triune God would work in the deepest part of human beings: in their loves. As Andrew Lincoln notes, "This continuing presence of Christ is to be experienced 'in your hearts.' As in the OT, so in Paul and now here in Ephesians, the heart is understood as the center of the personality, the seat of the whole person's thinking, feeling, and willing."[27] In complete de-

---

27. Andrew T. Lincoln, *Ephesians*, Word Biblical Commentary, vol. 42 (Waco: Nelson, 1990), 196.

pendence upon the Spirit's work in mediating Christ's presence, it is Christ's love that Paul petitions to be at the root of our human loves. "I pray that you, being rooted and established in love, may have power . . . to grasp how wide and long and high and deep is the love of Christ." This love of Christ—in the context of the triune God acting for and in us—is the great reality that Paul prays that we "grasp." But Paul knows that we cannot fully grasp it. For to pray for believers to grasp this is to pray that they "know this love that surpasses knowledge."

Yet, this experiential knowledge that surpasses understanding is a far cry from the common cultural view that since God cannot be fully known, whatever religious perspective "works" for the individual is true for him or her.[28] To the contrary, it is absolutely dependent upon Trinitarian particularities: that as ones united to Christ by the Spirit, believers can kneel before the Father. This is not a static reality—prayer and worship never are. The shape of this is constituted by "the love of Christ," shown in his self-sacrificial life and death. Adoption as God's children through Christ (Eph. 1:5) brings them before the cosmic Father in this passage ("from whom every family in heaven and on earth derives its name" [Eph. 3:15]), all in and through the Spirit, who strengthens the "inner being" of Christians by mediating Christ's presence (Eph. 3:16-17). This movement and reorientation of identity—reflected also in the reorientation of core desires in the quotes by Augustine, Gregory, and Calvin above—happen in and through worship: "The Church will become more what it ought to be as it experiences more of the one who mediates God's purposes in salvation, more of Christ's presence through the Spirit, and more of his all-embracing love that surpasses knowledge."[29] Meditation upon God's Word, for Christians, inserts them into a triune drama where the Spirit is reshaping God's people into the image of Christ, enabling them to embrace their identity as adopted sons and daughters of the Father. The movement of the triune God in and through God's people reorients their love so that it reflects the self-sacrificial love of Christ. Yet, worship is not just a "pep rally" for ethical action or evangelism—it is the real thing, the taste of the real life for which we were created, which *expresses* itself through love of God and neighbor in the world.

---

28. See Christian Smith and Patricia Snell, *Souls in Transition: The Religious and Spiritual Lives of Emerging Adults* (Oxford: Oxford University Press, 2009), 286-87.

29. Lincoln, *Ephesians*, 196.

## Desiring Christ, Desiring Worship

If we are created to be desiring creatures whose proper desire and end is to long for and delight in the triune God, then Augustine is right that, ultimately, it is Christ the Word whom we desire. For worship, this means that our preaching and sacraments, and our prayers and Scripture readings, participate in the Spirit's work of mediating Christ's powerful presence among his people. Although worship should include confession of sin and calls to repentance, worship is ultimately not just a stopgap, emergency measure to restore what was lost in the Fall. It is a taste of God's Word, nourishment for God's people in Christ. As Calvin writes concerning the Lord's Supper, "Now Christ is the only food of our soul, and therefore our Heavenly Father invites us to Christ, that, refreshed by partaking of Him, we may repeatedly gather strength until we shall have reached heavenly immortality."[30] Yet, Calvin affirms (influenced by Augustine) that even before the Fall, human beings were to feed upon the second person of the Trinity through the tree of life. The sacraments, for Calvin, cannot simply be about remembering forgiveness or the cross, because God actually created human beings to desire a physical, tasteable sign of his love. In language that reflects the movement described above of reorienting one's love and trust from oneself to God and his Word, Calvin describes how God "intended, therefore, that man, as often as he tasted the fruit of that tree, should remember whence he received his life, in order that he might acknowledge that he lives not by his own power, but by the kindness of God alone; and that life is not (as they commonly speak) an intrinsic good, but proceeds from God. Finally, in that tree there was a visible testimony to the declaration, that 'in God we are, and live, and move.'"[31] According to Calvin, this movement of tasting God's word in Christ is absolutely central in worship, given the Trinitarian reality of how God acts in and through worship: the sacraments have "the same office as the Word of God," namely, to "set forth Christ to us, and in him the treasures of heavenly grace," by the power of the Holy Spirit.[32] Thus, the office of the Word of God is to be an instrument of grace in uniting believers to Christ by the Spirit. As Calvin notes in his *Short Treatise on the Lord's Supper*, "Just as God has set all fullness of life in Jesus, in order to communicate it to us by means of him, so he has ordained his Word as instrument by which Jesus Christ, with all his

30. Calvin, *Institutes* 4.17.1.
31. Gen. 2:9, CTS.
32. Calvin, *Institutes* 4.14.17.

benefits, is dispensed to us."[33] As Brian Gerrish summarizes Calvin's position on the Word of God: "The word is not simply information about God; it is the instrument through which union with Christ is effected and his grace is imparted."[34] And Christ is the one, in Calvin's words, "through whom the Father's infinite goodness was more clearly and liberally poured out upon the earth and declared to men than ever before."[35] The triune God is the fountain of all goodness, and the children of the Father feed upon the life-giving Christ in Word and sacrament through the Spirit.

When considering how the triune God acts in and through corporate worship, and specifically in the ministry of Word and sacrament, we approach a mystery at the heart of the Christian faith. In this union with Christ by the Spirit—enacted by faith in Word and sacrament, displayed in discipleship and service—we approach the central mystery of worship and of the Christian life. After Jesus declares, "I am the true vine, and my Father is the vinegrower" in John 15:1 (NRSV) (one of the "I am" statements in John), he describes the centrality of abiding in Christ: "Abide in me as I abide in you. Just as the branch cannot bear fruit by itself unless it abides in the vine, neither can you unless you abide in me" (John 15:4 NRSV). This abiding means making our "abode" in Christ, making our "home" with him, just as he makes his home in us.[36] How do we abide in Christ? By having "my [Christ's] words abide in you," and in obedience that reflects the love of Christ: "If you keep my commandments, you will abide in my love, just as I have kept my Father's commandments and abide in his love" (John 15:7, 10 NRSV). Moreover, John 6 uses the same term for abiding (*menein*), suggesting the way in which this "making a home" can take place at the Lord's Supper: "Those who eat my flesh and drink my blood abide in me, and I in them" (John 6:56 NRSV). As our attention is moved from our resources, our self-made homes apart from Christ, and we direct our hearts to Christ by the Spirit in worship, we encounter, hear, taste, and see our true identity as children of the Father. In worship, we taste and see how God provides the ground for resting in his love. "As the Father has loved me, so I have loved you; abide in my love" (John 15:9 NRSV). God's love is not based upon our own initiative, but it nevertheless

---

33. Jean Calvin, *Calvin: Theological Treatises*, ed. J. K. S. Reid (Philadelphia: Westminster, 1954), 143.

34. B. A. Gerrish, *Grace and Gratitude: The Eucharistic Theology of John Calvin* (Eugene, OR: Wipf and Stock, 2002), 48.

35. Calvin, *Institutes* 4.16.6.

36. Frederick Dale Bruner, *The Gospel of John: A Commentary* (Grand Rapids: Eerdmans, 2012), 881.

bears the fruit of obedience ("You did not choose me but I chose you. And I appointed you to go and bear fruit" [John 15:16a NRSV]). Indeed, as ones united to Christ and grounded in God's love, when we obey this command we reflect the self-sacrificial service of Christ: "This is my commandment, that you love one another as I have loved you. No one has greater love than this, to lay down one's life for one's friends" (John 15:12–13 NRSV). Worship shifts our attention to the mystery of the triune drama of being united to Christ, dwelling in the home of his Word and his love as we bear fruit as his disciples; this is the mystery of the triune God working in and through Christian love, service, and witness in the world.

In sum, Christians find themselves shaped by various symbolic forces and symbolic narratives. What is salvation? What is the good news of Jesus Christ? What is the Lord's Supper? There is a Sunday school answer for each of these questions, and then there is a more probing answer that examines how our actions, habits, and narratives display a functional theology. Whether a congregation is "traditional" or "contemporary" in worship, the challenge is the same: how to move beyond a myopic perception of the gospel to embrace the depth and breadth of the good news of God's action in and through Jesus Christ. As adopted children of the Father who are filled with the Spirit and conformed to Christ through the Word, we are called to participate in the triune God's work; to cultivate a desire for Jesus Christ as our food and nourishment; to find our home and identity in Jesus Christ; and to abide in him.

Congregations are tempted to reduce the gospel in numerous ways, both implicitly and explicitly. For some, the gospel is justification and forgiveness of sins, and new life is an optional extra. For others, the gospel is an ethic of "radical discipleship," and there seems to be little need or room for receiving God's free pardon to sinners who cannot save themselves. In various ways, we are tempted to embrace resurrection victory without the cross, or the sacrifice of the cross without new life by the Spirit. Thankfully, we are not left to our own devices in moving toward the Lord in covenantal fellowship, away from communal idolatries. The Lord himself has given an instrument—the Lord's Supper—a physical, tasteable sign of his covenantal love. This Supper is a sign-action that displays the gospel and, together with the preached Word, draws us into the drama of God's work. Through the Word preached and received in the Lord's Supper, we encounter and receive Jesus Christ by the Spirit. In him, we find forgiveness and new life, justification and sanctification. In him, we receive nourishment and enter into loving fellowship.

A key assumption of this vision is that we human beings were created as fundamentally affectionate beings, made to delight in God and his Word. Before moving to the particularities of the doctrine of the Lord's Supper in chapter 3, we need to explore how our humanity relates to the Spirit's work: not simply humans as thinkers, but humans as deeply affectionate, embodied creatures who are longing for communion with Christ, their beloved.

CHAPTER 2

 ∾

# Embodied Perception and Delight in Christ

Humans are fundamentally affectionate beings. We are made to delight in God, to enjoy fellowship with him and with others as God's good creation. In the first chapter, we saw how this key claim emerges from biblical exegesis, early Christian voices such as Gregory of Nyssa and Augustine, and Reformers such as Calvin. But why does this claim about human beings really matter for the project of moving the functional theologies of congregations in a more biblical direction?

If congregations are to embrace the Lord's Supper as a God-given instrument for moving to live more deeply out of the gospel, as this book advocates, then something more than a doctrinal lesson is required. The doctrinal logic is relatively simple: Human beings were created to desire God and to delight and have fellowship with God. Sin has disrupted this communion, misdirecting our affections—and our sinful decisions flow from these misdirected affections. But the Christian life involves a process of dwelling and soaking in God's word in Christ, feeding upon it within the church in Word and sacrament, and bearing the fruit of our abiding union with Christ in acts of love in and to the world.

Unfortunately, it is possible for congregations to accept this "doctrinal logic" while maintaining a functional theology that tells a different story. In many Reformed congregations in the West, the body's senses are engaged relatively little in worship: the pattern of singing, a long sermon, and a very rare celebration of the Lord's Supper reinforces a fundamentally cerebral expression of faith. Modifying particular aspects of the Lord's Supper is unlikely to make a significant change in how such congregations view, and experience, the gift of salvation itself. The patterns and communal habits need to change. The body needs to be engaged more deeply. And the affections at the depth of our hearts need to be engaged.

In this chapter, I begin by showing the link between an affectionate anthropology and a recovery of the value of Christian practice and habit; but I also seek to set this in a theocentric context. To this end I draw upon the notion of "spiritual senses" to show how affectionate knowing participates in the triune work of God. Finally, I point to the holy fairs as an instructive example of how an affectionate anthropology, with a robust trust in the Trinity's work in and through worship, was manifested in an earlier era of Reformed theology and practice of the Lord's Supper. For readers who have visited Reformed congregations and think they know the Reformed worship tradition, this historical sketch will be full of surprises.

## Humans as Lovers

Thinking is important, and it is intertwined with our affections. In our era, we may assume that Descartes gets to the most basic level: "I think, therefore I am." Beyond René Descartes himself, contemporary consumer culture, saturated with social media, can reinforce variations of this: the products I buy, the friends I make, the messages I post on social media—they can all make me satisfied or discontented; I think, I produce, I buy, I post, therefore I am. My decisions, my thinking, come first. Then, I decide whether or not I am satisfied, whether or not I delight in what I have chosen.

But perhaps our affections are even more primary than all these "thinking" decisions. Perhaps Augustine is right, and in a different way, contemporary neuroscientists are also right: affections and habits are much more basic in forming human identity than our conscious thinking. Augustine claims that on a fundamental level all humans desire a "happy life" in some form: "Is it not the happy life itself that everyone wants? And is it not impossible to find anybody who does not want it?"[1] Thus, while humans choose all sorts of inadequate and sinful ends that do not bring true happiness, all people desire and direct their love toward a perceived good: "There is no one who doesn't love. The only question is what a person loves."[2] This does not flow from a neutral, dispassionate "decision" on a cognitive level. As Jean-Luc Marion exposits Augustine's anthropology, "My desire—or more exactly, that to which I respond and commit myself—knows better who I am than my (intentional) thought ever

---

1. Augustine, *Confessions*, Book 10, chapter 1, in Jean-Luc Marion, *In the Self's Place: The Approach of Saint Augustine* (Redwood City, CA: Stanford University Press, 2012), 85.
2. Augustine, *Sermon* 34, 2, in Marion, *In the Self's Place*, 96.

will."[3] Truly, every person is a thinker and a lover. But our conscious thinking can never fully catch up with the identity-forming action that we have in fact entered into as lover. According to Marion, in Augustine, the person is a lover, and "for the lover, the question never consists in deciding to love or not but always and only in orienting oneness in terms of desire, in determining what he loves." For "the *lover* loves so radically that loving decides everything about him and first of all his being."[4]

Recently, James K. A. Smith has sought to extend this broadly Augustinian instinct to discussions of Christian formation, the influence of the subconscious, and the powerful role of habits in human development. Smith, a philosophy professor, is not claiming that intellectual activity is unimportant. It is of crucial importance. But an "intellectualist" account of how humans function leaves us with a naïve view: if Christians think rightly, it will result in lives of discipleship. Smith argues that Christians involved in education need to be attentive to the *telos*, or end, of Christian discipleship, and how education might help form the desires, motivations, habits, and practices that seek after Christ's kingdom.[5] We live in a context where there are alternative cultural liturgies—those of the shopping mall, for example—that shape our desires in a particular way. They shape and orient our desires toward some vision of human flourishing. Unfortunately, these "secular" liturgies shape our affections—and thus our habits, decisions, and practices—in a way that sharply contrasts with the vision of Christ's kingdom.[6] Christian worship, then, can and should function as a counterliturgy to the secular liturgies for Christians, reorienting Christians toward the loves, habits, and practices of disciples of Christ.

## Perception, Narrative, and the Reordering of Affections

A key insight in Smith's work is the watershed importance of *perception*. Most of the time, when we go through our day, we do not consciously think about what we do: we walk to the kitchen, go to the fridge, pull out a bottle of milk— all in "automatic" mode, while our conscious mind is thinking about other things. Our way of going through the day is colored, or coded, with affec-

3. Marion, *In the Self's Place*, 84.
4. Marion, *In the Self's Place*, 96.
5. See James K. A. Smith, *Desiring the Kingdom: Worship, Worldview, and Cultural Formation* (Grand Rapids: Baker Academic, 2009), 47–62.
6. See Smith, *Desiring the Kingdom*, 75–79, 93–103.

tions—we have intuitive, bodily responses to a red light while driving, to a billboard with our favorite coffee drink, to a colleague who walks toward us with an angry face. The most significant aspect of how we respond to these situations is not our conscious thought—what Princeton professor Daniel Kahneman calls the "slow" or "effortful" processing in "System 2." "System 2 articulates judgments and makes choices"—indeed, in everyday life, "System 2 is who we think we are."[7] Yet the most influential aspect for most behaviors is level 1, the "fast," "automatic" thought that quickly *perceives* a situation in an af-fectively coded way. Indeed, System 2 "often endorses or rationalizes ideas and feelings that were generated by System 1."[8] In Smith's account, he claims that key to Christian formation is the *perception* of the world in an affective-coded way—what Smith calls "pre-cognitive, affective 'drivers' that orient our being in the world."[9] Unconscious processing is key for how we perceive and enter into the world. Smith notes that what "I 'take in'" in encountering a situation is "governed and shaped by affective dispositions I bring to the encounter."[10] This means that the unconscious act of "perception" is critical to our judgments of what is true, beautiful, and good.

Yet these affective drives and desires governing perception are not flatly "hardwired," such that one's experiences and conscious deliberation have no effect upon perception. To draw upon the language of David Brooks in *The Social Animal*, the conscious mind (level 2) is not the "dictator" of the mind, but its workings are not insignificant either.[11] Rather, one of the key things that the conscious mind can do is direct *attention* in a particular direction, and see itself as part of a larger story or narrative, acting in a particular script.

Consider a helpful example from Brooks. In *The Social Animal*, Brooks gives a fictional story of a married couple, Harold and Erica, with accompany-ing analysis informed by recent brain science. In one episode, Erica, a company CEO, has dinner with a celebrated business leader. "She'd followed this guy's

---

7. Daniel Kahneman, *Thinking, Fast and Slow* (New York: Farrar, Straus and Giroux, 2013), 415.

8. Kahneman, *Thinking, Fast and Slow*, 415.

9. James K. A. Smith, "Secular Liturgies and the Prospect for a 'Post-Secular' Sociology of Religion," in *The Post-Secular in Question: Religion in Contemporary Society*, ed. Philip S. Gorski et al. (New York: New York University Press, 2012), 171.

10. James K. A. Smith, *Imagining the Kingdom: How Worship Works* (Grand Rapids: Baker Academic, 2013), 34.

11. David Brooks, *The Social Animal: The Hidden Sources of Love, Character, and Achieve-ment* (New York: Random House, 2012), 373. Hereafter, page references from this work will be given in parentheses in the text.

career for years on the covers of business magazines, and when they'd met at a charity event he'd asked her to join his board of directors" (276). After a "business lunch" in her hotel suite, Erica and the business celebrity both welcomed an adulterous encounter. Erica did not engage in much level 2, conscious "slow thinking" to lead to this decision; rather, it was conditioned upon the story she saw herself acting in. "It really wasn't the aridity of her own marriage at that point or her profound loneliness that made her sleep with him that day. It was mostly the novelty of having sex with a *Forbes*-cover boy and the excitement of having an experience she would always remember" (277).

About an hour after this sexual encounter that she had welcomed, Erica was overwhelmed with sensations of pain, shame, and regret. "That night, she felt rancid in every way. Thoughts and images swarmed across her brain, not only of that afternoon's event, but also randomly associated terrible moments from her past. Her remorse seethed, and she could do nothing to will it away" (278). Neither Erica's original decision for adultery nor her later revulsion was simply the result of a battle between "selfish and primitive passions" and "the enlightened force of reason" (279).

From this illustration, Brooks observes that "most of our moral judgments, like Erica thrashing about that night in agony, are not cool, reasoned judgments, they are deep and often hot responses. We go through our days making instant moral evaluations about behavior, without really having to think about why. We see injustice and we're furious. We see charity and we're warmed" (280). With Erica, in her response to her adultery "she almost felt as if she were two different people"—because she *perceived* the act so differently after the event than she had leading up to it (280). She was caught between acting in two different stories. In one story, she acted as if family, country, and work were "sacred." These were her conscious, stated values. Indeed, "if you had asked her about the old values, she would have told you that of course she still embraced them" (292). But instead, long before she found herself in that hotel room, "she had become a different person without realizing it." The decision to commit adultery "didn't even feel like a decision. It was just the culmination of a long unconscious shift" (292). For years now, she had started to act in a different story—seeing herself as "as a hustling young Horatio Alger girl" who was "consumed" with the quest to rise the ladder of the business world. Through thousands of small actions, through the movement of her affections and desires from the story of the "old values" to this new story, Erica started to act in a drama that made committing adultery with a business celebrity the obvious action to take, acting in accord with the character of this new story. But after the act, the first story gave her a deeply affective way to

34

view this act as not merely an innocent one of climbing the corporate ladder but as a deep betrayal of the person of the "old values" that she claims to hold. After the event, "she told herself a story about herself. It was the story of drift and redemption—of a woman who'd slid off her path inadvertently and who needed anchors to connect her to what was true and admirable. She needed to change her life, to find a church, to find some community group and a cause, and above all, to improve her marriage, to tether herself to a set of moral commitments" (293). In other words, she needed to rediscover a set of practices and habits that could help her to live by this old script once again. She had to move beyond one emotionally charged story of her life to another in order to rediscover her true story.

While Brooks's fictional account is meant to illustrate the analysis of contemporary brain science on human behavior, in broad terms it helps to expose the centrality of loves, practices, and desires for human identity. We are not just what we "think," or even what we "want" at the moment we update our social media status. As Augustine, Calvin, Jonathan Edwards, and other theologians have long testified, humans are created as desiring creatures, affective creatures—they will be known by their loves, and shaped by their habits, which bear fruit in human action.

Extending Erica's story for a moment beyond Brooks's analysis, we might ask: If Erica were to ask a pastor to help her "tether herself to a set of moral commitments," how might the pastor respond? In a sense, Erica's story is one of a lack of integration between two stories, two dramas and scripts that she entered into: one that valued family and the "old values," and the second that valued upward mobility above all. To truly respond to Erica's query, the pastor should not just offer a onetime prayer for her to "change her life," or make a single commitment. The pastor should point her toward a new way of life—incorporation into a community of Word and sacrament, with its shared habits of prayer, worship, Bible study, service, and witness. Indeed, as Smith rightly argues, the "narrative practice" that internalizes the Christian story above all is worship.[12] And all this takes place in and through a people—a community for Erica to attach herself to. Yet, in all this, from a Christian perspective, it is not just a human practice that will lead to change. It is the Holy Spirit's work in uniting Erica to Christ and his people, bringing her gradually—yet decisively—to recognize and participate in the drama of being a child of God. In all these practices and particularities, the Spirit can reshape Erica's loves, her affections, and her actions.

12. Smith, *Imagining the Kingdom,* 38.

## Learning to Love in Practice, in Habit, in Community

When Jesus speaks about the central aspects of the identity and obedience to which he calls us, he speaks of the love at the core of a person's identity.[13] "'Love the Lord your God with all your heart and with all your soul and with all your mind.' This is the first and greatest commandment. And the second is like it: 'Love your neighbor as yourself.' All the Law and the Prophets hang on these two commandments" (Matt. 22:37–40). The loves of the heart are expressed in actions, in the fruit of obedience or disobedience. "No good tree bears bad fruit, nor does a bad tree bear good fruit. Each tree is recognized by its own fruit. People do not pick figs from thornbushes, or grapes from briers. A good man brings good things out of the good stored up in his heart, and an evil man brings evil things out of the evil stored up in his heart. For the mouth speaks what the heart is full of" (Luke 6:43–45).[14]

In light of this view of the person, the Christian tradition has often emphasized that a key for reorienting one's loves toward Christ's kingdom is redirecting *attention* toward God's word in Christ. This redirection of attention is absolutely necessary if Christians are to dwell in—and act in—the story of God rather than their own self-serving stories. Redirecting attention, through formative practices such as prayer and worship, helps us to *perceive* the world differently and act in the world, which is charged with God's presence and action.

But this redirection of attention to God and his word is difficult. It does not happen through a onetime act of the will, but in the practices of prayer and worship over a lifetime. Calvin speaks in words reflective of much of the Christian tradition about meditative prayer when he considers the psalmist's declaration

> I meditate on your precepts
> and consider your ways. (Ps. 119:15)

The mind is like a sieve, with a tendency toward distraction; this makes us "lose sight of the law of God."[15] Thus, if the heart is to be shaped by the desire

---

13. "Anyone who loves their father or mother more than me is not worthy of me; anyone who loves their son or daughter more than me is not worthy of me. Whoever does not take up their cross and follow me is not worthy of me. Whoever finds their life will lose it, and whoever loses their life for my sake will find it" (Matt. 10:37–39).

14. Also see Matt. 7:16–20; John 15:1–16.

15. Calvin's commentary on Psalm 119:15, CTS.

for God and his Word, we must "consider attentively the ways of God"—and "cheerfully and proficiently set our minds upon [them]."[16] This engages our deep affections, for "the commencement of a good life" is not in the acquisition of possessions or being the hero in a worldly script, but it "consists in God's law attracting us to him by its sweetness."[17]

As Matthew Myer Boulton has shown in some detail in *Life in God*, Calvin draws deeply upon the ancient ascetic traditions of prayer and meditation in his theology and in his practical reforms in Geneva. Calvin critiques monasticism—especially the monasticism of his own day. Yet, "for Calvin, monastics are mistaken only insofar as they make elite, difficult, and rare what should be ordinary, accessible, and common in Christian communities: namely, human lives formed in and through the church's distinctive repertoire of disciplines, from singing psalms to daily prayer to communing with Christ at the Supper."[18] Thus, "Calvin positions himself not only *against* monasticism as a critic, but also alongside monasticism as a fellow heir to the church's practical treasury"—a treasury of formative practices emerging from Scripture that provides a "rule for regulating life well," involving "renouncing our former life" with its "impiety and worldly desires."[19] For Calvin, this involved reviving aspects of monasticism's practical treasury, including regular prayer, worship, singing the psalms, discipline, and celebrating the Lord's Supper. In particular, the words of Scripture were emphasized in the daily lives of the Genevans. As Scott Manetsch has shown in a detailed social-historical study of the ministers of Geneva during and after Calvin's reforms, "between 1536 and 1609, the language and message of the Bible was nearly omnipresent in Geneva's religious life as it was proclaimed in sermons, recited in catechism, sung in the Psalter, studied in the *Congregation*, discussed in the marketplace, and read devotionally in households."[20] As Boulton points out, through his various reforms, Calvin sought a particular type of Christian formation: to cultivate *pietas* among the Christians in Geneva, which Calvin defined as "that reverence joined with love of God which the knowledge of his benefits induces."[21] *Pietas* is not just a "theoretical" knowledge for Calvin, but, as Boul-

16. Calvin's commentary on Psalm 119:15, CTS.

17. Calvin's commentary on Psalm 119:15, CTS.

18. Matthew Myer Boulton, *Life in God: John Calvin, Practical Formation, and the Future of Protestant Theology* (Grand Rapids: Eerdmans, 2011), 13.

19. Calvin, commentary on Titus 2:12, in Boulton, *Life in God*, 25.

20. Scott M. Manetsch, *Calvin's Company of Pastors: Pastoral Care and the Emerging Reformed Church, 1536–1609* (New York: Oxford University Press, 2015), 305.

21. Calvin, *Institutes* 1.2.1. On these reforms in Geneva, see Boulton, *Life in God*, 29–58.

ton describes, it is "a divine gift, a gracious way for disciples to participate in a life of communion with Christ."[22] As I have argued elsewhere, "*Pietas* is profoundly existential" for Calvin, for "it involves knowledge of God's paternal kindness in a way that brings delight and moves believers to action."[23] Specifically, for Calvin, *pietas* is animated in believers by the Spirit as they receive the gifts of justification and sanctification in union with Christ—experienced in practices such as prayer, the sacraments, and acts of service and justice as part of one's love of neighbor.[24] As Boulton shows, the reverence and love of God involved in *pietas* implicate both "dispositions and actions, doctrines and practices, reverence and righteousness, and so point toward a holistic, integrated way of life."[25] In the words of Calvin, *pietas* "is the beginning, the middle, and the end of the Christian life."[26]

Protestants, in particular, have a tendency to underestimate the significance of actual concrete practices that take the form of habits in the Christian life. This can emerge from a legitimate concern: Christ's person and work are fully sufficient for salvation—thus, there is a persistent concern about the danger of "legalism" and "works righteousness" in speaking about rituals. A ritual can become a "dead ritual," a habit, an "empty habit." Thus, even when spiritual disciplines are emphasized among contemporary Protestants (such as in the importance of personal devotions and prayer), that emphasis is usually accompanied by a suspicion of repetition and ritual. They assume that prayer needs to be spontaneous to avoid emptiness and be "authentic."

Reformers such as Calvin advocated simplicity in worship to keep believers from being overwhelmed with an ever-increasing multiplication of "ceremonies" that could obscure the heart of worship. Yet, for Calvin, this was part of a program to reform and renew these ascetic traditions, not to jettison them. Calvin and many contemporaneous and later Protestants continued to emphasize the importance of regular prayer, Scripture study, celebration of the Lord's Supper, and worship. Thus, a commitment to the sufficiency of Christ's saving work can be fully compatible with an emphasis on the importance of habit, regularity, and repetition in Christian practice.

22. Boulton, *Life in God*, 50.
23. J. Todd Billings, *Calvin, Participation, and the Gift: The Activity of Believers in Union with Christ* (Oxford: Oxford University Press, 2008), 36.
24. See Billings, *Calvin, Participation, and the Gift*, chaps. 4–5.
25. Boulton, *Life in God*, 50.
26. Calvin's commentary on 1 Tim. 4:8, in Boulton, *Life in God*, 50.

## Is Counterformation Enough?

But are worship and education as "counterformation" really enough for congregations today who are shaped by powerful forces that can undermine their allegiance to Christ? If Christian worship is a form of counterformation in contrast to the many secular liturgies in our culture, how could Christian disciples ever be formed? These are very real questions that point to the limits of our necessary talk of habit and practice; if Christian habits are simply a human practice, apart from a mighty work of the Spirit of God in and through the church in the world, then counterformation is a dead end. For if we are subject to formative liturgies that shape us to be a kingdom of consumers rather than a kingdom of Christ for most waking hours of the day, how could the Christian formative "liturgy" ever compete with these many other cultural liturgies? In viewing worship as counterformation to other cultural liturgies, there is a danger in assuming that all liturgies are equally efficacious, equally formative: that twenty minutes of commercials necessarily shape us as much as twenty minutes of communal prayer. But that would be a mistake: it would assume that we act in a closed, immanent system in which God is not active. Ironically, that would imply that prayer and worship are not the site for the Spirit's transformative work, but are simply sites of self-transformation by humans trying to improve themselves.

In response, Smith gives a nuanced account of "thick" and "thin" practices, in which not all practices (or liturgies) are equally formative.[27] Brushing one's teeth is not as "formative" a practice as taking a weekly trip to the shopping mall. Moreover, although he does not go into great detail, Smith emphasizes in *Imagining the Kingdom* that practices are the means through which the Spirit works—thus, it is not a closed, immanent system.[28] The Spirit works in and through worship, in and through Christian practices, to form Christian identity in deep ways.

While Smith's response is helpful, the challenges here are significant. It is helpful to draw upon a phenomenology of affective knowing and works that draw upon contemporary brain science (as in the David Brooks example above), but there are dangers in simply importing such anthropological notions of practice as well. Will Willimon reflects on this problem in a trenchant *Christian Century* article, "Too Much Practice." Willimon expresses his "regrets" about a theological movement that he helped to initiate, "a communal

27. Smith, *Desiring the Kingdom*, 80–88.
28. For example, see Smith, *Imagining the Kingdom*, 152–62.

tradition that gives us the skills, habits and practices that enable us truthfully to know the world in the way of Christ and subversively to resist the toxic pressures of the world's godlessness." However, Willimon is now concerned that "talk of 'practices' may be a way of avoiding talk of God." It can deflect "our attention from the living God." Instead, "the true God can never be known through our practices but comes to us only as a gift of God, only as revelation." We need to recover a sense of the agency of God, such that "Christian practices are not primarily what we do. Rather, our practice of the faith is something that God does for us, in us, often despite us."[29]

## The Spiritual Senses:
## The Spirit Enabling Affective Human Perception of God

Thankfully, many earlier Christian theologians brought together an anthropological portrait of human beings as fundamentally affective creatures with the centrality of the triune God acting through human practices of prayer, meditation on Scripture, worship, and discipleship. In particular, I would like to draw upon an important tradition that has not received the wide attention that it deserves: the "spiritual senses" tradition.

"Spiritual senses" is a wide-ranging tradition of thought that spans the eras of the church's history; it occurs in the Orthodox East as well as among Roman Catholics and Protestants in the West. A recent collection of studies on the spiritual senses included material on Gregory of Nyssa, Augustine, Bonaventure, Jonathan Edwards, John Wesley, and even contemporary philosopher Alvin Plantinga—and this is a very small sampling of the tradition.[30] While the tradition on this point is diverse, there are common features amidst the diversity of approaches. This tradition develops the scriptural theme that human senses are utilized in knowing God.[31] For example, the psalmist gives the imperative to "taste and see that the LORD is good" (Ps. 34:8); the prophets "hear" God's word; Jesus teaches that "the pure in heart . . . will see God" (Matt. 5:8); Paul uses the image of sight, "for now we see only a reflection as

---

29. Will Willimon, "Too Much Practice," *Christian Century* 127, no. 5 (March 9, 2010): 22–25.

30. See William J. Abraham, "Analytic Philosophers of Religion," in *The Spiritual Senses: Perceiving God in Western Christianity*, ed. Paul L. Gavrilyuk and Sarah Coakley (Cambridge: Cambridge University Press, 2014), 285–88.

31. For this list, I draw and expand upon the material in Gavrilyuk and Coakley, *The Spiritual Senses*, chap. 1.

in a mirror; then we shall see face to face" (1 Cor. 13:12), and smell, "for we are to God the pleasing aroma of Christ among those who are being saved and those who are perishing" (2 Cor. 2:15). In 1 John 1:1–2, the senses of hearing, sight, and touch are used to speak of apprehending Jesus Christ, the incarnate one: "That which was from the beginning, which we have heard, which we have seen with our eyes, which we have looked at and our hands have touched—this we proclaim concerning the Word of life. The life appeared; we have seen it and testify to it, and we proclaim to you the eternal life, which was with the Father and has appeared to us." In Jesus Christ, the eternal Word has taken on human flesh—flesh that can be seen and touched. Nevertheless, if God is not corporeal, how can we see God? This is a mystery and a paradox that John 1:18 expresses: "No one has ever seen God, but the one and only Son, who is himself God and is in closest relationship with the Father, has made him known."

The "spiritual senses" tradition builds upon these features of the biblical witness and thus speaks about a "non-physical mode of perception" for perceiving God.[32] Frequently, it notes the way in which biblical language for the Spirit very often relates to perception—for example, when Jesus speaks to Nicodemus about being "born of the Spirit," he uses the imagery of sight: "no one can see the kingdom of God without being born from above" (John 3:6; 3:3 NRSV). In addition, this tradition frequently occurs with a theological anthropology that emphasizes human beings as affective creatures, and the significance of worship, prayer, and meditation upon Scripture in the development of spiritual sight in this light, even as the vision of God is far from "face to face" in this life, "for now we see in a mirror, dimly" (1 Cor. 13:12 NRSV). At times, the Spirit is spoken about as giving an additional, sixth sense to perceive the things of God in revelation.

Drawing upon a broad Puritan tradition of the Spirit bringing a sixth spiritual sense, Jonathan Edwards provides a helpful example of the way in which this tradition can hold together a commitment to human beings as affective beings, the importance of habit and practice, with a thoroughly Trinitarian account of "perception" that takes place by the Spirit. In *A Treatise concerning Religious Affections* (1746), Edwards gives an anthropology in which affections, as "the more vigorous and sensible exercises of the inclination and will of the soul," are essential for the way in which humans exist in the world.[33] While affections, emerging from the will's inclination, are distinct from a pure "no-

32. Gavrilyuk and Coakley, *The Spiritual Senses*, 3.
33. *WJE* 2:96. Hereafter, page references from this work will be given in parentheses in the text.

tional" knowledge, to know rightly and fully one needs the accompanying affections that display an inclination toward that object or person. Thus, one could have a certain knowledge of honey by "only looking on it," but that is quite different than "the sweet taste of honey" (*WJE* 2:206). In tasting the sweetness of honey, one is inclined to take delight in it. Edwards brings this insight about knowledge and the senses to his meditation upon Scripture, since "the work of the Spirit of God in regeneration is often in Scripture compared to giving a new sense, giving eyes to see, and ears to hear, unstopping the ears of the deaf, and opening the eyes of them that were born blind, and turning from darkness to light" (*WJE* 2:206). Thus, for Edwards, in regeneration the Spirit brings, adds to, and makes fruitful our other faculties of knowing, without which we cannot properly know God. For if we do not respond to God with delight and worship, it simply indicates that we have not really come to know God. Knowledge of God involves concepts, but it can never be reduced to concepts—it necessarily involves an affective response. Moreover, affections generated by the Spirit overflow into action—the fruit of our response to God in acts of love.[34] After quoting Luke 6:44 that "Every tree is known by his own fruit," Edwards notes that "Christ nowhere says, Ye shall know the tree by its leaves or flowers, or ye shall know men by their talk, or ye shall know them by the good story they tell of their experiences . . . but by their fruits ye shall know them" (*WJE* 2:407). Christian practices of worship and testimony are indispensable. But ultimately, in Edwards's account, it is only by the Spirit that affections are made "gracious," resulting in a life of love of God and neighbor. The Spirit gives the sixth sense to perceive God, and this knowledge of God—which includes an affective response—overflows in a godly life.

For Edwards, this sixth sense becomes a way to speak about the affective human creature becoming caught up in worshipful knowledge of the triune God, through the Spirit's regenerating work. This "new inward perception" is generated by the Spirit, who acts not only *upon* regenerate Christians but also *within* them: "The Spirit of God is given to the true saints to dwell in them, as his proper lasting abode; and to influence their hearts, as a principle of new nature, or as a divine supernatural spring of life and action" (*WJE* 2:205; 2:200). Edwards notes that the New Testament portrays the Holy Spirit as dwelling in them "as his temple, his proper abode, and everlasting dwelling place (I Corinthians 3:15, II Corinthians 6:16, John 14:16-17)." As such, the Spirit is "so united to the faculties of the soul, that he becomes there a principle or spring of new

---

34. For Edwards, "gracious and holy affections," which are produced in believers by the Spirit's power, "have their exercise and fruit in Christian practice." *WJE* 2:383.

nature and life" (*WJE* 2:200). Thus, the Spirit, "dwelling as a vital principle in their souls," brings the regenerate into fellowship with the triune God: "The Spirit of God so dwells in the hearts of the saints, that he there, as seed or spring of life, exerts and communicates himself, in this his sweet and divine nature, making the soul a partaker of God's beauty and Christ's joy, so that the saint has true fellowship with the Father, and with his Son Jesus Christ, in thus having the communion or participation in the Holy Spirit" (*WJE* 2:201). Thus, "participation in the Holy Spirit" provides an entryway to "fellowship" with the Father and the Son. Specifically, using the language of delight, Edwards notes that the Spirit "dwells in the hearts of the saints" in a way that makes them partake of "God's beauty and Christ's joy." The indwelling Spirit enables true religious affections, flowing forth in "worshiping God in prayer, and singing praises" (*WJE* 2:121).

Note that in Edwards's account, all this is completely dependent upon the Spirit, not the "natural" capacities of the person in themselves. The sixth sense, enabling this joyful perception and communion with the triune God, is empowered solely by the Holy Spirit in regeneration. In this way, humans—who are created to find joyful, worshipful delight in God—are being restored by the Spirit, and the sixth sense restores the use of their various capacities toward this end. Yet, this God-empowered regeneration does not bypass bodily human practices. To the contrary, Edwards's account suggests that a thick set of Christian practices (prayer, worship, the Lord's Supper, love of neighbor) is essential to experiencing this joyful fellowship, even though the practices are not the (effective) cause of the fellowship. For example, he speaks of the way in which preaching and the "ordinances" (baptism and the Supper) have "a tendency deeply to affect the hearts of those who attend these means" (*WJE* 2:121). God is free to give surprises outside of these means. But these ordinary "means" of Christian practice are still central. Moreover, for the regenerate, habituated Christian, practice is central. "Christian practice is the sign of signs," the "great evidence, which confirms and crowns all other signs of godliness. There is no one grace of the Spirit of God, but that Christian practice is the most proper evidence of the truth of it" (*WJE* 2:141). Christian practice and habits are the fruit of the Spirit's reviving work, a work that enables an affective perception of God that flows forth in obedient action.

My point here is not to argue for Edwards's specific account of anthropology, or the spiritual sense. In many ways, Edwards's account was largely synthetic of a seventeenth-century Reformed tradition that included a number of variations, and certain aspects of his specific account may have better alternatives in other theological accounts, whether contemporaneous or of a different era.[35] My point is to draw upon the contours of Edwards's account as an example of the ways in which an affective anthropology—with a strong emphasis on the importance of Christian practice—can go hand in hand with a robust Trinitarian account of divine action. Moreover, in using the "spiritual senses" theme, Edwards keeps a focus on *perception* as key to the process of coming to know the triune God. In this Spirit-enabled communion, Christians come to "taste and see" the kingdom. In Edwards's words, "the knowledge which the saints have of God's beauty and glory in this world . . . is a foretaste of heavenly happiness, and an earnest of their future inheritance" (*WJE* 2:133).

As the constructive account of this book unfolds, we will return repeatedly not only to Scripture but also to various representatives of the catholic-Reformed tradition, to enliven our imagination with concrete theological possibilities that tend to elude the vision of many modern Christians. The goal is to move, by the Spirit, toward a renewal of our *perception*—our perception of God's kingdom in Christ—in a way that exposes and calls into question other allegiances. Whether the Supper is celebrated weekly or quarterly or even annually, it is certainly not less than a Christian formative practice—and a Christian practice that is celebrated with certain precognitive judgments that manifest themselves in habits and patterns. These practices are repeated week by week or month by month, and they are both shaped by the Spirit's enlivening work in our lives and entail the means the Spirit uses to reshape our perception of the world. To be a Christian is *more* than embracing a specified set of practices. Edwards signals this in pointing out that preaching and the Supper do not automatically bring about benefits. To be a Christian is to encounter the triune God, and to experience the indwelling Spirit who unites us to the Son, bringing us into our new identity as adopted children of God. But while being a Christian is always more than embracing a set of practices, it is never less. As Edwards suggests, a saving encounter with the triune God necessarily leads to a worshipful embrace of fellowship with God and fortitude in the love of others. The Spirit generates affective perception of the beauty and goodness of God in Christ, such that Christians are drawn back to preaching, the Supper, prayer, and worshipful songs—activities that the Spirit then uses to further conform believers to their true identity in Christ.

This book focuses upon a particular aspect of this renewed affective per-

---

35. For example, William J. Wainwright argues that John Smith (1618–1652), the Cambridge Platonist, holds a more philosophically coherent account of the spiritual senses than Edwards, due at least partly to the influence of John Locke's epistemology upon Edwards. See William J. Wainwright, "Jonathan Edwards and His Puritan Predecessors," in Gavrilyuk and Coakley, *The Spiritual Senses*, 224–40.

ception and knowledge of God in Christ; the Lord's Supper is the "true icon" of the good news of Jesus Christ. In the Supper, we encounter God's word in Christ in a form that we can "taste and see," in a way that presents the "clearest promises" of God for sensory, material creatures like us.[36] In the Supper, believers enact their role in the Trinitarian drama of the gospel, as ones who are nourished by Christ through the power of the Spirit as adopted children of the Father. If this is possible, what would it look like in the context of Reformed convictions about worship? How can the Spirit generate affective knowledge of God and the gospel through a repeated, habituated action like the Lord's Supper? To explore these questions, we examine a historical example.

### The Catholic-Reformed Piety of Holy Fairs

The Reformed tradition is often portrayed as heady, abstract, and dispassionate in worship. Indeed, Brian Gerrish is right that at times during the modern era, Reformed worship has suffered from "an arid intellectualism that turns the worshipping community into a class of glum schoolchildren."[37] Some of this relates to the question of how Word is related to sacrament, a question we will take up in the next chapter. But first, it is crucial for us to consider an important counterexample to this contemporary sense of Reformed worship, to get a sense of some of the affection-oriented worship that had preaching and the Lord's Supper at its heart.

The focus of this example is the "holy fairs," which were important in the Scottish Reformed tradition (in both Scotland and North America) from the 1620s until their decline in light of the Enlightenment critique during the late eighteenth and early nineteenth century.[38] Holy fairs were large four-to-five-day outdoor festivals culminating in the celebration of communion. The week of the festival included communal times of singing, the hearing of preaching, and a day of public fasting. In addition, preparations took place privately "in family worship, secret prayer, self-examination, personal covenanting and

---

36. Calvin, *Institutes* 4.14.5.

37. B. A. Gerrish, *Grace and Gratitude: The Eucharistic Theology of John Calvin* (Eugene, OR: Wipf and Stock, 2002), 83.

38. As Leigh Eric Schmidt notes, aspects of the holy fair continued in America's later revivalism, but it generally lost its distinctive eucharistic focus and its catholic-Reformed theological cast. In parts of Scotland, the phenomena of "holy fairs" continued well into the twentieth century. See Leigh Eric Schmidt, *Holy Fairs: Scotland and the Making of American Revivalism*, 2nd ed. (Grand Rapids: Eerdmans, 2001), 169–212.

meditation."[39] On the day of communion, participants wore their finest clothes and the celebration took place at long tables covered with clean, white linens.[40] Each had a place at Christ's table. Rich and poor, male and female, celebrated together—no one was to receive superior or inferior wine and bread.[41] Psalms and hymns were sung; tears of joy were shed at the table. Some fainted in their excitement; all celebrated.[42] These gatherings deeply engaged the affections and the senses, as they centered on a message of passionate communion with Christ by the Spirit's power. While the festivals themselves were characteristic of the Scottish tradition, there were broadly similar developments among English Puritans and in the Dutch Reformed tradition's *Nadere Reformatie* (further Reformation).[43] While these latter two movements are not often discussed by Reformed theologians, I will note their significance at various points of this book. This initial portrait will focus on how the holy fairs bring together an affective anthropology with a concern for Christian practices in a way that is attentive to the action of the triune God.[44]

The festival—from the preaching, to the focus of the devotional practices, to the mode of celebrating the Supper—was centered upon the triune action of God at the Supper. As historian of the fairs Leigh Eric Schmidt notes, these Scottish Presbyterians affirmed with Calvin, John Knox, and their Scots Confession that Christ was present through the Spirit at the Supper—"a presence that was real, powerful, overwhelming."[45] This was not asserted as a mere abstraction; a set of embodied, habitual practices made this presence of Christ by the Spirit the pinnacle for many of the participants—as historians have observed from examining their spiritual journals.

39. Schmidt, *Holy Fairs*, 71.

40. Schmidt, *Holy Fairs*, 82–83.

41. Schmidt, *Holy Fairs*, 105.

42. For a helpful overview of the ritual actions of the holy fairs, see Schmidt, *Holy Fairs*, chap. 2.

43. For an overview of similar themes in the Dutch Reformed tradition, see Arie de Reuver, *Sweet Communion: Trajectories of Spirituality from the Middle Ages through the Further Reformation* (Grand Rapids: Baker Academic, 2007). For an account that compares the similarities and differences between English Puritan and Reformed movements and the *Nadere Reformatie*, see Joel Beeke, "The Dutch Second Reformation," *Calvin Theological Journal* 28, no. 2 (1993): 298–327. For an illuminating study of the affective eucharistic piety of English Puritan Isaac Ambrose, see Tom Schwanda, *Soul Recreation: The Contemplative-Mystical Piety of Puritanism* (Eugene, OR: Wipf and Stock, 2012), 35–196.

44. There were variations in the holy fairs according to when and where it was practiced, but I give a brief synthetic sketch here to point to key characteristics.

45. Schmidt, *Holy Fairs*, 19.

Preparation for the communion festival was not for a head trip, a dispassionate mental act of remembrance. Rather, in the fasting, meditation upon Scripture, self-examination, and other acts, believers sought to direct their affections to Christ as the host of the feast. With this fasting, in the words of the Westminster Directory, congregations were encouraged to have "total abstinence, not only from all food but also all worldly labour, discourses and thoughts, and from all bodily delights."[46] Yet, the fasting and penitence were not to "make satisfaction to divine justice for the least of sin," as American Presbyterian preacher James McGready (1763–1817) emphasized. Rather, fasting, along with tearful repentance, was to "empty thy stomach" to "make ready to feast with thy Redeemer." He continued that those who were parched and hungry would feast "at Christ's table on the hidden manna" and be "refreshed with the new wine of Canaan."[47]

As communion on Sunday approached, the gathered would prepare with singing, prayer, and listening to more preaching. Warnings were issued about unworthy partaking of the Supper, and adults would need to receive tokens from their church elders to partake at the table. The preaching also spoke about union with Christ. At times, this could utilize the language of theophanies, such as Mount Sinai or the burning bush. McGready framed this in terms of attention and sight in "A Sacramental Meditation": "As Moses did at the burning bush, turn aside and see this great sight, here you may behold all the perfections of God shining with amiable brightness in the face of Jesus Christ."[48] This sanctified "sight," enabled by rebirth by the Spirit, emerges from and deepens the affections of the heart for Christ:

> The real Christian, the new born child of God, loves to see Jesus and behold his glory, and with joy, delight, and wonder, to admire and adore his soul attracting beauty and loveliness; and for this reason—he is the centre of his love, his portion, his inheritance, and the soul and substance of his happiness. Christ, in his esteem, is the fairest among ten thousand and altogether lovely [Song of Sol. 5:10, 16] . . . he is dearer to his soul than life itself, with all its pleasures and comforts; and his greatest happiness on earth, is to *"see Jesus"*—to have sweet communion and fellowship with him, and to feel his

46. Schmidt, *Holy Fairs*, 77.
47. McGready, quoted in Kimberly Bracken Long, *The Eucharistic Theology of the American Holy Fairs* (Louisville: Westminster John Knox, 2011), 78.
48. McGready, quoted in Long, *Eucharistic Theology*, 72.

love shed abroad in his heart; yea, the very heaven after which his soul longs and pants [Ps. 42:1], is to "*see Jesus*"—to see him forever and be like him.[49]

Obviously, this sanctified "sight" is not a mere intellectual apprehension, but one that relates to the deepest of human affections and desires for God. Communion, or "conversation," with Christ at the Supper is intimate for McGready. "The sacrament of the Supper is one of the most affecting institutions of heaven, and one of the nearest approaches to God that can be made on this side of eternity, in which believers are permitted to hold intimate conversation with our blessed Jesus."[50]

One of the most common ways in which preachers connected this anthropology of desire with union with Christ at the Supper was through speaking of the church as the bride of Christ, and the table as a foretaste of the wedding banquet. Drawing upon a long catholic tradition, the Song of Solomon was frequently preached at holy fairs as a poem about Christ's love for the church, as the betrothed lover of Christ. (This was also a widespread practice in the Dutch "further reformation.") Like McGready, Presbyterian preacher Gilbert Tennent (1703–1764) used the language of Song of Solomon to extol Christ as the bridegroom of believers, who "is the perfection of beauty, the chiefest among ten thousand" (see Song of Sol. 5:10).[51] This was used to speak about the "ravishing Beauty and charming Glory of Christ," for "through faith they sit under the Shadow of this blessed Apple Tree, and taste his pleasant Fruits. O! How infinitely amiable is the Person of Christ to the enlightened Understanding!"[52] This reaches its culmination in the sermon immediately before the celebration of communion, sometimes called the "action sermon," where the preacher would seek to "woo" the congregation to the sacrament. Tennent's approach is characteristic when he speaks of Christ the lover who "bears with many Afronts, Delays, Refusals, and yet repeats his Love addresses; which considering his Majesty and our meanness is very admirable."[53] After speaking of how Christ is a desirable husband, Tennent asks, "Will you not then, poor Sinners, give your Consent to be espoused to this beautiful Jesus?"[54]

49. McGready, quoted in Long, *Eucharistic Theology*, 72–73. Scripture references in brackets are added to highlight McGready's allusions.
50. McGready, quoted in Long, *Eucharistic Theology*, 72.
51. Tennent, in Long, *Eucharistic Theology*, 93.
52. Tennent, in Long, *Eucharistic Theology*, 95.
53. Tennent, in Long, *Eucharistic Theology*, 95.
54. Tennent, in Long, *Eucharistic Theology*, 93.

Not surprisingly, when communicants spoke about their experience at the Supper, "time and again the most joyous and fulfilling experiences that these evangelicals had . . . were expressed in the diction of the Song of Songs."[55] This shows the way in which, through meditation upon Scripture and hearing the preaching focusing upon the Song of Solomon, this scriptural book provided a narrative for understanding their experience of union with Christ at the Supper. Reflecting on the experience, one communicant invokes Song of Solomon 5:16, "His mouth is most sweet yea He is altogether lovely," adding "my heart was greatly inflam'd with love to him and made to rejoice & delight in him." Another: "When I came to the Lords Table, he was pleased to give me much of his gracious presence; & I may say, he took me into his banqueting house, and his banner over me was love" (cf. Song of Sol. 2:4). This is far from dispassionate "biblical exegesis," but the result of internalizing and dwelling upon this scriptural motif so that the table has become a taste of the "marriage feast" of their beloved husband, Christ.[56]

*Perceived* in this way, the call to feast at Christ's table taps into deep affections—as one communicant expressed of this call: "I could scarce walk, I was swallowed up in love & Enflamed affection for the Redeemer."[57] One communicant wrote about her struggles following the death of her husband and "my heavy Charge of seven fatherless Children."[58] At the Saturday night service before communion, she had a "kind visit of heaven," and again scriptural passages (including Song of Solomon) provided the grammar for framing her experience:

> I had Cause to say, It is the voice of my Beloved, Behold he commeth—Skipping over the Mountains & leaping over the Hills: and I believe he never leapt over higher hills. I was so much ravished with his Love, that I scarce knew where I was, Mean while there was a Scripture brought to my mind with irresistible power, 1 Sam. 1.15. The woman went away & did eat & was no more sad. By free Grace I found a blessed change on my frame, and my Soul was Swallowed in the Love of God. On the morrow I went to the Table of the Lord, & found it a good day.[59]

55. Schmidt, *Holy Fairs*, 162.
56. Schmidt, *Holy Fairs*, 162.
57. Schmidt, *Holy Fairs*, 162.
58. Journal of Elizabeth Blakader, in Schmidt, *Holy Fairs*, 48.
59. Journal of Elizabeth Blakader, in Schmidt, *Holy Fairs*, 48.

There is no doubt that not only for the preachers but also for participants such as these, an anthropology of "humans as lovers" combined with a theology of union with Christ involved a dramatic, powerful sense of Christ's presence at the table. Immersed in a tapestry of scriptural passages that spoke to this reality, the *perception* of participants was attentive to the triune God's action through Word and sacrament.

The holy fairs were a feast for the senses, but in them the sense-oriented activities were directed toward repentance, nourishment in Christ, and celebration of the church's identity as the bride of Christ. Even the setting of the celebration at great, long tables was designed to give it "some faint resemblance" to "the heavenly city of Jerusalem," in the words of McGready. For "when our Lord's table is spread in the wilderness, and he holds communion with his saints, I think it is rational and scriptural to suppose that the angels are hovering over the table and the assembly, rejoicing with Christ over the dear bought purchase of his blood, and waiting to bear joyful tidings to the heavenly mansions."[60]

The frequent singing of psalms and hymns at the holy fairs was aimed in this affective direction as well. Scottish Presbyterian John Willison, in a popular manual, instructs that singing "helps excite and accentuate the graces; it is the breath or flame of love or joy; it is the eternal work of heaven, the music of saints and angels there." This singing was intended to "raise and elevate the heart."[61] This vision of hymnology emerged from a deeply Reformed view of the Lord's Supper as a covenantal meal.[62] Willison himself composed over one hundred sacramental hymns.[63]

The rituals, preaching, visual displays, and even preparation of the elements at holy fairs brought together instincts about humans as affectionate, embodied, habituated creatures with a desire to meditate upon God's word in Scripture, and to be nourished by Christ through the Spirit at the table.[64] In all these ways the holy fairs defied the common stereotypes—among not only laypeople but also scholars—about the nature of Reformed worship, and Reformed theology and practice of the Lord's Supper in particular. As Schmidt

---

60. McGready, in Schmidt, *Holy Fairs*, 101.

61. Willison, quoted in Schmidt, *Holy Fairs*, 97.

62. See Hughes Oliphant Old, *Themes and Variations for a Christian Doxology: Some Thoughts on the Theology of Worship* (Grand Rapids: Eerdmans, 1992), 122–28.

63. See Schmidt, *Holy Fairs*, 97.

64. Manuals widely used for communion, such as John Willison's, gave instructions for the preparation of the bread and wine that involved grinding and squeezing as signs of Christ's passion, and other aspects of preparation emphasizing the nourishment and refreshment of the Lord's Supper. (See Schmidt, *Holy Fairs*, 90.)

notes, "The history of these Reformed Protestant festivals serves as an important corrective to those scholars within religious studies who continue to use Protestantism as their antiritualistic other. From Mary Douglas and Jonathan Z. Smith to Catherine Bell and Arnold Eisen, Protestantism stands as the arch devaluator of ritual, the great source of a modern bias against ceremony and practice."[65] Schmidt provides several quotes from Catherine Bell to show how misguided this characterization is in light of the holy fairs. For Presbyterianism, Bell writes, rituals become "a matter of outward, empty forms, disconnected from personal intention and sincerity." For "Presbyterianism rejects the notion of any divine presence in the sacraments."[66] It would be hard to think of a description that is more distant from the actual theology and practice of the holy fairs.

I do not deny that much recent Reformed worship—and practice of the Supper—has been cognitivist rather than properly affective, more interested in abstract ideas than in the way God may work through bodily, material means. But the common move of projecting this present experience back onto the Reformation and post-Reformation period is extremely misguided. We misdiagnose the cause of our modern malady if we place it on Reformation and post-Reformation thought and practice.

## Diagnosing the Present:
## An Anemic *Perception* of the Gospel and the Supper

For many readers in the contemporary West, this portrait of holy fairs will seem strangely foreign—not only because of various differences in cultural particularities, but also because of the strong connections made between the gospel and the Lord's Supper, as well as the affective, bodily emphasis upon the powerful presence of Christ at the Supper by the Spirit. Many contemporary Christians in the broadly evangelical tradition—whether connected with a denomination or not—are heirs to nineteenth- and twentieth-century forms of revivalism that were subsequent to the Reformed movements described above. Celebrating the Lord's Supper was no longer the pinnacle of Christian worship and Christian identity. At times, revivalism became primarily concerned with how to generate the highest numbers of the "converted," and focused on certain affective states as an end in themselves.

65. Schmidt, *Holy Fairs*, xxvi.
66. Catherine Bell, *Ritual: Perspectives and Dimensions*, rev. ed. (Oxford: Oxford University Press, 2009), 188–89.

An important aspect of this transition took place as the eucharistic theology animating the holy fairs went into decline in the late eighteenth and
early nineteenth century. In general, Schmidt records that "the Enlightenment
transformed much of Scottish life and thought." Specifically, "Enlightenment
rationalism would also threaten traditional Reformed views of the Eucharist;
Christ's real presence in the sacrament, for example, would be increasingly
challenged as memorialistic doctrines or even more skeptical ones gained as-
cendancy."[67] As Robert Burns's poem of 1785 (popular in Scotland, Ireland, and
America), "The Holy Fair," satirically expressed, the festivity was inherently
suspect, as shown by the presentation of three women (Fun, Superstition,
and Hypocrisy) in attendance. Their religion was tied to "Auld [old] Orthodoxy" and "Poor gapin, glowrin Superstition," which for Burns was "past redemption."[68] Not surprisingly, observes Schmidt, "not only the doctrines of
the evangelical Presbyterians, but also their rituals were challenged by the
incoming tide of the Enlightenment. To those who shared in this cultural
reorientation, few aspects of the popular religious culture would look more
glaringly unenlightened than the festal communions."[69] An influential source
for this was a widely reproduced anonymous letter, written by "Blacksmith,"
addressed to Scottish ministers, which critiqued the "low superstition" of "our
worship," and sought to root out its "indescencies and follies."[70]

Blacksmith argued for reforms in worship catered to "the rational people" rather than "the common people"; he condemned enthusiastic forms of
prayer, and singing and preaching that led "the mob to the highest pitch of
enthusiasm."[71] In particular, for reformers of the festival like Blacksmith, its
deep affective elements—"the weeping, fainting, groaning, trembling, and rejoicing of the newly converted and the freshly revived"—were "incompatible"
with "middle-class respectability, decorum, and self-control."[72] In addition, the
practice of holy fairs, with its sequence of fasting and preparation for several
days, was said to "contract an idle disposition of mind" and "get into a *bad habit
of* body." Why? "Our idle days . . . do hurt true religion: the people lose many
laboring days by them, and the country is deprived of the fruit of their indus-
try."[73] True religion for Blacksmith was not only rational and nonemotional,

---

67. Schmidt, *Holy Fairs*, 171.
68. Quoted in Schmidt, *Holy Fairs*, 172.
69. Schmidt, *Holy Fairs*, 171.
70. Schmidt, *Holy Fairs*, 180.
71. Schmidt, *Holy Fairs*, 179–81.
72. The words of Schmidt, *Holy Fairs*, 199.
73. Quoted in Schmidt, *Holy Fairs*, 193.

but also oriented toward cultivating the habits of economic productivity. The followers of this reforming trend also became embarrassed at the "indelicacy" and "licentiousness" of the imagery in the Song of Solomon, and hymnists and preachers moved away from utilizing the spiritual marriage imagery and toward what Schmidt calls "a desexualized piety."[74] The influence of Blacksmith and others led to proposals to abandon the seasonal communion festivals, at times claiming that communion should be practiced at more regular intervals (quarterly) or more frequently. Eventually, these reforms "put an end to sacramental festivity."[75] Yet, as Schmidt notes, "what some of them—the Blacksmith or members of the Clydesdale Synod, for example—had been after all along was not so much more frequent communions as less festal ones. They wanted circumscribed, controlled, convenient sacraments, essentially parochial events instead of regional festivals."[76]

The decline of these sacramental festivals in America corresponded with the rise of a new, modern form of revivalism, characterized by the "new measures" of Charles Finney. Although Finney used the practice of four-day festivals as a rationale for his protracted revival meetings, the new revivalism "was a poor conserver of tradition." "With new rituals and often with new theological emphases, nineteenth-century revivalism shared little in the Calvinism and sacramentalism that had informed the festal communions."[77] Revivalism was no longer focused on union with Christ and the Lord's Supper. It was focused on using "new measures" to produce results in generating conversions, as fit with Finney's hyper-Arminian, semi-Pelagian theology.[78] Finney was also pragmatic in a way that would become characteristic of American revivalist Christianity—always on the search for something new. As Finney said, "The object of our measures is to gain attention, and you must have something new. As sure as the effect of a measure becomes stereotyped, it ceases to gain attention, and you must try something new."[79] For Finney, the search for "new measures" that produce results was an alternative to what earlier preachers had

---

74. Schmidt, *Holy Fairs*, 198.

75. Schmidt, *Holy Fairs*, 190.

76. Schmidt, *Holy Fairs*, 191.

77. Schmidt, *Holy Fairs*, 207.

78. Contemporary Arminian scholars, such as Roger Olson, do not see Finney as a true Arminian, but much more of a Pelagian. Finney accepted "a vulgarized version of Arminianism that is closer to Semi-Pelagianism." Roger E. Olson, *Arminian Theology: Myths and Realities* (Downers Grove: IVP Academic, 2009), 27.

79. Charles G. Finney, *Lectures on Revivals of Religion*, Lecture 11 (New York: Revell, 1868), 173.

seen as a need to wait on the Spirit's timing in bringing conversions.[80] Rather than wait on "God's timing," one needed to implement "new measures" to put pressure on sinners to convert. The most famous example of these measures (which became the norm for revivalism) was the "anxious bench"—a place, usually in the front of the assembly, "to which Finney called people to prayer or to be admonished about the condition of their souls." This "measure" was designed to put pressure on those who might be near conversion to make their decision. As Mark Noll notes, "The anxious bench led to the modern evangelistic practice of coming to the front at the end of a religious service to indicate a desire for salvation."[81] The anxious bench was a formative, habitual practice that put the human will—and the human ability to manipulate it—at the center of the functional theology of salvation.

At this moment of great cultural transition, John Williamson Nevin of Mercersburg Seminary provided a theological critique of the new measures, and also sought to recover a robust "Calvinist" sacramental theology. Nevin viewed the anxious bench as "spiritually dangerous"; in the way it was often being used, it was "more suited to ruin souls than to bring them to heaven."[82] Rather than the person focusing on God and a genuine call to repentance, the question becomes "will he go to the anxious bench, which is something different altogether." The problem with the anxious bench is that it involves having one's "attention diverted" toward the human action of going to the bench, and away from "the High and Holy One with whom he is called to make his peace."[83] Stated differently, according to Nevin, the anxious bench inserts participants into a drama based on their own heroic will rather than on the saving action of the triune God. In place of this practice, in *The Anxious Bench*, Nevin commended the renewal of catechetical instruction and the return to an emphasis upon Word and sacrament as means of grace and ways to counterbalance the destructive direction of the revivalism of the new measures.[84]

For our purposes, neither Calvin's Geneva nor the era of the holy fairs should be approached as a "golden age" to be slavishly imitated and repristi-

---

80. See Mark A. Noll, *A History of Christianity in the United States and Canada* (Grand Rapids: Eerdmans, 1992), 176.

81. Noll, *History of Christianity*, 176.

82. John Williamson Nevin, *The Anxious Bench*, in *Reformed and Catholic: Selected Theological Writings of John Williamson Nevin*, ed. Charles Bricker and George Bricker (Eugene, OR: Pickwick, 1978), 59.

83. Nevin, *The Anxious Bench*, 60.

84. See Hans Schwarz, *Theology in a Global Context: The Last Two Hundred Years* (Grand Rapids: Eerdmans, 2005), 63–64.

nated. Calvin's eucharistic vision was not fully implemented in Geneva, and the liturgical forms he provided were generally lackluster in comparison to his biblical and doctrinal vision of the Supper.[85] With the holy fairs, the exalted place of partaking the Supper was generally set against a backdrop of great fear of unworthy partaking; moreover, as regional, seasonal gatherings, the holy fairs did not celebrate the Supper with frequency and in the congregational context that most naturally fits the Supper as nourishment for the covenant community. Nevertheless, the holy fairs are an illuminating historical example of the way a Reformed eucharistic theology with broadly catholic points of emphasis had considerable vitality in ways that counter common recent generalizations: that Reformed eucharistic theology was intellectualistic and rationalistic; that it was inherently blind to the power of ritual and habit; that in denying transubstantiation and gnesio-Lutheran sacramental doctrines, it functionally denied the presence of Christ at the Supper for the communicants. The fact that the holy fairs persisted for over two hundred years is a direct counterexample to these claims.

Yet, theologians seeking a path toward sacramental renewal have very rarely noted the significance of this movement. Recent sacramental proposals in the evangelical and Reformed traditions tend to jump back to Calvin and the Reformers, perhaps stopping along the way to examine Nevin and the Mercersburg movement.[86] However, the holy fairs movement (along with similar movements in English Puritan and Dutch *Nadere Reformatie* contexts) is deeply instructive and provides a window into post-Reformation Reformed thought and practice. The movement itself shows how an affective anthropology can go hand in hand with a strong emphasis upon God's Word and the triune action of God in uniting believers to Jesus Christ. It shows that the Reformed tradition, which is concerned with fidelity to Scripture, need not be "intellectualistic," but can participate in habitual, formative practices that both deepen and express a delight in God's Word and ways. It shows that an emphasis upon transformed, affective perception—made possible by the

---

85. See Sue Rozeboom, "The Provenance of John Calvin's Emphasis on the Role of the Holy Spirit regarding the Sacrament of the Lord's Supper" (diss., University of Notre Dame, 2010), 342–71.

86. For example, see George Hunsinger, *The Eucharist and Ecumenism: Let Us Keep the Feast* (Cambridge: Cambridge University Press, 2008); Martha L. Moore-Keish, *Do This in Remembrance of Me: A Ritual Approach to Reformed Eucharistic Theology* (Grand Rapids: Eerdmans, 2008); Leonard Vander Zee, *Christ, Baptism and the Lord's Supper: Recovering the Sacraments for Evangelical Worship* (Downers Grove: InterVarsity, 2004); and Brad Littlejohn, *The Mercersburg Theology and the Quest for Reformed Catholicity* (Eugene, OR: Pickwick, 2009).

Spirit—is not only a broadly catholic theme but also one that can thrive in the Reformed tradition.

The reasons for the decline of these fairs are instructive as well. As noted above, in the nineteenth century two unhappy alternatives emerged for Reformed Christians in the West: an intellectualistic form of memorialism and a human-centered revivalism. Both diverge from the affective perception of the gospel explored in this chapter. Human beings were created to delight in God and his Word. The triune God has fellowship through the means of Word and sacrament with his people, and nourishes a hungry people with Christ by the Spirit. In this gospel vision, the Spirit enables a sixth sense, empowering humanity with a God-exalting delight and knowledge of God in Christ, overflowing in concrete, embodied acts of love. Thus, the Spirit shapes not only the thinking of believers, but also their habits and their loving through the Word in practices of prayer, memorization of Scripture, and worship. Through Word and Spirit, the affections of believers are redirected toward Christ, their beloved, and the triune God shapes these disciples to bear witness to Christ and his reign through love of God and neighbor. In part 2 we will examine the doctrinal contours of this theological vision, a vision of Christ made known to us in the breaking of the bread.

# PART 2

A Catholic and Reformed Theology of the Supper

Part 1 has shown how the wager of this book is rooted in a dynamic theological and experiential drama: the drama of the triune God uniting his people to Christ and one another by the Spirit through his instruments of Word and sacrament. Specifically, through the Supper, the Father's adopted children delight in a fore-taste of heavenly fellowship with Christ, their spouse. We have not started with traditional confessional convictions in part 1, but with a broader set of claims related to the action of the triune God, an affective anthropology, and the deep connections between one's functional theology of salvation and the Supper.

In part 2 I continue making the case for the book's wager, moving to a treatment of more traditional questions related to the Supper, in particular: Is the Supper a means, or "instrument," of grace? How should we speak about the presence of Christ at the Supper? What are we to think of the considerable ecclesial divisions connected to theologies of the Supper?

In chapter 3 I articulate an account of the Lord's Supper that is confessionally Reformed, and yet seeks to inhabit a larger catholic tradition. Readers of various ecclesial backgrounds will find themselves agreeing with some points and disagreeing with others. My intent is to frame these Reformed convictions in a clear yet generous way that seeks to be ecumenical in a bottom-up rather than top-down manner. I suspect that many nondenominational, evangelical, and mainline Protestants will be able to affirm its basic structure, even as there are points of ongoing difference. In addition, this chapter makes the case that the Reformed confessional tradition can embody and extend the vision for the Supper that this book puts forth in part 1. The Reformed tradition has not always done this. At times it has been stoic rather than affective, and at other times it has preferred a mental act of remembrance at the Supper to an embodied encounter with Christ and his people at the table.

These reflections are extended in chapter 4, raising an important issue, even if it is more abstract than other sections of the book: Can a Reformed sacramental theology embrace the ontological reality of God's action through the sacraments? Is it just talk, or does the triune God really act at the Supper? This chapter responds to recent theologians who have argued that a Reformed sacramental vision cannot coherently uphold the reality of divine action. It ends with a constructive vision, extending beyond the bare claims of the Reformed confessions to utilize John Calvin's theology as a supplement in answering these charges. Indeed, this brings us back to a vision reflected in part 1, extended into broad ontological terms: that as we come to recognize the "desolation" of life "in ourselves," we hunger to feed upon God's Word, feeding upon Christ—his promises, his consolation, his commands. Since finding our nourishment in God's Word is central to our existence as Christians, we not only need to hear God's Word proclaimed but also need to touch and taste it in the sacraments as the "clearest promises" of God. The Lord's Supper, in particular, is a "true icon" of the gospel—of union with Christ by the Spirit, and the gifts of forgiveness and new life received in this union. Through the Supper, our Lord provides nourishment for our hunger in directing us to God's word in Scripture, which makes known to us Jesus Christ, the eternal Word.

CHAPTER 3

∾

# Reformed Doctrine and the Promise of the Supper

The Supper is a sign and action of oneness with Christ and oneness in Christ's body, the church. But the visible church is sadly divided. At times Christians cooperate with persons of other communions, despite the ongoing ecclesial separations. Yet at other times Christians demonize other Christians, bearing false witness to their theology and practice, generating an enmity that leaves the world with a sour taste about "those combative Christians."

It would be tempting to throw up our hands, give up on the task of clarifying Christian doctrine, and try to take solace in the slogan "doctrine divides, mission unites." But as we saw in part 1, all Christians have a functional theology—functional theologies are unavoidable. If we are to be nourished in God's Word, we cannot avoid the fact that it makes claims on our lives and communities, and that these claims extend even to the "divisive" area of sacramental theology. Perhaps the central problem is not with doctrine, or even with particular doctrinal traditions as aids to the interpretation of Scripture, but with the way we inhabit these traditions.

This chapter seeks to inhabit the Reformed confessional tradition in a broadly catholic way. First, I explore the possible "ecumenical reach" of the Reformed confessional tradition. Then, I outline my approach to the legitimate concerns for living into the God-given oneness of the church in an age of ecclesial division. Finally, I provide a confessional sketch of the Reformed tradition on the Supper in a way that connects to the Trinitarian vision and affective anthropology of part 1.

## The Lord's Supper in the Reformed Tradition: Considering Its Ecumenical Reach

Does a Reformed confessional account of the Lord's Supper necessarily exclude the concerns of Christians who are not Reformed? I do not think so. Indeed, in many ways the Reformed confessional tradition can mediate between the eucharistic theology of various ecclesial and theological traditions. Many Christians who do not identify as Reformed will still be able to adopt substantial parts, if not the whole, of the catholic-Reformed proposal in this book.

In their Reformation context, many of the Reformed confessions sought to hold together the concerns of various competing Protestant sacramental traditions. For example, as Lyle Bierma has argued, the Heidelberg Catechism was formulated in the relatively diverse Palantine region to be able to be affirmed by Philippist Lutherans as well as "Calvinist" and Zwinglian Reformed Christians.[1] In a similar way, Calvin himself, as a second-generation codifier of the Reformed tradition, did not seek to present a new, "original" doctrine of the sacraments. For the most part, he consolidated and synthesized from first- and second-generation Reformers to develop a sacramental theology that was faithful to Scripture and Reformation insights yet was agreeable to the widest possible range of Protestants. Calvin sought to find sacramental unity both with Lutherans and with Zwinglians. Thus, in seeking commonality with the Lutheran tradition, Calvin subscribed to Melanchthon's revised Augsburg Confession (1540), which states that "the body and blood of Christ are truly exhibited with the bread and wine."[2] Yet, on the other hand, Calvin was willing to make considerable compromise in his preferred language about the Lord's Supper in order to sign the Agreement of Zurich with Bullinger (the *Consensus Tigurinus*).[3] In both cases, Calvin sought to harmonize the language of differing Protestant traditions with his own.

1. Lyle D. Bierma et al., *An Introduction to the Heidelberg Catechism: Sources, History, and Theology* (Grand Rapids: Baker Academic, 2005), 78–80.

2. See Timothy George, "John Calvin and the Agreement of Zurich (1549)," in *John Calvin and the Church: A Prism of Reform*, ed. Timothy George (Louisville: Westminster John Knox, 1990), 44–45. Calvin not only subscribes to this formulation, but he also repeatedly uses the term *exhibere*, meaning "to exhibit," "to present," or "to offer," in his various writings on the Lord's Supper. The term itself has a conciliatory sense, as it was used by Melanchthon and Bucer in the Wittenberg Concord in 1536. See Sue A. Rozeboom, "Calvin's Doctrine of the Lord's Supper and Its Early Reception," in *Calvin's Theology and Its Reception: Disputes, Developments, and New Possibilities*, ed. J. Todd Billings and I. John Hesselink (Louisville: Westminster John Knox, 2012), 152.

3. See J. Todd Billings, *Calvin, Participation, and the Gift: The Activity of Believers in Union with Christ* (Oxford: Oxford University Press, 2008), 96–100.

Certainly, Calvin's eucharistic thought has an identifiable character and train of development. We can affirm with Thomas Davis that Calvin moved "from denying the Eucharist as an instrument of grace to affirming it as such, [while developing] a notion of substantial partaking of the true body and blood of Christ over his career."[4] On the other hand, Wim Janse shows how identifiably Lutheran, Bucerian, and Zwinglian strands of Calvin's theology persist in his "mature" eucharistic thought.[5] This occurred because, in dialogue with various interlocutors and seeking unity among Protestants, Calvin incorporated insights from competing schools of sacramental thought.[6] In a similar way, the Reformed confessions arose from numerous influences, including the preferred theological language of a range of Reformers.

Yet, in important ways, Calvin was unsuccessful in forging the unity that he sought. Calvin's compromise with Bullinger fueled criticism from Lutherans that Calvin was just a Zwinglian after all. And Calvin's commonality with Melanchthonian Lutheranism did not lead to significant sacramental unity with Lutherans in his lifetime.

In the history of reception, however, Calvin's sacramental theology has shown more promise. In cases where limited Protestant ecumenical agreement has taken place, his theology has often had a mediating role—opening the possibility to newly formulated statements that differ from Calvin but are nevertheless indebted to his sacramental theology. For a modern example, consider the declaration emerging from Lutheran, Reformed, and Union churches in Germany in the face of the threat of National Socialism in 1937. Michael Welker summarizes key points of this common declaration, including that Jesus Christ is the giver and the gift in the Supper, communicating himself to those with faith, and that the Lord's Supper is "a communal meal, a meal that grounds community."[7] Negatively, as a result of the declaration, "two misplaced concentrations have been increasingly edged out of the picture"—a "concentration on 'the elements' in themselves," and a "concentration on an abstract 'ubiquity' of Christ."[8] For those familiar with Calvin's sacramental

---

4. Thomas J. Davis, *The Clearest Promises of God: The Development of Calvin's Eucharistic Teaching* (New York: AMS Press, 1995), 7–8.

5. Wim Janse, "Calvin's Eucharistic Theology: Three Dogmatic-Historical Observations," in *Calvinus sacrarum literarum interpres: Papers of the International Congress on Calvin Research*, ed. Herman J. Selderhuis (Göttingen: Vandenhoeck & Ruprecht, 2008), 60–61.

6. Janse, "Calvin's Eucharistic Theology," 51–67.

7. Michael Welker, *What Happens in Holy Communion?*, trans. John F. Hoffmeyer (Grand Rapids: Eerdmans, 2000), 92, 99.

8. Welker, *What Happens in Holy Communion?*, 100.

theology, it is easy to see reflections of his thought in ecumenical declarations like this one—a declaration that was instrumental in bringing Reformed, Lutheran, and a limited range of other Protestants into full communion in the Evangelical Church in Germany.[9]

Moreover, for centuries, many outside the bounds of self-identified "Reformed" circles could affirm key parts, if not all the key claims, in the Reformed confessions. Anglicans who value their heritage in the Reformation are likely to find significant commonality here, particularly if they draw upon the thought of Thomas Cranmer (1489–1556) and the Thirty-Nine Articles (1801) that reflect—to a significant degree—a Genevan strand of the Reformed confessions.[10] Lutherans are likely to find many commonalities and some differences, though they may find seeds for Lutheran-Reformed rapprochement in the Geneva-leaning Reformed confessions, as the example from the Evangelical Church in Germany above shows.

Many other traditions of Christians will find commonalities here as well. Baptists seeking to enrich their theology of the Supper are likely to draw upon Calvinists like Charles Spurgeon, and Pentecostal theologians often gravitate toward the Reformed tradition on the Supper.[11] Moreover, it is no accident that recent proposals for the renewal of sacramental theology among evangelical Protestants have often championed the Reformed confessional tradition, and Calvin in particular.[12] The importance that the Reformed tradition places

9. Welker's account has significant parallels with Gerrish's portrait of Calvin's eucharistic theology in the use of the language of gift, the role of faith and the community, as well as the critique of a preoccupation with the elements themselves and a doctrine of the ubiquity of Christ's body. See B. A. Gerrish, *Grace and Gratitude: The Eucharistic Theology of John Calvin* (Eugene, OR: Wipf and Stock, 2002), especially chap. 5.

10. On the connection and degree of commonality between Calvin's eucharistic theology and that of Cranmer, see B. A. Gerrish, *Thinking with the Church: Essays in Historical Theology* (Grand Rapids: Eerdmans, 2010), 249–54. On the Thirty-Nine Articles, Gerrish considers them "cautiously Calvinistic" on the Lord's Supper, yet the Anglican catechism of 1662 is clearly reflective of Calvin's theology of the Supper, "faithfully Calvinistic" in Gerrish's view. See Brian A. Gerrish, *Old Protestantism and the New* (Edinburgh: T. & T. Clark, 2000), 126.

11. For documentation of this point for a number of key Pentecostal theologians, see Chris E. W. Green, *Toward a Pentecostal Theology of the Lord's Supper: Foretasting the Kingdom* (Cleveland, TN: CPT Press, 2012), 17–18, 22, 26–27, 38–42, 62, 298. For examples of Baptist retrievals of Spurgeon's theology of the Supper, see Tim Grass and Ian Randall, "C. H. Spurgeon on the Sacraments," in *Baptist Sacramentalism*, ed. Anthony R. Cross and Philip E. Thompson (Carlisle, UK: Paternoster, 2003), 55–75; Peter J. Morden, "The Lord's Supper and the Spirituality of C. H. Spurgeon," in *Baptist Sacramentalism 2*, ed. Anthony R. Cross and Philip E. Thompson (Eugene, OR: Wipf and Stock, 2008) 175–96.

12. See Leonard Vander Zee, *Christ, Baptism and the Lord's Supper: Recovering the Sac-*

upon the sacraments as a sign of God's promise to be received in faith is particularly significant for evangelicals. Many nonconfessional Christians in global evangelicalism will be unlikely to accept a eucharistic theology that is seen as downplaying the significance of faith or the preaching of the gospel. Yet, the Reformed confessions retain this emphasis, along with a powerful sense of the triune God working through the Supper as the Spirit's instrument. For many, something like a catholic-Reformed sacramental theology may be one of the few viable paths for moving toward a sense of Christ's presence at the Supper through the Spirit. As we have noted about the holy fairs and the *Nadere Reformatie* in the last chapter, this emphasis upon Christ's powerful presence by the Spirit at the Supper can go along with a theology and practice that have much in common with global evangelicalism: a high sense of Scripture's authority and the call to repentance and faith, combined with an embodied, affective, Spirit-based sense of worship and communion with God. A historical example of how these features can be manifested in a nonconfessional form is the Stone/Campbell (Disciples of Christ) movement. Historically, both conservative and mainline strands of the Stone/Campbell movement largely reflect the eucharistic theology of Calvin and the Reformed confessions, even though it is a nonconfessional movement.[13] In addition, many other nonconfessional Protestant movements will find much in a Reformed confessional account that reflects their concerns, even as it reveals areas of difference.

### Exchange of Gifts: An Ecumenical Vision

My doctrinal project in this book is ultimately an ecumenical one—to celebrate and, in modest ways, move toward greater Christian unity, as Christ prays for the church that they may all be one, as he and the Father are one (John 17:21). This oneness is a theological reality based in Christ and our union with him, and Christians are called to seek to live into this unity more and more.

However, my approach is distinct from many forms of modern ecumenism. With Cardinal Avery Dulles, I assume that differences in theological traditions need not be insular points of separation, but can provide creative

---

*raments for Evangelical Worship* (Downers Grove: InterVarsity, 2004); John Jefferson Davis, *Worship and the Reality of God: An Evangelical Theology of Real Presence* (Downers Grove: IVP Academic, 2010).

13. See Timothy Hessel-Robinson, "Calvin's Doctrine of the Lord's Supper: Modern Reception and Contemporary Possibilities," in Billings and Hesselink, *Calvin's Theology and Its Reception*, 173-78.

points of illumination.[14] In this new mode of ecumenism, the central goal is not to compromise doctrinal distinctives in order to develop broad "consensus statements." Instead, Dulles writes, "Unlike some recent models of dialogue, ecumenism of this style leaves the participants free to draw on their own normative sources and does not constrain them to bracket or minimize what is specific to themselves. Far from being embarrassed by their own distinctive doctrines and practices, each partner should feel privileged to be able to contribute something positive that the others still lack."

So, "with this mentality, Catholics would want to hear from the churches of the Reformation the reasons they have for speaking as they do of Christ alone, Scripture alone, and faith alone, while Catholics tend to speak of Christ and the Church, Scripture and tradition, grace and cooperation, faith and works." While ecumenical convergence statements such as *Baptism, Eucharist, and Ministry* are significant, they are starting points rather than ending points for ecumenical dialogue. When they are taken as an ending point, all theological traditions are reduced and diminished in their contribution. As a starting point, though, they move beyond historic caricatures and anathemas to open the dialogue to discover a genuine conversation. As John Paul II argued, ecumenical dialogue should be seen as an "exchange of gifts" that can "complement each other."[15] This is not done by smashing and reshaping each distinct gift to make all gifts look the same; rather, the gifts of each tradition remain different anyway, even after convergence statements. The exchange of gifts is accomplished by using theological and ecclesial distinctives for catholic and ecumenical ends.

It may be helpful to clarify the ecumenical approach of my project by contrasting it with a significant recent work by George Hunsinger, *The Eucharist and Ecumenism: Let Us Keep the Feast*. While Hunsinger, a Presbyterian, says that "every tradition in the church has something valuable to contribute," his book is organized around an attempt to develop consensus around historically thorny issues such as "real presence," eucharistic sacrifice, and the place of the episcopal office in the orders of ministry.[16] While he draws from certain aspects of the Reformed confessions and Reformers such as Calvin and Vermigli, he does so in a way that prioritizes these contemporary ecumenical

14. Avery Dulles, "Saving Ecumenism from Itself," *First Things*, no. 178 (December 2007): 23–27.

15. John Paul II, *Ut Unum Sint: On Commitment to Ecumenism*, quoted in Dulles, "Saving Ecumenism from Itself," 26.

16. George Hunsinger, *The Eucharist and Ecumenism: Let Us Keep the Feast* (Cambridge: Cambridge University Press, 2008), 2.

categories. Thus, he develops a theology of "transelementation" by which the Reformed should confess "real presence"; they should "affirm, without equivocation, that the consecrated bread has become the body of Christ and the consecrated cup the blood of Christ."[17] He also insists that Reformed churches move away from their historic understanding and practice of the office of elder, and accept the office of the bishop.[18] Of course, he calls for concessions and compromise from Roman Catholic and Orthodox communions as well, which would require the overcoming of very significant obstacles.[19]

Hunsinger's book is commendable as a bold thought experiment, a creative attempt to revisit the possibility of consensus in a way reflective of much mid-twentieth-century ecumenism. He seeks to find a solution to make shared communion possible—so that the sacrament of Christian unity might not be a painful sacrament of division. (Official Roman Catholic teaching does not permit its clergy to administer communion to Protestant Christians, with extremely rare exceptions;[20] among Protestants, the teaching varies, but many Protestants welcome all who are baptized or who confess faith in Christ to the table. Orthodox Christians do not open Holy Communion to Protestants or Roman Catholics, though there are provisions for Roman Catholics to welcome Orthodox to the Mass.)[21] Hunsinger's attempt to move toward a shared table—and shared ecclesial fellowship—among Roman Catholic and certain traditions of Protestant Christians is a contribution in its own right. However, as a general approach to ecumenical discussion on the Eucharist, the approach raises serious problems. By framing the discussion as he has, the gifts of his own tradition are buried. Unlike Hunsinger, the Reformed tradition

17. Hunsinger, *Eucharist and Ecumenism*, 315.

18. Hunsinger, *Eucharist and Ecumenism*, 325.

19. For more on the significant changes that Hunsinger's approach would require of Roman Catholic and Orthodox communions, see Will Cohen, "The Thing of It: An Orthodox Response to Hunsinger's Not-So-High Sacramental Theology," *Pro Ecclesia* 19, no. 3 (2010): 247–55, and Paul D. Molnar, review of *Eucharist and Ecumenism*, by George Hunsinger, *Scottish Journal of Theology* 65, no. 1 (2012): 121–25.

20. There are strict guidelines for these exceptions in canon law: "If the danger of death is present or if, in the judgment of the diocesan bishop or conference of bishops, some other grave necessity urges it, Catholic ministers administer these same sacraments licitly also to other Christians not having full communion with the Catholic Church, who cannot approach a minister of their own community and who seek such on their own accord, provided that they manifest Catholic faith in respect to these sacraments and are properly disposed." Code of Canon Law 844.4, Vatican web site, http://www.vatican.va/archive/ENG1104/_P2T.HTM.

21. On the Orthodox position of closed communion, Hunsinger has a very helpful overview of the literature. See *Eucharist and Ecumenism*, 226–28.

sought to reframe the traditional debate about "real presence," with its heavy focus upon the "moment" of the prayer of consecration and on the elements in themselves. Instead, the Reformed confessional tradition sought to recover a sense of the whole assembly participating in Christ by the Spirit in the overall celebration of the Supper itself. This is a gift of the Reformed tradition for the ecumenical conversation, but it is obscured in Hunsinger's book, since his starting point accepts the very categories the Reformed tradition sought to critique and reframe.[22] In a consensus-seeking approach such as this, the gifts of all traditions involved are frequently truncated, and the resulting document does not reflect an organic unity inherent in these worshiping traditions, but a speculative attempt to find commonality in terms that are often not true to any of the traditions.

Rather than looking for agreements that affirm a lowest common denominator on points of dispute, I pursue a different approach to ecumenism, agreeing with Dulles's assessment that there has been a "reconfessionalization in the ecumenical landscape."[23] Thus, in order to present its own distinctive gifts in the ecumenical conversation, each tradition should work, in an unembarrassed way, from its "own distinctive doctrines and practices." This means that all participants need to dig deeply into their respective traditions. Yet, they also need to engage and enter into them in a way that is open to the voice of others, and avoids caricaturing other traditions—even if that is what their tradition has done in the past. The result is that—even in the midst of real and serious disagreements—we can actually find overlapping territory, if not common ground, in surprising places.

An illustration might be helpful here. I recall attending a worship seminar with four panelists—a Roman Catholic nun, a conservative Reformed pastor, and two nondenominational pastors. In the discussion, the two evangelical pastors raised concerns about how to integrate a concern for social justice into the weekly worship of congregations. They felt that they were facing a new problem and were unclear about how to approach addressing it, besides writing new praise songs for worship. The Catholic nun spoke about the natural law tradition, and the way in which concern for the poor and oppressed is integrated—in a characteristically Catholic way—into various aspects of Catholic worship through this tradition. The Reformed pastor spoke about ways to draw upon the connection that Bucer and Calvin made between the

22. For more on this point, see Billings, "Eucharist and Ecumenism: Review," *Journal of Reformed Theology* 6 (2012): 89–90.
23. Dulles, "Saving Ecumenism from Itself," 25.

Lord's Supper and almsgiving—thus between fellowship with Christ, his church, and sharing with the poor. Now, the Catholic nun and the Reformed pastor were not saying the same thing. Nothing about their response indicated a "convergence" of their views on disputed matters. But it was clear that they had much more in common with each other than with the two nondenominational pastors. They already had resources in their theological and liturgical traditions for addressing the question of how the gospel directly implicates Christians in a concern for justice and action on behalf of those in need. In my view, ecumenism today needs to focus more on being "deep" rather than just being "wide." When we dig deeply into our historic Christian traditions—in a way that remains charitable and generous to those outside of them—we will hit the ecumenical water table; all disagreements are not resolved there, but in our deep place of inhabiting the tradition, we find unexpected commonality with those who have dug deeply into other traditions.[24]

Accordingly, I do not seek a solution to doctrinal differences by brokering a consensus agreement among "theological experts" from different traditions on Holy Communion as a "sacrifice," or specific issues in eucharistic metaphysics. Rather, I seek to show how, in working within a broadly Reformed confessional framework on the Lord's Supper, there are many gifts to be given and received in seeking to interpret Scripture faithfully and live deeper into a multifaceted gospel today. Indeed, in digging deeply into the Reformed tradition on this point—in a way animated by generosity and a concrete desire for Christian unity—I believe we will discover a deep catholicity in the Reformed tradition and surprising areas of commonality with other Christian traditions. Christians who are not Reformed are likely to rediscover their own traditions—and shared Christian traditions—in a new way. Conversation and friendship between Christians of different traditions can be expansive and illuminating when the participants inhabit their own traditions deeply, generating a grassroots form of ecumenism.

In addition, the Reformed confessions on the Lord's Supper were written with intentional ambiguity on various technical points because not all theological differences were seen to rise to a level of "confessional disagreement." Thus, for example, the Heidelberg Catechism was written to bypass confessional disagreements between Philippist Lutherans, Zwinglians, and Calvinists. Some, like the Belgic Confession, were approved by Calvin and bear

---

24. For a further development of the example in this paragraph, see J. Todd Billings, "The Problem with Mere Christianity: We Jettison 'Nonessential' Theology at Our Own Peril," *Christianity Today*, February 2007, 46–47.

the distinctive mark of Genevan theology. Others, like the Second Helvetic Confession, bear the marks of Bullinger's theology. Some bear the mark of students of Calvin, such as John Knox in the Scots Confession (1560). Thus, there is a range of perspectives included within each Reformed confession, and different confessions also have different points of emphasis.

Because of this indeterminacy on various points, one can hold to the key features of a Reformed confessional account and then develop them in different directions. Thus, while the rest of the book will continue to draw upon the Reformed confessions, when specific theological issues arise I will draw upon various theologians in the Reformed tradition to explore particular implications or problems that a confessional document does not seek to resolve. As I do so, I will develop a Genevan "strand" of the Reformed tradition, while recognizing that there are other ways to develop the Reformed tradition on the Lord's Supper as well. Various aspects of this Genevan strand were on display on a functional level in the snapshot of the holy fairs in the last chapter; I develop a similar strand—in a way that brings an affective anthropology and Trinitarian soteriology to the basic framework here about the Lord's Supper— in a constructive account for today.

## A Confessional Sketch of the Lord's Supper
## in the Reformed Tradition

*The Lord's Supper, as a sacrament, is fundamentally a divine promise offered through covenantal signs and seals.*[25] From beginning to end, the Supper is constituted by God's word, God's promise. Ontologically speaking, the Reformed confessions frequently use the covenantal terms "signs" and "seals" to refer to the sacraments, just as Paul spoke of circumcision (Rom. 4:11), since he refers to baptism as a "spiritual circumcision" (Col. 2:10-11 NRSV), and the Lord's Supper is frequently referred to in covenantal terms (e.g., "this is my blood of the covenant" [Matt. 26:28; Mark 14:24]; "the new covenant in my blood" [Luke 22:20; 1 Cor. 11:25]).[26] The covenantal context, derived from biblical exegesis, is key for the Reformed confessional tradition. As various questions

25. My format of presenting doctrinal "theses" is inspired, in part, by Gerrish's articulation of "six Calvinistic propositions" in *Grace and Gratitude*, 135-39. While the purpose and content of our theses differ, I am indebted to his articulate framing of the issues.

26. For more on the exegetical issues in seeing the relation between Paul's "spiritual circumcision" and baptism, see James V. Brownson, *The Promise of Baptism: An Introduction to Baptism in Scripture and the Reformed Tradition* (Grand Rapids: Eerdmans, 2006), 136-42.

arise about the function and status of the sacraments, the covenantal categories—such as "sign and seal"—are repeatedly drawn upon in the Reformed confessions. The Belgic Confession presents this in a characteristic yet fulsome manner: God "has ordained sacraments for us to seal his promises in us, to pledge good will and grace toward us, and also to nourish and sustain our faith. God has added these to the Word of the gospel to represent better to our external senses both what God enables us to understand by the Word and what he does inwardly in our hearts, confirming in us the salvation he imparts to us."[27]

Note that the Belgic uses two other terms that are covenantal in focus, particularly in their interplay together: God's "promise" and God's "pledge." On a fundamental level, following Luther, the sacraments were conceived of as God's *promise* in the gospel—not first and foremost as a human act of merit, or even as a human act of obedience. Rather, like the preaching of the Word, which declares God's promise in Christ, the sacraments call forth faith. The promise is in fact a "pledge [of] good will" toward believers, since it is not an abstract declaration by God, but a promise of God toward his covenant people.

*Faith, kindled by the Spirit, is necessary to receive the gift offered in the Supper, though the gifts in the Supper are truly offered to all who partake.* Since the Lord's Supper is a sign and seal of God's covenantal promises ("holy signs and seals of the covenant of grace" in the Westminster Confession), it calls forth faith just as the preaching of God's promise does.[28]

This does not mean that there is nothing offered by God in the Supper, or that the Supper is simply a subjective act that produces a sense of Christ's presence. Rather, as the French Confession of 1559 states about the table: "God gives us really and in fact that which he there sets forth to us; and that consequently with these signs is given the true possession and enjoyment of that which they present to us. And thus all who bring a pure faith, like a vessel, to the sacred table of Christ, receive truly that of which it is a sign."[29] Faith is like a receiving vessel, which adds nothing in itself. Yet faith is necessary to receive what is offered. After stating that believers receive "the true body and true blood of Christ, our only Savior," at the Supper by the Spirit, the Belgic emphasizes the instrumental and receptive character of faith, explaining that "we receive these by faith, which is the hand and mouth of our souls."[30]

The issue of faith as a condition for receiving the Supper raises the ques-

27. Belgic Confession, article 33, in *Our Faith*, 58.
28. Westminster Confession of Faith, in *BC*, 206.
29. "The French Confession of 1559," article 37, in *Reformed Confessions of the Sixteenth Century*, trans. Arthur C. Cochrane (Louisville: Westminster John Knox, 2003), 157.
30. Belgic Confession, article 35, in *Our Faith*, 62.

tion of how to interpret the "unworthy manner" of receiving the Supper that Paul speaks about in 1 Corinthians 11:27–32. While these issues will be explored later in the book, it is important to recognize that from a confessional perspective, bringing the "pure" or "true faith" does not require perfection. Indeed, as the Heidelberg Catechism repeatedly notes, "true faith" is a trust in God and his Word, not our own righteousness; thus, those welcomed to the table are "those who are displeased with themselves because of their sins, but who nevertheless trust that their sins are pardoned."[31]

*The Supper is a testimony of our faith, but first and foremost, it is a gift to be received. While believers feed upon Christ in the Christian life generally, the gift received in the Supper is to be cherished and desired.* In light of Reformation disputes about how to interpret the feeding upon Christ's flesh in John 6, some Reformed confessions have an emphasis that seems to make "eating" synonymous with the act of having faith in Christ. For example, the Second Helvetic Confession, emerging from Bullinger's Zurich, gives this impression in interpreting John 6: "'The bread which I shall give for the life of the world is my flesh' (John 6:51) and 'the flesh' (namely what is eaten bodily) 'is of no avail. It is the spirit that gives life' (v. 63)."[32] In contrast, true eating takes place when "we receive Christ by faith."[33] Along with this, this Zurich-based theology emphasized the act of partaking of the Supper as a sign of one's own faith.[34] Yet, even Zurich's Second Helvetic Confession combines the emphasis on faith with emphasis on the gift offered and received at the Supper itself.[35] Thus, feeding upon Christ takes place in the Supper, though not exclusively in the Supper. As Calvin states with more clarity than the Second Helvetic, Christ's discourse in John 6 relates to "the uninterrupted communication of the flesh of Christ," yet there is "nothing said here that is not figuratively represented, and actually bestowed on believers, in the Lord's Supper."[36]

Like confessions emerging from Zurich, the Reformed confessions gen-

31. Heidelberg Catechism, question and answer 81, in *Our Faith*, 99.

32. Second Helvetic Confession, 21, in *BC*, 143–44.

33. Second Helvetic Confession, 21, in *BC*, 144.

34. See Jan Rohls, *Reformed Confessions: Theology from Zurich to Barmen* (Louisville: Westminster John Knox, 1998), 235.

35. Second Helvetic Confession, 21, in *BC*, 144.

36. From Calvin's commentary on John 6: On the one hand, the "discourse does not relate to the Lord's Supper, but to the uninterrupted communication of the flesh of Christ, which we obtain apart from the use of the Lord's Supper." Yet, on the other hand, Calvin says, "I acknowledge that there is nothing said here that is not figuratively represented, and actually bestowed on believers, in the Lord's Supper; and Christ even intended that the holy Supper should be, as it were, a seal and confirmation of this sermon." Calvin, John 6, CTS.

erally incorporate the theme of the Supper as a sign of one's own faith, but they combine it with a strong emphasis on the "gift" character of the Supper. For example, the Geneva Catechism says the sacraments "are also signs and marks of our profession. That is to say, by them we declare that we are of the people of God, and make our confession of our Christianity."[37] A similar emphasis is found in even much later confessions, such as the Westminster Standards. Yet, the emphasis in the Reformed confessions is that baptism and the Lord's Supper are signs of God's promise in Jesus Christ and God's action by the Spirit in uniting believers to Christ, not primarily signs that signify the human response of faith.[38] Faith enables the reception of the gifts offered at the Supper, and faith needs to be nourished, not simply to be testified to through the Supper. In the words of the Geneva Catechism, faith "must be nourished continually, and increase more and more every day. To nourish, strengthen, and advance it, the Lord instituted the sacraments."[39] Thus, by faith and through the Spirit, Christ "makes us partakers of his substance, that thus we may have one life with him."[40]

One objection to what the Reformed confessions claim at this point is: Does not the feeding upon Christ not only within but outside of the Supper make the Supper superfluous? Part of the response to this will be explored below, as the confessions speak of the necessity of material, sensible signs in receiving the gospel promise. In addition, however, it is important to recognize the significance of the symmetry of God's promise in the gospel and God's promise in the sacraments: both portray union with Christ by the Spirit as the source for forgiveness, new life, and a new identity in Christ. The material signs and acts of the Supper are to be valued precisely because the gospel promises that what they hold forth are to be valued. If one considers episodes in the history of reception such as the holy fairs, this theme that one feeds upon Christ in the whole Christian life, not just within the Supper, does not lead to a devaluing of the Supper, but to a heightened valuing of it. In the Supper, the heart of the gospel is displayed and offered—and the heart of Christian identity is both revealed and enacted. For example, with the spiritual marriage imagery prominent in the holy fairs and the *Nadere Reformatie*, spiritual marriage with Christ was experienced in the Christian life generally, not just

37. Quoted from Rohls, *Reformed Confessions*, 235.

38. This emphasis on God's promise as the signified is present, though less emphatic, in Zurich-based confessions such as the First and Second Helvetic Confession. See Rohls, *Reformed Confessions*, 182–83.

39. Catechism of the Church of Geneva (1545), in *Tracts and Treatises of John Calvin*, vol. 2, trans. Henry Beveridge (Eugene, OR: Wipf and Stock, 2002), 85.

40. Catechism of the Church of Geneva (1545), 2:91.

received at the Supper. Yet, precisely because it was central to the Christian life, the material sign of God's love at the banquet of the Supper was cherished and fervently desired. Their vibrant reflections on the Supper presuppose that the Supper is brought up into the larger drama of God's action, an instrument of the bridegroom to give his bride a taste of the communion that is the focal point of the Christian life.

*The Lord's Supper is a site for the action of the triune God—where God acts in and through the Supper, using the Supper as an instrument of grace.* This claim in the Reformed confessions contrasts with Zwingli, who claims that since "grace is effected and present before the sacrament is administered," then "the sacraments are given as a public testimony to that grace which is already present." Indeed, Zwingli says, "all sacraments, so far from conferring grace, neither impart nor bestow it."[41] The Spirit needs no material "vehicle" to generate and build up faith.[42] In his denial of the Lord's Supper as a means of grace, Zwingli departs from the Reformed confessions. As Rohls notes, "even the early Swiss confessions do not follow Zwingli in this view of the sacraments."[43] While most (but not all) Reformed confessions affirm the sacraments as "instruments" and "means" of grace, no significant Reformed confession denies this, which would restrict the sacraments to a human testimony to past grace received, as Zwingli does.[44] In this book, I will be working with the view expressed in the majority of Reformed confessions—that the sacraments are means and instruments of grace, received through the Spirit by faith.

In this view, the Reformed confessions give a robust account of the action of the triune God working in and through the sign-act of the Supper. Indeed, this emphasis is so strong in the confessions that Nicholas Wolterstorff has suggested that it represents a move in the church's eucharistic reflection away from the categories of "presence" and "sign-agency" in theologians such as Aquinas, toward an emphasis upon the sacraments as "action" through divine agency.[45]

---

41. Translations from Gottfried W. Locher, *Zwingli's Thought: New Perspectives* (Leiden: Brill Academic, 1997), 217.

42. "Moreover, a channel or vehicle is not necessary to the Spirit, for He Himself is the virtue and energy whereby all things are borne, and has no need of being borne." Ulrich Zwingli, *On Providence and Other Essays*, ed. Samuel Macauley Jackson and William John Hinke (Durham, NC: Labyrinth Press, 1983), 46.

43. Rohls, *Reformed Confessions*, 182.

44. Rohls, *Reformed Confessions*, 181–82.

45. See Nicholas Wolterstorff, "Sacraments as Action, Not Presence," in *Christ: The Sacramental Word—Incarnation, Sacrament, and Poetry*, ed. David Brown and Ann Loades (London: SPCK, 1996), 103–22.

Wolterstorff is not denying that the Reformed confessions use the conventional, Augustinian language of sign and signified, but he notes the emphasis upon how God acts in and through the eating and drinking at the table. Confessions such as the Belgic are heavy in their emphasis on divine action through the sacraments: God "has ordained sacraments for us to *seal* his promises in us, to *pledge* good will and grace toward us, and also to *nourish* and *sustain* our faith."[46] For sacraments are "visible signs and seals . . . by means of which God works in us through the power of the Holy Spirit."[47] This language of the sacraments as "means" and "instruments" for the Spirit's work is widespread in Reformed confessions,[48] expressing a view of divine action through material means vividly expressed in confessions such as the Bremen Consensus: the sacraments are "powerful signs and seals of God's grace, through which God not only visibly informs us of the divine will, but also assures us in the most certain way, strengthens and increases our faith, offers and gives Christ with all his benefits to the faithful."[49] God informs, assures, strengthens, increases, offers, and gives all *through* the visible signs and seals of the sacraments. God uses the sacrament as an instrument through which to act, a means of grace to be received by faith through the Spirit.

At this point the Reformed tradition may offer a gift to the ecumenical community at large. Calvin himself was willing to affirm the language of "real presence" for the Lord's Supper, but he preferred to speak in the more active, Trinitarian (and more directly biblical) terms of "true participation in Christ" by the Spirit at the Supper.[50] This dynamic emphasis on the triune God's action is reflected in the Reformed confessions.

*The substance and "matter" of God's promise signified in the Supper is Jesus Christ.* At the heart of the Lord's Supper, according to the Reformed confessions, is that the Word and promise of God that is signified is none other than Jesus Christ himself—the whole person of Jesus Christ, in his body and his blood.[51] Even for confessions emerging from Zwingli's Zurich, the signs do

---

46. Belgic Confession, article 33, in *Our Faith*, 58.
47. Belgic Confession, article 33, in *Our Faith*, 59.
48. See the survey of Rohls, *Reformed Confessions*, 181–85.
49. Translation from Rohls, *Reformed Confessions*, 184.
50. See Billings, *Calvin, Participation, and the Gift*, 128–29, and Joseph Tylenda, "Calvin and Christ's Presence in the Sacrament—True or Real," in *Calvin's Ecclesiology: Sacraments and Deacons*, ed. Richard C. Gamble (New York: Garland, 1992), 215–25.
51. Rohls gives a helpful gloss on how the terms "body and blood" in the Reformed confessions do not stand "for two different materials—that is, two parts of Christ. Instead they designate the whole person of Christ sacrificed for us, the person along with his work" (Rohls, *Reformed Confessions*, 225). At times this is explicit in the confessions: "In the Lord's Supper the

not simply signify the faith of the believers—the bread and wine signify the body and blood of Christ.[52] Indeed, for the Second Helvetic, the "substance and matter of the Sacraments" is "Christ the Savior."[53]

In this way, the Reformed confessions teach that the sacrament does not signify the faith of believers, even though the sign and signified are received by faith. To the contrary, the sign-action of the Lord's Supper signifies Jesus Christ. The gift of the Supper is the gift of Jesus Christ, not the human action of faith. "So they are not empty and hollow signs to fool and deceive us, for their truth is Jesus Christ, without whom they would be nothing."[54] In the stronger language of the Scots Confession, "we utterly condemn the vanity of those that affirm sacraments to be nothing else but naked and bare signs."[55] Far from being a bare sign, the sign-act of the Supper is such that "the bread which we break is the communion of Christ's body and the cup which we bless the communion of his blood." For "we confess and believe that the faithful . . . do so eat the body and eat the blood of the Lord Jesus that he remains in them and they in him."[56] Jesus Christ is the signified, the matter, of the Supper—and thus union and communion with Christ are also its fruit.

*God not only signifies but also truly exhibits, offers, and communicates Jesus Christ in the Supper through the Spirit to believers by faith.* Not only is Jesus Christ the signified of the sacrament, but the Spirit shows, offers, and communicates Jesus Christ to believers at the Supper. In the words of the Irish Articles, Christ's body "is really and substantially presented unto all those who have grace to receive the Son of God, even to all those that believe in his name."[57]

While the manner of eating is beyond human comprehension, it is enabled by God's Spirit. "Now it is certain that Jesus Christ did not prescribe his sacraments for us in vain, since he works in us all he represents by these holy signs, although the manner in which he does it goes beyond our understanding and is incomprehensible to us, just as the operation of God's Spirit

---

Lord truly offers His body and His blood, *that is, Himself,* to His own to enjoy" (First Helvetic Confession, in Rohls, 225, emphasis added).

52. "In the Lord's Supper, the outward sign is bread and wine, taken from things commonly used for meat and drink; but the thing signified is the body of Christ which was given, and his blood which was shed for us, or the communion of the body and blood of the Lord." Second Helvetic Confession, 19, in *BC*, 139.

53. Second Helvetic Confession, 19, in *BC*, 138.

54. Belgic Confession, article 33, in *Our Faith*, 59.

55. Scots Confession, 21, in *BC*, 44.

56. Scots Confession, 21, in *BC*, 44.

57. Translation in Rohls, *Reformed Confessions*, 236.

is hidden and incomprehensible."[58] Given this qualification, the Belgic can speak emphatically that "Yet we do not go wrong when we say that what is eaten is Christ's own natural body and what is drunk is his own blood—but the manner in which we eat it is not by the mouth, but by the Spirit through faith."[59] This "manner" of eating—by the Spirit, through faith—is essential for rightly framing how Christ is communicated to believers, according to the Reformed confessions. But, in a way later reflected in the emphatic account of Christ's presence by the Spirit in the holy fairs, the confessions make strong claims about the way in which believers feed upon Christ at the Supper.

In the Lord's Supper, according to the Heidelberg Catechism, Christ "wants to assure us, by this visible sign and pledge, that we, through the Holy Spirit's work, share in his true body and blood,"[60] indeed, to "assure us that by the communication of his body and blood, our souls are nourished, in the hope of eternal life."[61] By the Spirit, God signifies, assures, and seals his promise of union with Christ in the Supper. The Spirit also offers, presents, and communicates Christ's body and blood, as a gift, at the Supper. Some of this is displayed in a term used in a number of Reformed confessions, and frequently in Calvin's writings: *exhibere*.[62] While it has the English cognate "to exhibit," as Sue Rozeboom has demonstrated, it means more "than 'to present,' as in 'to show,' as the English implies. It means 'to present,' as in 'to offer,' 'to proffer,' 'to hand over.'"[63] Melanchthon's revised Augsburg Confession, to which Calvin subscribed, uses the same terminology: "the body and blood of Christ are truly exhibited [*vere exhibeantur*] with the bread and wine."[64] In the English of the Irish Articles (1615), "the body and blood of Christ is not only signified and offered, but truly exhibited and communicated."[65]

---

58. Belgic Confession, article 35, in *Our Faith*, 62–63.

59. Belgic Confession, article 35, in *Our Faith*, 63.

60. Heidelberg Catechism, question and answer 79, in *Our Faith*, 97.

61. Heidelberg Catechism, question and answer 75, in Rohls, *Reformed Confessions*, 227.

62. Forms of the term *exhibere* are used in the Bern Articles (1532) and the Genevan Catechism (1541). The Westminster Catechism speaks of "the grace which is exhibited in or by the sacraments," and the Irish Articles (1615) say that "the body and blood of Christ is not only signified and offered, but truly exhibited and communicated" (Rohls, *Reformed Confessions*, 236).

63. Sue A. Rozeboom, "Calvin's Doctrine of the Lord's Supper," in *Calvin's Theology and Its Reception*, 152.

64. See Joseph Tylenda, "The Ecumenical Intention of Calvin's Early Eucharistic Teaching," in *Reformatio Perennis: Essays in Honor of Calvin and the Reformation in Honor of Ford Lewis Battles*, ed. B. A. Gerrish (Eugene, OR: Pickwick, 1981), 35.

65. Translation from Rohls, *Reformed Confessions*, 236.

Therefore, according to these confessions, the Supper communicates far more than a mental remembrance of Christ or a mental sense of Christ's presence. By the Spirit, the Supper presents a material sign that displays the gospel promise, and when received in faith, assures, nourishes, and enlivens the recipients through the gift that is offered. This happens "spiritually"—not in the sense that it is in one's own head or the product of one's own faith, but "by the Spirit." For, in the words of the Scots Confession, "this union and conjunction which we have with the body and blood of Christ Jesus, in the right use of the sacraments, is wrought by operation of the Holy Ghost."[66]

*At the Supper, believers both remember and commune with Jesus Christ by the Spirit. But, in recognition of the ascension, they also await the second advent of Christ.* The Reformed confessions are clear and emphatic in claiming that the bread and cup are not empty signs but are attached to God's promise in Jesus Christ—thus believers feed upon Christ as the substance of the Supper by the Spirit. But this set of claims is held together with another affirmation: that Jesus Christ has ascended, and is seated at the right hand of the Father. Exegetically speaking, this affirmation emerges not only from the New Testament ascension narrative (Acts 1:9–11; Luke 24:50–53; Mark 16:19) and Christ's exaltation to the Father's right hand (Eph. 1:20; Col. 3:1; Heb. 1:3), but also from Paul's account of the Lord's Supper itself: "For as often as you eat this bread and drink the cup, you proclaim the Lord's death until he comes" (1 Cor. 11:26 NRSV). "Until he comes"—in the same passage where Paul insists upon a partaking of Christ at the Supper (11:24–25, 27–29), he insists that the Supper itself awaits the parousia, the second advent and bodily return of Christ. Christ is present at the Supper, but there is also a sense in which Christ is absent—and the final culmination of his kingdom is longed for in and through the Supper. The Reformed confessions attend to this paradox.

While the language about the session (seating of Christ at the Father's right hand) and the ascension is very common in the Reformed confessions, the French Confession (1559) gives a good example of how the paradox is frequently articulated:

> We confess that the Lord's Supper, which is the second sacrament, is a witness of the union which we have with Christ, inasmuch as he not only died and rose again for us once, but also feeds and nourishes us truly with his flesh and blood, so that we may be one in him, and that our life may be in common. Although he be in heaven until

66. Scots Confession, 21, in *BC*, 44.

he come to judge all the earth, still we believe that by the secret and incomprehensible power of his Spirit he feeds and strengthens us with the substance of his body and of his blood. We hold that this is done spiritually, not because we put imagination and fancy in the place of fact and truth, but because the greatness of this mystery exceeds the measure of our senses and the laws of nature. In short, because it is heavenly, it can only be apprehended by faith.[67]

Note the way the confession affirms that Christ "feeds and nourishes us truly with his flesh and blood," yet Christ is in heaven until he comes again. In this way, a taste of heaven is enabled by the Holy Spirit—which is not simply an appeal to "imagination and fancy," but "because the greatness of this mystery" cannot be comprehended. Rather than Christ coming to descend to inhabit the elements, the emphasis of the Reformed confessions is upon an ascent to heaven to feed upon Christ. At times, this articulation of Christ's ascension and the ascent of believers at the Supper has been expressed liturgically in the *sursum corda*, "Lift up your hearts!," and the prayer of epiclesis, an invocation of the Spirit at the Supper. The Reformed confessions also connect Christ's session in heaven to a Chalcedonian concern in maintaining the distinction of Christ's two natures, which, although "without division," are also "without mixture" and "without confusion." This concern led the Reformed confessions to reject formulations of Christ's body as "ubiquitous," drawing upon the patristic axiom "that which is not assumed is not healed" to suggest that Christ's body is circumscribed like our own bodies. Yet, "Jesus Christ remains always seated at the right hand of God the Father in heaven—but he never refrains on that account to communicate himself to us through faith."[68]

The material sign-act of the whole celebration of the Supper is essential to the gracious character of the Supper; yet, the elements do not enclose Christ's presence, but they are instruments of the Spirit to hold forth Christ. In light of the last section, the confessions draw a few implications from this Spirit-enabled feeding upon Christ at the Supper. On the one hand, the confessions highly value the Supper as a sign-act—"a ceremony or external sign or a work, through which God offers us that which is attached to the same ceremony—namely, the divine promise."[69] The confessions show no interest in turning the sacrament

---

67. "The French Confession of Faith 1559," article 36, in *Reformed Confessions of the Sixteenth Century*, 156–57.

68. Belgic Confession, article 35, in *Our Faith*, 63.

69. The Bremen Consensus, in Rohls, *Reformed Confessions*, 223.

into merely a mental act of meaning making, for its sense-oriented character is essential to its very purpose—in terms of both giving a visual "icon" of the gospel and the use of the senses in eating and drinking. The Heidelberg Catechism gives a characteristic account of this sense-oriented experience:

> First, as surely as I *see with my eyes the bread of the Lord broken for me and the cup shared with me*, so surely his body was offered and broken for me and his blood poured out for me on the cross.
>
> Second, as surely as I *receive from the hand of the one who serves, and taste with my mouth the bread and cup of the Lord*, given me as sure signs of Christ's body and blood, so surely he nourishes and refreshes my soul for eternal life with his crucified body and poured-out blood.[70]

This emphasis on sense experience is based in a view of human knowing that is embodied. As embodied human beings, we cannot truly and fully know God's promises without a bodily form for doing so. The Belgic Confession is characteristic on this point:

> We believe that our good God,
> mindful of our crudeness and weakness,
> has ordained sacraments for us
> to seal his promises in us,
> to pledge good will and grace toward us,
> and also to nourish and sustain our faith.
>
> God has added these to the Word of the gospel
> to represent better to our external senses
> both what God enables us to understand by the Word
> and what he does inwardly in our hearts,
> confirming in us
> the salvation he imparts to us.[71]

God graciously condescends to the limited, circumscribed character of human knowing to further enable understanding of God's Word and the reality of union with Christ that the Spirit works in and through believers. In this, God

---

70. Heidelberg Catechism, question and answer 75, in *Our Faith*, 95 (emphasis added).
71. Belgic Confession, article 33, in *Our Faith*, 58.

graciously represents and confirms the salvation that he gives. If Calvin's theology—which so deeply influenced the Belgic—is to be a clue to interpreting the phrase "crudeness and weakness" here, we should note that Calvin does not attribute this need for a material, sacramental sign simply to "humanity's fallen condition," as is sometimes assumed.[72] As noted in chapter 1, in his Genesis commentary Calvin suggests that prefallen human beings had a need for a material sign of God's love to know and live in fellowship with God. Calvin interprets the tree of life as God's accommodation to unite Adam to himself, an external sign of God's promise, for by these signs God "stretches out his hand to us, because, without assistance, we cannot ascend to him."[73] Before the Fall, humanity needed not only God's word but also the physical, external signs of God's promise to "seal his grace to man."[74]

Thus, when Calvin speaks of the sacraments as being necessary because of our "weakness" in apprehending God's promise, this "weakness" is not a contingent handicap, a crutch for immature Christians. The "weakness" is, at least in part, a dimension of the created goodness of humanity. We were created to know God by means of physical, material signs. We were also created to hear God's word, as God spoke to humans in the garden. But part of the created structure for a human way of knowing God, according to Calvin, involves not just hearing but also seeing, touching, and tasting.

On the other hand, while affirming the need for material, sensible signs of God's promise, the Reformed confessions repeatedly reject the notion that the elements "enclose" or "contain" Christ's presence. Some of this is in Reformation protest to the Fourth Lateran Council's doctrine of local presence in the elements and transubstantiation, as it claims that Christ's "body and blood are truly *contained* in the sacrament of the altar under the forms of bread and wine; the bread being changed (*transsubstantiatio*) by divine power into the body, and the wine into the blood."[75] Key Reformed confessions condemn the

<hr>

72. This is a lapse in Moore-Keisha's otherwise insightful account: "Although Calvin implied that our need for the visible and tangible is a symptom of humanity's fallen condition, we do not have to agree with his negative judgment in order to affirm with him this fact of human nature as we know it." Martha L. Moore-Keish, *Do This in Remembrance of Me: A Ritual Approach to Reformed Eucharistic Theology* (Grand Rapids: Eerdmans, 2008), 29.

73. See Gen. 2:9, CTS.

74. See Gen. 3:22, CTS.

75. See Canon 1, "Medieval Sourcebook: Twelfth Ecumenical Council: Lateran IV 1215," Fordham University, http://www.fordham.edu/halsall/basis/lateran4.asp (emphasis added).

adoration of the elements, which they associated with the doctrine of transubstantiation in particular.[76]

This objection to local presence in the elements need not emerge from a metaphysical dualism or an anthropology that devalues the senses. Rather, its best articulations emerge from the paradox explored in the last section—the emphasis upon Christ's ascension, session, and the Holy Spirit's mediation of Christ. If Christ is contained in the elements, then the receiver is having an immediate experience of Christ. This would fail to recognize that we await Christ ("until he comes") and that Christ is presently mediated always by the Spirit. Union with Christ at the Supper is real, but it is by the Spirit. "Through the Holy Spirit, who lives both in Christ and in us, we are united more and more to Christ's blessed body. And so, although he is in heaven and we are on earth, we are flesh of his flesh and bone of his bone. And we forever live on and are governed by one Spirit, as the members of our body are by one soul."[77]

According to the Reformed confessions, to adore the elements is misguided on several levels: it misses the true role of the bread and cup—namely, as *instruments* to hold forth Christ—and instead worships the creation rather than the Creator. But just as importantly, localizing Christ's presence in the elements also obscures what a true taste of "heaven" by the Spirit should be like: that union with Christ is always communal, as believers "live on and are governed by one Spirit, as the members of our body are by one soul."[78] In this account, Holy Communion should not focus primarily upon objects, such as the bread and the cup, but upon the sign-action of enacting a communal meal. Indeed, this communal feast is a foretaste of heaven by the Spirit. In the words of the Westminster Confession, Christ gave the Supper as a "bond and pledge" to believers' "communion with him, and with each other, as members of his mystical body."[79] The traditional Reformed prohibition of a "private" celebration of Holy Communion emphasizes that the koinōnia with the body and blood of Christ at the Supper that Paul speaks of in 1 Corinthians 10:16 is always horizontal and communal as well as with Christ himself. "Because there is one bread, we who are many are one body, for we all partake of the one bread" (10:17 NRSV). For the confessions, local presence in the elements is a dangerous diversion of attention—making us focus upon objects (the elements) rather than the sign-action of a communal celebration.

76. Confessions making this connection include the Heidelberg Catechism, Westminster Confession, and the Scots Confession. See Rohls, *Reformed Confessions*, 228.

77. Heidelberg Catechism, question and answer 76, in *Our Faith*, 96.

78. Heidelberg Catechism, question and answer 76, in *Our Faith*, 96.

79. Westminster Confession, chap. 31.1.

*As a result of God's action in and through the Supper, believers are empowered to mutual love in the church and love of neighbor, bearing fruit in acts of witness, mercy, and justice in the world. These actions flow from the joy and gratitude generated by the Spirit in sanctification.* As a result of the strong emphasis on *koinōnia* with both Christ and Christ's ecclesial body in the Supper, the Reformed confessions accent the horizontal and ethical aspects of the Supper without downplaying the significance of fellowship with Christ by the Spirit. The Belgic Confession states it succinctly: "In short, by the use of this holy sacrament we are moved to a fervent love of God and our neighbors."[80] This emerges from the interpretation of 1 Corinthians 10:16-17 noted in the previous paragraph, but also from a larger theme: that the Supper is a sacrament of union with Christ, which necessarily relates to both justification and sanctification.

Although the Belgic does not use Calvin's phrase "the double grace" to speak about union with Christ, the basic structure of the double grace is built into the confession itself. In article 22, it introduces the notion of union and communion with Christ, in which "the Holy Spirit kindles in our hearts a true faith that embraces Jesus Christ, with all his merits, and makes him its own, and no longer looks for anything apart from him."[81] This is followed by an exposition of justification in article 23, and sanctification in article 24. The Belgic is emphatic that justification and sanctification are distinct yet inseparable gifts—for all who are united to Christ by faith through the Spirit receive both. Because by faith believers are united to Christ, receiving forgiveness through the declaration of Christ's righteousness and the regeneration of the Spirit that "makes us new creatures, causing us to live a new life," then "it is impossible for this holy faith to be unfruitful in a human being."[82] Thus, since the Lord's Supper "is a spiritual table at which Christ communicates himself to us with all his benefits," it is no surprise that it relates not only to justification but also to sanctification.[83]

The Belgic Confession is not unique in these claims—as I have explored elsewhere, there is a similarly rich theology of union with Christ in the Heidelberg Catechism and the Westminster Standards as well.[84] The Heidelberg Catechism is particularly helpful in unpacking what is involved in the concrete

---

80. Belgic Confession, article 35, in *Our Faith*, 64.
81. Belgic Confession, article 22, in *Our Faith*, 46.
82. Belgic Confession, article 24, in *Our Faith*, 48.
83. Belgic Confession, article 35, in *Our Faith*, 63.
84. See J. Todd Billings, "Union with Christ and the Double Grace: Calvin's Theology and Its Early Reception," in Billings and Hesselink, *Calvin's Theology and Its Reception*, 65-67.

outworking of sanctification, which the Supper fuels. For the Heidelberg Catechism, in light of the third use of the law—as instruction for the Christian life—believers are to display a costly love of neighbor. This emerges from the gift of new life by the Spirit, which entails "wholehearted joy in God through Christ and a love and delight to live according to the will of God by doing every kind of good work."[85] This leads to works that "are done out of true faith, conform to God's law, and are done for God's glory."[86] Flowing from this affective gratitude delighting in God and his ways, the Heidelberg Catechism gives an exposition of the Ten Commandments that unfolds their positive directives, not simply their prohibitions. Not only should one not take the Lord's name in vain, but one's words and works should bear witness to the Lord, so that we "may properly confess God, pray to God, and glorify God in all our words and works."[87] Not only is murder prohibited, but "by condemning envy, hatred, and anger God wants us to love our neighbors as ourselves, to be patient, peace-loving, gentle, merciful, and friendly toward them, to protect them from harm as much as we can, and to do good even to our enemies."[88] Not only is stealing prohibited, but positively the new life in Christ should mean "that I do whatever I can for my neighbor's good, that I treat others as I would like them to treat me, and that I work faithfully so that I may share with those in need."[89] These acts of mercy and works of justice for the good of others—even our enemies—are a manifestation of the new life that comes in union with Christ. This new life brings "joy," "love," and "delight" that manifest themselves in action.[90] It is this new life that is signified, confirmed, and edified by the Spirit in the instrument of the Lord's Supper.

This sketch gives a brief sense of what the Reformed confessions affirm about the Lord's Supper and how they articulate their characteristic positions. There are points of ambiguity—both because the confessions want to accommodate a range of possible positions, and because the nature of confessional documents does not permit extensive elaboration and doctrinal development.

Yet, it should be clear that this confessional account fits well with key parts of the portrait in part 1: it is Word-centered and covenantal, and it recognizes a symmetry between God's promise in the gospel and God's promise at

---

85. Heidelberg Catechism, question and answer 90, in *Our Faith*, 102.
86. Heidelberg Catechism, question and answer 91, in *Our Faith*, 102.
87. Heidelberg Catechism, question and answer 99, in *Our Faith*, 106.
88. Heidelberg Catechism, question and answer 107, in *Our Faith*, 109.
89. Heidelberg Catechism, question and answer 111, in *Our Faith*, 110.
90. Heidelberg Catechism, question and answer 90, in *Our Faith*, 102.

the Supper, such that participants come to fervently desire the Supper as the focal point and enactment of the heart of the Christian life more generally. The confessions give a powerful sense of Christ's presence at the Supper, hand in hand with an emphasis upon the Spirit's work and the significance of faith in receiving this gift; the anthropology is not content with abstract knowledge of the gospel, but it relates to our bodily senses, our affections, and our deepest desires; at the center of it all is the triune God's action in uniting believers to Christ by the Spirit. This involves not only the reception of forgiveness through Christ's work, but also the reception of new life by the Spirit, imparting joy and love that are expressed in actions of witness, love, and mercy in the world. As the project of this book continues, the convictions expressed in this confessional portrait will be utilized in an expansive way, as we engage in biblical exegesis, theological exploration, and pastoral appropriation of the ways in which the Lord's Supper and the gospel are multidimensional and multifaceted in terms of remembrance (chap. 5), communion (chap. 6), and hope (chap. 7). But before that exploration, we need to expand upon this catholic-Reformed confessional account in addressing important issues related to the reality of the triune God's saving action, and particular issues related to the triune God's action in and through the Lord's Supper.

CHAPTER 4

ॐ

# Does God Really Act through the Sacraments?

Does God really act through the sacraments? This question pushes us to examine how the sacraments relate to ontology, what is real or true. "Ontology," the study of being, may seem to be an abstract affair, and, certainly, abstractions are unavoidable in discussing it. Yet, when we probe deeply into what is really "true" or "real," the questions about our framework for reality itself (ontology) are not far away. After evangelical professor John Jefferson Davis visited thirty-five different worship services in a wide variety of congregations while on his sabbatical, he was left with "disturbing questions" that were ultimately ontological ones: "Where is God in all this? What are we really doing here? Is there a vivid consciousness of the presence of the living, holy God among his people at these services?"[1] Davis sensed that there was confusion on the first two questions, and that the consciousness of the third was often missing. Davis witnessed congregations that said the right words and performed the right actions but lacked a sense that *God* was actively a part of their worship. Others had a small or truncated view of God: God was part of the furniture on Sunday and played his role, but the triune God—Father, Son, and Holy Spirit—certainly was not "the center of the universe as the ultimately and eternally real."[2] God was present to authorize and confirm what the pastor said, or to hear the worship of the people; but the congregations did not live in a sense that the triune God was actually enabling their worship, that the Spirit was praying through those who are in Christ to the Father. The issue here is

1. John Jefferson Davis, *Worship and the Reality of God: An Evangelical Theology of Real Presence* (Downers Grove: IVP Academic, 2010), 35–36.
2. Davis, *Worship and the Reality of God*, 23. I am using Davis's language about "Trinitarian theism" here as a contrast with a deficient, more deistic ontology.

84

not the sincerity of the worship or the particular style of worship. The issue is the underlying ontology.

Ontologies are rarely named, but that does not make them any less significant. Ontology often operates under the surface, shaping our understanding of what is real. On a basic level, Davis felt that what was considered "real" and "present" had somehow eclipsed the work of the triune God—that many were functioning with ontological views of reality that were "modern" in deistic or materialist modes, or "postmodern" in consumerist and relativistic modes, rather than shaped by a vision of an active triune God.[3] We may say the right words in worship, but if our background theories are thoroughly shaped by one of these "competing ontologies," then we cannot really experience the central reality of worship: that *"Jesus Christ is risen from the dead; Jesus is still alive today, and is present here with us in the power of the Spirit to enjoy communion with his people."*[4]

Christians of a variety of traditions would heartily affirm that congregations need to recover a sense of the action of the triune God in and through worship generally, and in and through the sacraments in particular. Yet, there is no generic "Christian ontology," and *how* different traditions would answer the question of what is ultimately most "real" varies dramatically. As it pertains to the Lord's Supper, the traditional ontological question is: How is Christ present at the Supper? Or, how can the Supper communicate the reality of Christ's personal presence? But further underlying questions also affect how the words and melodies of worship will be embraced in worship: Is "salvation" just about an immaterial soul, or also about our bodies? Does the Spirit work through material means? How does God relate to the creation? If we believe that the triune God's work is real, and that sacramental renewal is desirable, these are questions that are raised. As noted in the last chapter, I do not seek a "consensus statement" that resolves all the debates on these matters between different Christian traditions. Yet, since the catholic and Reformed vision that chapter 3 presents is utterly dependent on an ontology in which the triune God acts in and through the material world through Word and sacrament, an ontological supplement to chapter 3 is in order. The particularities of sacramental doctrine can be undermined by broader assumptions about what is real: if our functional theologies indicate that God is not really active in and through the communal, aural, and material means of Word and sacrament, then talk of God's presence in corporate worship has become hollow and shallow.

3. Davis, *Worship and the Reality of God*, 21.
4. Davis, *Worship and the Reality of God*, 12; emphasis in original.

In this chapter we begin with a challenge and end with a constructive proposal. The challenge comes from a number of recent voices (in Radical Orthodoxy—hereafter "RO"—and Hans Boersma) who share my concern for sacramental renewal. However, they claim that the catholic-Reformed tradition lacks the proper ontology to truly undergird an account of Christ's sacramental presence at the Supper and a Trinitarian ontology that affirms the reality of God's presence. The analysis in the first few sections requires some philosophical "heavy lifting" that some readers may find difficult. If so, I would encourage them to skip to the final two sections of this chapter,[5] where I present a constructive theological proposal, before moving on to part 3 of the book. In my constructive account, I draw upon Calvin's thought to give more specificity to a Reformed sacramental ontology than the confessions alone could provide, building upon the portrait in chapter 3. All this will be toward the end of showing how a catholic and Reformed account of the Supper can be used by God to bring congregations into a more multifaceted sense of the gospel.

## A Genealogy of Decline: The Fall from "the Sacramental Ontology"

In the contemporary West, Christians in a wide variety of traditions find that sacred, sacramental rites are not approached with the respect and reverence of earlier ages. Why is this the case? Has contemporary Christianity become largely "de-sacramentalized"? In seeking to diagnose what they see as a de-sacramentalized present, figures in RO give a grand narrative of decline. This grand narrative is a "genealogy"—a story accounting for origins—that sees Thomistic metaphysics as a high point of promise. After this high point, late medieval metaphysics declines into "nominalism" and the theology of Duns Scotus, which then poisons the traditions of the Reformation (Reformed and Lutheran) and generates the acids of rationalistic modernity.[6] As fascinating as

---

5. "The Reformed Tradition and the Ontological Status of the Sacraments" and "Moving beyond Reductions of the Gospel and the Supper."

6. I use the term "nominalism" in a sense that reflects the contemporary discussion of RO and Boersma, in spite of hesitancies that I have about the historical usefulness of the term (see note 13 below). In this context, nominalism refers to a position in the medieval debates about universals—whether a universal term, such as "human being," corresponds with a universal property of what it means to be human in the mind of God (in a broadly Platonic conception), or in the thing itself (in an Aristotelian conception), or whether the term "human" is not used because it corresponds to a knowable universal, but it is a "nominal," conventional name that

it would be to speculate that a fourteenth-century scholastic debate could be at the origins of eighteenth- and nineteenth-century rationalism, this genealogy is problematic in numerous ways. In this chapter, after presenting a word of appreciation for the goals of these movements, I give a summative account of how and why the genealogy is misleading, particularly when used as a lens for describing and critiquing the ontology undergirding a catholic-Reformed tradition's account of the Lord's Supper and salvation in union with Christ.

Positively, as contemporary movements in theology, authors connected to RO and Boersma (who does not identify with RO) have provided much fodder for the academy's and the church's reflection. They have engaged in a theology of "retrieval" of voices such as Augustine's and Thomas's in a way that shows their relevance to contemporary discussion and debate. They have engaged in a sustained critique of the "secular" in a way that overcomes the modern tendency in systematic theology for theology to be subordinate to one or another social science.[7] In the process, the church and the Eucharist, along with the church's social-political engagement, have received renewed attention and focus. The doctrine of the incarnation has been championed as key for reinvigorating our engagement not only with Scripture,[8] but also with history, the social sciences, and philosophy.[9]

However, when it comes to the particular ways these authors approach historical "retrieval"—particularly as it relates to ontology—the problems are manifold. When particular historical figures are championed as heroes in their genealogy, they are often described in a way that lacks plausibility for historians who examine these figures in their historical context.[10] At other times, broad

---

we use to describe that group. As we will see, nominalist thinkers will have their own ways of affirming a type of communion and participation in God, but in terms of the grounds for doing this, they start with a more pragmatic theory of language.

7. John Milbank, *Theology and Social Theory: Beyond Secular Reason*, 2nd ed. (Oxford: Wiley-Blackwell, 2006); Hans Boersma, "Theology as Queen of Hospitality," *Evangelical Quarterly* 79, no. 4 (2007): 291–310.

8. Hans Boersma, *Heavenly Participation: The Weaving of a Sacramental Tapestry* (Grand Rapids: Eerdmans, 2011).

9. For example, see the essays in John Milbank, Catherine Pickstock, and Graham Ward, eds., *Radical Orthodoxy: A New Theology* (London: Routledge, 1998).

10. For an articulate summary of the ways in which Aquinas has been decontextualized in the use of his thought by Radical Orthodoxy, see Paul J. DeHart, *Aquinas and Radical Orthodoxy: A Critical Inquiry*, Routledge Studies in Religion 16 (New York: Routledge, 2012). In particular, DeHart shows not only how particular claims that RO attributes to Aquinas are problematic, but also the way a Heideggerian gloss leads RO astray in its interpretation. See DeHart, 189–94. In the words of medievalist John Marenbon, the Aquinas of RO "has almost nothing to do with the

generalizations are made about "*the* sacramental ontology of the Great Tradition" that dramatically underestimate the diversity in medieval and Reformation thought, and also point to an assumption common in RO and Boersma: that in sacramental metaphysics there is one golden key to unlock a truly sacramental theology and practice.[11] Rather than recognizing a variety of ways to affirm Christ's presence at the Supper, these theologians begin with their golden key and read all other traditions in light of it. When other traditions do not possess this golden key, it is bemoaned as an egregious departure from "the sacramental ontology." All who are without the golden key are assumed to have no access to a sacramental ontology that can bear the weight of truly upholding Christ's presence at the Supper.

In contrast to a golden key, I think a more helpful image is a catholic "water table" in which one can dive deeply enough into a tradition to discover catholic commonality with other traditions, even if in distinctive ways.[12] In terms of upholding a Trinitarian ontology that can bear the weight of Christ's presence at the Supper, I sense that the search for a single golden key is helpful for neither the academy nor the church. While recognizing the problem that Davis identifies of modern congregations lacking a sense of the reality of God in worship, and in the Supper in particular, I do not see the solution that "everyone needs to become a Thomist" as workable or helpful. Instead, theologians and congregations of various traditions need to do the hard work of returning to God's word in Scripture and entering into their own characteristic traditions in a way that is open to the insights of the broad and diverse voices of the catholic tradition. A golden key approach moves against the generosity and dialogical insight provided by such an approach to catholicity. In what follows, I seek to show how the catholic-Reformed tradition responds to genuine concerns about the reality of the triune God's action in and through the Supper, but in a framework that is first and foremost covenantal in its framing of the Supper, for biblical-exegetical reasons. It has points of commonality with the Thomistic vision advocated by RO and Boersma, but it also

---

Aquinas of history." John Marenbon, "Aquinas, Radical Orthodoxy and the Importance of Truth," in *Deconstructing Radical Orthodoxy: Postmodern Theology, Rhetoric, and Truth*, ed. Wayne J. Hankey and Douglas Hedley, new ed. (Aldershot, UK, and Burlington, VT: Ashgate, 2005), 62.

11. While I have this general concern about Hans Boersma's "sacramental tapestry," his practice of referring to "*the* sacramental ontology" and the overgeneralized concept of "*the* sacramental ontology of the Great Tradition" (emphasis added) is particularly revealing about his proposal. See Boersma, *Heavenly Participation*, 22–23, 52, 59, 61, 75, 94, 103, 105.

12. For an exposition of this catholic "water table" approach to ecumenical engagement, see pp. 64–69.

has points of difference that do not undermine its claim about divine action in worship and the sacraments, but undergird it in a distinctively Trinitarian and covenantal way.

But first, we need to assess the genealogy of decline presented by RO and Boersma. In portraying this "grand narrative" of decline from the alleged high point of a Thomistic metaphysic, they are forced to make three very problematic moves.

First, by blaming the rationalism of the Enlightenment on scholastic debates that took place four to five centuries earlier, they must claim that the divergence of Scotus and "nominalism" from Thomas is much greater than a contextual approach to this history will allow. As Richard Cross has argued in detail, RO dramatically misreads Scotus and "nominalism."[13] Scotus was not giving an ontological account that undermined sacramental theology or the participation of the sign in the thing itself, but was giving a semantic theory that "is wholly consistent with the view that creatures somehow participate in divine attributes."[14] Even if this more nuanced account of Scotus attested by historians is rejected, the genealogical account of one aspect of Scotus's thought undermining a whole medieval ontology of participation is not historically plausible, for "the processes of history are almost infinitely more complex than this."[15] Moreover, the fact that the impugned Scotus taught a very high sacramental theology (of transubstantiation)—in Scotus's view, higher than

13. Some of this misreading develops from an overly loose use of the term "nominalism" itself. It is often construed as a much more homogeneous movement than close historical investigation will permit, and defined in ways that even major "nominalists" would disagree with. As noted above, I use the term here because it is used by Boersma and RO, but I seek to use it cautiously. For a historical argument that calls into question the accuracy and even the historical usefulness of the category of "nominalism," see William J. Courtney, "Nominalism and Late Medieval Religion," in *The Pursuit of Holiness in Late Medieval and Renaissance Religion,* ed. Charles Trinkaus with Heiko A. Oberman, Studies in Medieval and Reformation Thought, vol. 10 (Leiden: Brill, 1974), 26–59.

14. Richard Cross, "'Where Angels Fear to Tread': Duns Scotus and Radical Orthodoxy," *Antonianum* 76, no. 1 (2001): 7–41, here 19.

15. Richard Cross, "Duns Scotus and Suarez at the Origins of Modernity," in *Deconstructing Radical Orthodoxy,* 66. Cross's methodological point that critiques RO's genealogical method of explaining modernity is worth considering in full: "Clearly *something* happened between (say) Aquinas and Christian Wolff. But the right answer is that *many* conceptual innovations occurred in this period, and perhaps that not even all of these together were sufficient for Wolff's unadulterated rationalism. On the level of the implicit causal conditions for modern metaphysics, it is not likely to be plausible to answer that there was just one fundamental shift that explains subsequent development. As a general rule, the processes of history are almost infinitely more complex than this."

Thomas Aquinas's theology—should also make us hesitate before affirming such a genealogy of sacramental decline.[16]

Second, seeing the pernicious "seed" of the Enlightenment in "nominalism" leads them to downplay or ignore the actual worship of congregations emerging from the Reformation. These authors quickly assume, in a top-down way, that if the Thomistic ontology is missing, then God and humanity are polarized and there is no real participation of the sign (of the bread and wine) in the signified (Christ). Consequently, they have paid very little attention to the social-historical, not to mention theological, development of the sacramental theologies of congregations worshiping in the tradition of the Reformation.[17] But as we saw in our sketch of the holy fairs, for centuries congregations who held to a Reformed confessional account had a lively, vivid, and powerful sense of Christ's presence at the Supper and the Spirit as working in and through the sign-act of the Supper. In addition, the reassessment of Reformed scholasticism in recent decades has shown that it was not, on the whole, part of a gradual movement toward Enlightenment rationalism. To the contrary, the movement was at once catholic and Reformed, retrieving from the church fathers and medieval theologians a Reformed confessional framework and safeguarding their work against rationalism by seeing theology as a "pilgrimage" toward the God who is fully known only by himself.[18] Rather than looking for the origins of the Enlightenment in a dubious reading of fourteenth-century texts, and using those to claim that those with a vivid sense of Christ's presence at the Supper did not really have that (such as Reformed congregations in the seventeenth and eighteenth centuries), these authors would do better to look contextually at the actual movement of the Enlightenment itself: that Enlightenment movements departed from the theology of divine mystery in

16. See Richard Cross, *Duns Scotus* (New York: Oxford University Press, 1999), 139–41.

17. An exception to this is the ambitious work by Brad S. Gregory, *The Unintended Reformation: How a Religious Revolution Secularized Society* (Cambridge, MA: Belknap Press of Harvard University Press, 2012). Gregory's account parallels, in important ways, the genealogy of RO for modernity. For our purposes, the central weakness of Gregory's argument is that it misreads early Reformed figures as advocating a theology of "univocity" rather than Thomistic "analogy" in the God-human relation. As the next few pages will show, such a characterization is inaccurate as an account of Reformation or post-Reformation Reformed theology.

18. On this, the archetypal/ectypal distinction is crucial. For an account of the argument against Reformed scholasticism as leading toward Enlightenment rationalism (in relation to this distinction), see Willem J. Van Asselt, "The Fundamental Meaning of Theology: Archetypal and Ectypal Theology in Seventeenth-Century Reformed Thought," *Westminster Theological Journal* 64 (2003): 322–24.

Reformed scholasticism, critiquing the convivial, embodied practice of the holy fairs through a movement toward "rational religion."[19]

Third, in reading the Reformation as largely captive to the mistakes of late medieval Scotist ontology, RO and Boersma misinterpret the sacramental theology and soteriology of the Reformation. They present an important objection to the project of the present book on this point, so I will outline some of the specific claims of RO and Boersma and then offer a response that builds upon the Reformed confessional portrait of chapter 3.

At the core, the Reformers are characterized by RO and Boersma as largely inheriting a univocal, nominalist theology, which—because the golden key is missing—is destined to give an unstable ontology of "participation." On the one hand, "the main historical target of Radical Orthodoxy is not the Reformation but rather late Scholasticism."[20] For "late medieval thought tended to back off from the metaphysics of participation, and the notion of the cosmos as sharing in, displaying to a certain degree, the divine essence."[21] In this account, Duns Scotus becomes a "crucial" figure in "the general shift away from a focus upon the metaphysics of participation."[22] With these late medieval ontological tendencies, the reality of God supposedly becomes dichotomized from that of creatures, so that divine and human attributes are not seen as related analogically (as with Thomas), but univocally (as with Scotus—where there is allegedly no correspondence or participation between "love" or "power" for God, for example, and the terms applied to human beings). This leads to a dualistic approach that polarizes God and humanity, and the sign and signified of the sacraments, so that divine and human agency are polarized against one another. While Milbank sees Luther as more guilty than Calvin of advocating a "univocalist and nominalist" metaphysic, he thinks that Calvin's support of justification by faith alone pushes his thought in a nominalist direction, and that a univocal ontology becomes widespread in seventeenth-century Reformed theology.[23] But Milbank thinks that even Calvin fails to "truly grasp a participatory ontology" in his doctrine of justification, his Christology, and his sacramental theology.[24] In all these, Calvin would have been better served

19. See the analysis at the end of chap. 2.

20. John Milbank, "Alternative Protestantism," in *Radical Orthodoxy and the Reformed Tradition: Creation, Covenant, and Participation*, ed. James K. A. Smith and James H. Olthuis (Grand Rapids: Baker Academic, 2005), 26.

21. Milbank, "Alternative Protestantism," 27.

22. Catherine Pickstock, "Modernity and Scholasticism," *Antonianum* 78 (2003): 5.

23. Milbank, "Alternative Protestantism," 30–31.

24. Milbank, "Alternative Protestantism," 33–35.

by an "analogical, participatory" ontology than the "univocalist or nominalist currents" that are more often "associated" with the Reformed.[25]

Undergirding this account is a very suspicious reading of the Reformation doctrine of justification by faith. According to Milbank, justification as "imputation"—the declaration of Christ's righteousness—was an outworking of a nominalist vision that sees the creation "univocally 'alongside' God, as if God and creation were both individual entities."[26] In a similar way, Hans Boersma asserts that "the imputation—according to the Reformers, a forensic declaration—was external or nominal in nature. Luther's notion that the believer was at the same time righteous and sinner (*simul iustus et peccator*) gave strong evidence of the nominal character of salvation."[27] Moreover, Boersma asserts that although Calvin had "a strong sense of the sanctifying grace of the Holy Spirit," yet "he, too, maintained that justification was a nominal or external juridical declaration rather than an internal transformation worked by the Holy Spirit."[28] As a part of this, Boersma claims Calvin opposed "nature and grace" in a way that a sacramental ontology would not.[29]

Concordant with this line of interpretation, RO theologians Graham Ward and Simon Oliver interpret Calvin's eucharistic theology in light of his alleged nominalist metaphysic.[30] Although the historical case for considering Calvin to be a theological "nominalist" is extremely weak,[31] Ward and Oliver assume this and consequently assert that even though Calvin uses the language of "participation" in the "substance" of Jesus Christ at the Supper, he does so assuming a metaphysical dualism that anticipates the individualism of modernity, where "spiritual" experiences are validated by the self.[32] On a fundamental

---

25. Milbank, "Alternative Protestantism," 35.

26. Milbank, "Alternative Protestantism," 32.

27. Boersma, *Heavenly Participation*, 92–93

28. Boersma, *Heavenly Participation*, 93.

29. Boersma, *Heavenly Participation*, 94.

30. See Simon Oliver, "The Eucharist before Nature and Culture," *Modern Theology* 15 (1999): 331–53; Graham Ward, "The Church as the Erotic Community," in *Sacramental Presence in a Postmodern Context*, ed. L. Boeve and L. Leijssen (Sterling, VA: Peeters, 2001); Graham Ward, *Cities of God* (London: Routledge, 2001), 161–67.

31. As I have argued in detail elsewhere, attempts to argue that Calvin had teachers who taught him theological forms of nominalism—who are then reflected in his later theology—fail on historical-contextual grounds. See my *Calvin, Participation, and the Gift: The Activity of Believers in Union with Christ* (Oxford: Oxford University Press, 2008), 24–35.

32. See Ward, "Church as the Erotic Community," 179–88. Also see Oliver, "Eucharist before Nature and Culture," 342–47; also see Catherine Pickstock, *After Writing: On the Liturgical Consummation of Philosophy* (Oxford and Malden, MA: Wiley-Blackwell, 1997), 162–63.

level, Calvin's alleged "dualism" between God and humanity, earthly and heavenly realities, makes his notion of a true union with Christ and participation in God unthinkable in his theology.

## Beyond the "Golden Key" Approach to Ontology: Responding to Misreadings and Locating the Reformed Tradition

In responding to these criticisms for the sake of the current catholic-Reformed project, we need to work at several levels. First, as noted above, Milbank, RO, and Boersma advocate much that is of historical value. Like them, I agree that figures such as Augustine are profoundly fruitful for contemporary retrieval; indeed, they have helped to revive valuable contemporary discussions of participation in God and Christ, and even deification. (On that point, both Luther and Calvin affirm a soteriology of deification that functions in a way that does not threaten their forensic account of justification.[33]) The problem with RO and Boersma is not that they seek to retrieve (*ressourcement*) from premodern sources; the problem is that as they do so, they create an implausible genealogy of modernity, mischaracterizing the theology of the Reformation and the origins of modernity.[34]

Second, while RO and Boersma focus much of their criticism on Calvin (to be addressed in the next point), a contextual history of the broader and later Reformed tradition gives their "Scotist/nominalist genealogy" approach very little plausibility for generalizing about the Reformed tradition and its theological trajectory. While Calvin is certainly a significant second-generation codifier of the Reformed tradition, he was one among several significant reformers in his own day; in the seventeenth and eighteenth century, he was not drawn upon as the sole authority or fountainhead of the Reformed tradition, but one among several reformers, as part of a range of theological sources drawn upon by the later Reformed tradition that included other reformers and patristic and medieval texts.[35] When one considers the broader

---

33. See J. Todd Billings, "The Contemporary Reception of Luther and Calvin's Doctrine of Union with Christ: Mapping a Biblical, Catholic, and Reformational Motif," in *Calvin and Luther: The Continuing Relationship*, ed. R. Ward Holder (Göttingen: Vandenhoeck & Ruprecht, 2013), 165–82; J. Todd Billings, "United to God through Christ: Calvin on the Question of Deification," *Harvard Theological Review* 98, no. 3 (July 2005): 315–34.

34. The French neologism *ressourcement* has no direct English equivalent, but as it has been used theologically, it signifies a movement of retrieval and return to core theological sources for the sake of contemporary renewal.

35. See Richard A. Muller, "Demoting Calvin: The Issue of Calvin and the Reformed Tra-

Reformed tradition, the genealogy that asserts that the Reformed tradition was "Scotist" and univocal rather than analogical and Thomistic falls flat. The Reformers, along with later figures in Reformed orthodoxy, were eclectic philosophically, using philosophy in ad hoc ways for the exposition of Scripture. Used toward this end, there was "a positive interest in Thomistic as opposed to Scotist formulations" in early Reformed thought and "no ground for claiming a nearly universal acceptance of Suarezian metaphysics" of univocity, as Brad Gregory and Milbank imply.[36]

Specifically, while seventeenth-century Reformed theologians would reference the opinion of Scotist-influenced Spanish Jesuit Francisco Suárez (1548–1617), they already occupied a tradition that had developed a Thomistic theology of analogy in a Reformed mode decades earlier. From the time of Girolamo Zanchi's *De natura Dei* (1577), along with Andreas Hyperius's *Methodus theologiae* (1567), Reformed theologians including Lambert Daneau and Theodore Beza continued to deny a doctrine of univocity and embrace an alternative favoring Aquinas.[37] Indeed, in Reformed orthodoxy, Reformed theologians engaged Aquinas directly, not simply through Catholic contemporaries such as Suárez and Cajetan, and their overall tendency was to reject the more Scotist-oriented approach of Suárez. As Richard Muller summarizes after a documentation of Reformed orthodoxy on this issue, "after Zanchi and Daneau had established a Thomistic line of argument, specifically referencing Thomas Aquinas as distinct from later Thomists like Cajetan, denying univocity and affirming analogy, the majority of Reformed writers held to the basic denial of univocity of being."[38] There were ongoing debates about how, exactly, to conceive of the alternative to univocity, but most Reformed writers "echoed Aquinas by grounding the analogy in a doctrine of participation and arguing an analogy of proportionality: God is being *essentialiter*, creatures have being by participation. Indeed, the foundational arguments against univocity of being rest on the assumption of creaturely dependence and a metaphysics of participation."[39] For our purposes, Muller's survey and analysis of Reformed orthodoxy on this point show how the genealogy of Milbank, Gregory, and,

---

dition," in *John Calvin, Myth and Reality: Images and Impact of Geneva's Reformer; Papers of the 2009 Calvin Studies Society Colloquium*, ed. Amy Nelson Burnett (Eugene, OR: Wipf and Stock, 2011).

36. Richard Muller, "Not Scotist: Understandings of Being, Univocity, and Analogy in Early-Modern Reformed Thought," in *Reformation and Renaissance Review* 14, no. 2 (2012): 145. Compare with Gregory, *The Unintended Reformation*, 53. See Milbank, "Alternative Protestantism," 35.

37. See Muller, "Not Scotist," 131.

38. Muller, "Not Scotist," 145.

39. Muller, "Not Scotist," 145.

presumably, Boersma is not plausible: while there is diversity in seventeenth-century Reformed theology on this point, a majority of theologians who addressed it affirmed a Thomistic "metaphysics of participation" that Milbank, Gregory, and Boersma all assume is missing.[40]

Finally, while RO and Boersma use Calvin as a target for the Reformed tradition on ontology, they neglect important aspects of Calvin's project and theology that would reframe their criticisms and concerns. Admittedly, Calvin, because he was first of all a biblical theologian, did not present a Thomistic view of participation with the clarity of Zanchi and some later in Reformed orthodoxy.[41] Yet, as neither a Scotist nor a Thomist, he clearly affirms a Trinitarian ontology that undergirds his view of salvation and the sacraments, based upon his biblical exegesis and use of earlier tradition.

Thus, to fit Calvin's doctrine of salvation and the sacraments into a "grand narrative" of the spread of a nominalist or Scotist metaphysic is to introduce a foreign and unhelpful framework for understanding Calvin's ontology. For Calvin, the doctrine of justification by faith—with its forensic emphasis—was not the outworking of a nominalist metaphysic: it was the result of biblical exegesis. If such a move would not be permitted by Milbank's metaphysic, as Milbank himself suggests, that simply points to the ways in which his ontology flattens the particularities of Scripture, rather than vice versa.[42] Instead of conforming biblical exegesis to a philosophical account of ontology, reformers such as Calvin prioritized biblical exegesis and utilized quite eclectic philosophical resources in the exposition and defense of biblically derived claims.[43]

---

40. Boersma does not specifically address Reformed orthodoxy on this point, but these later developments serve as a significant counterexample to the "grand narrative" he portrays in his account of the decline in a "sacramental ontology."

41. See Billings, *Calvin, Participation, and the Gift*, 190–95.

42. See Milbank, "Alternative Protestantism," 32.

43. In claiming that the Reformation doctrine of justification is "exegetically derived," I am not assuming that the Reformers simply received the Bible's teaching apart from a particular culturally embedded context. Rather, I am referring to the most widespread account of theological method given by the Reformers themselves, as well as in Reformed Orthodoxy: a *loci communes* approach, which starts with biblical exegesis and then moves to exposition that may draw upon philosophical distinctions for the sake of clarity, analysis, etc. This is why the Reformation is so philosophically eclectic, using philosophy for various ends, as the teaching of Scripture leads. Thus, for the vast majority of sixteenth- and seventeenth-century Reformation and post-Reformation theologians, they were not simply "Thomists" or "Scotists" but were first of all biblical theologians, and their philosophical development of the themes varied according to the issue. See Richard A. Muller, *After Calvin: Studies in the Development of a Theological Tradition* (New York: Oxford University Press, 2003), 130.

Likewise, it is a serious distortion to read the emphasis on the external righteousness of Christ as simply "nominal" in nature, as Boersma does, leading to a "nominal character of salvation." Far from being "nominal" or "name-only," Luther's mature account of justification is as forensic divine action that is never separated from the ontological reality of being united to Christ in a spiritual marriage by faith.[44] Moreover, Luther insisted upon Christ's external righteousness not because he was bound to a "nominalist" system but because of his biblical exegesis—an exegetical point that Thomist-trained and Thomist-leaning reformers such as Vermigli agreed with as well.[45] For Luther and Calvin, the declaration of God's Word in justification is not a fiction, or simply an abstraction, but an action—an enactment of God's own covenantal promise in Christ. Calvin spoke of this as the "double grace" of union with Christ, such that the regenerating and renewing Spirit is always given with the gift of justification. To suggest that a forensic notion of justification leads to a "nominal character of salvation" obscures this essential insight, not only because justification is not merely "nominal," but also because for Calvin and, to a large extent, the early Lutheran and Reformed tradition, salvation always involves the gift of new life and regeneration as well.[46]

## Creation, Participation, and Restoration in Calvin

For our purposes, the most significant question arising from the "golden key" authors above—usually posed to Calvin, specifically—is this: Does Calvin teach a dualism between God and humanity, along with "nature and grace," that nullifies the possibility of a true union with Christ at the Supper, and a participatory union with the triune God in salvation?

I have responded to a similar question at length in my first book,

---

44. See Billings, "The Contemporary Reception," 176–78.

45. On Vermigli's affirmation and use of the notion of Christ's external righteousness and imputation, see Frank A. James III, "Roman Commentary: Justification and Sanctification," in *A Companion to Peter Martyr Vermigli*, ed. Torrance Kirby, Emidio Campi, and Frank A. James III (Leiden: Brill Academic, 2009), 309–10. On his Thomist-leaning approach, see Luca Baschera, "Aristotle and Scholasticism," in *A Companion to Peter Martyr Vermigli*, 152–56.

46. While Calvin is clearer about and emphasizes more "the double grace," there is an analogous tradition in Luther, Melanchthon, and the early Lutheran confessions that emphasizes the doctrine of justification as one leading to good works. For historical analysis on this point, and the development of a pneumatology in the early Lutheran tradition in relation to the Reformed tradition, see Billings, "The Contemporary Reception," 177–80.

*Calvin, Participation, and the Gift.* I will give a brief summative response drawing on aspects of that earlier work here, but also explain how this relates to the Reformed confessional account of the Lord's Supper and the issues of sign and signified. For ultimately, on the issue of the Lord's Supper, the question for the present project is whether a Reformed confessional account of the sacrament of the Supper assumes a dualism between God and creation that would undermine its claims about union with Christ and communion with God.

Does Calvin, as a representative of the Genevan strand of a Reformed confessional theology, affirm a "dualism" between God and creation? When Calvin is read in his historical context, the answer must be an emphatic no. Throughout the course of Calvin's theological development as a reformer, he develops an emphatic and multifaceted theology of union with God in creation and redemption, clearly affirming that God's grace restores and fulfills created human nature rather than opposing nature and grace. Specifically, the saving work of the triune God restores, renovates, and heightens the primary participation that humanity was given in creation and that was disrupted through the Fall and sin.

Through his extensive work in biblical exegesis, along with his appropriation of aspects of the theology of church fathers such as Augustine, Irenaeus, and Cyril of Alexandria, Calvin developed a biblical theology that does not fit neatly into "Thomist" or "Scotist" categories, yet provides extensive ground for the reality of union with Christ by the Spirit, entailing a union and intimate communion with God. This account has a Trinitarian character for Calvin.[47] "Just as he [Christ] is one with the Father, let us become one with him."[48] In their union with Christ, believers are "participants not only in all his benefits but also in himself." Indeed, "day by day, he grows more and more into one body with us, until he becomes completely one with us."[49] Moreover, believers are "fully and firmly joined with God only when Christ joins us with him."[50] Yet, this union with Christ is impossible without a participation in the Spirit, who unites the believer to Christ.[51] Indeed, through the Spirit we

47. The rest of this paragraph is drawn from *Calvin, Participation, and the Gift,* 52–53.

48. My own translation of "et quemadmodum unus est in patre, ita nos unum in ipso fiamus." Note the parallel of "oneness" and mutual indwelling between the Trinitarian oneness (Father and Son) and economic oneness (Christ and believers). Calvin, Sermon on 1 Samuel 2:27–36, *CO* 29:353.

49. Calvin, *Institutes* 3.2.24.

50. Calvin, *Institutes* 2.16.3.

51. Calvin, *Institutes* 3.1.2. For an account of the crucial role of the Spirit in Calvin's Trin-

"come to a participation in God (*in Dei participationem venimus*)."[52] Through Christ and the Spirit, believers are gathered "into participation in the Father."[53] Since the "perfection of human happiness is to be united to God," this union takes place in redemption.[54] "We are united to God by Christ," Calvin writes. "We can only be joined to Christ if God abides in us."[55] In this way, "men are so united to Christ by faith that Christ unites them to God."[56] Yet, being united with God does not make believers "consubstantial with God," as if they were a fourth member of the Godhead, but rather it takes place in Christ, by "the grace and power of the Spirit."[57] Calvin also speaks of a coming beatific vision, a "direct vision" of the Godhead, "when as partakers in heavenly glory we shall see God as he is."[58] This final, temporal end is in fact "the end of the gospel," which is "to render us eventually conformable to God, and, if we may so speak, to deify us."[59]

This language is a far cry from "dualism." Obviously, Calvin uses strong language to affirm the reality of union with Christ by the Spirit and a strong sense of oneness between God and humanity in redemption, while maintaining a Creator-creature distinction. This union is real, and in some sense "ontological"—but it is not an ontological fusion between God and humanity or between Christ and the believer. It is a relational reality of communion with the triune God, made possible through the real and powerful work of this same triune God.

To address the concerns of Boersma and RO, it is necessary to see how this relational oneness in redemption is a restoration of the communion

---

itarian doctrine of participation, see Philip Walker Butin, *Revelation, Redemption, and Response* (New York: Oxford University Press, 1995), 79–92.

52. My own literal translation. Beveridge renders the overall passage "By means of him [the Spirit] we become partakers of the divine nature (*in Dei participationem venimus*), so as in a manner to feel his quickening energy within us." Calvin, *Institutes* 1.13.14. John Calvin, *Institutes of the Christian Religion*, trans. Henry Beveridge (Digireads.com Publishing, 2014); *Joannis Calvini: Opera Selecta*, vol. 3, ed. P. Barth and G. Niesel (Eugene, OR: Wipf and Stock, 2011), 128.

53. Calvin, *Institutes* 1.8.26.

54. Calvin, *Institutes* 1.15.6.

55. Calvin, 1 John 4:15, CC; CO 47:145.

56. Calvin, 1 John 4:15, CTS; CO 47:145. Cf. commentary on Jeremiah 31: "We shall at length be really and fully united to Thee [Almighty God] through Christ our Lord."

57. Calvin, *Institutes* 1.15.5.

58. Calvin, *Institutes* 2.14.3.

59. Calvin, 2 Peter 1:4, CTS; CO 55:446. Calvin's willingness to speak of deification, at this point, is in response to the statement in 2 Pet. 1:4 about believers becoming "participants of the divine nature."

with God at creation. To accomplish this, I will briefly draw upon Calvin's theology of creation in his *Institutes* and *Commentaries*, along with some philosophical distinctions he makes in his neglected work *The Bondage and Liberation of the Will*. Calvin, in language that is consonant with the Reformed confessions yet more elaborated, teaches that God made creation good, in communion with God.[60] In fact, Adam was "united to God," and his righteousness was through "participation in God."[61] Humanity was thus created to be in communion with God, united to God—but in a particular way: looking not to itself, but to God in active trust. As Calvin says in his Genesis commentary, God gave man the tree of life in the garden so that, "as often as he tasted the fruit of that tree, [he] should remember whence he received his life, in order that he might acknowledge that he lives not by his own power, but by the kindness of God alone; and that life is not (as they commonly speak) an intrinsic good, but proceeds from God. Finally, in that tree there was a visible testimony to the declaration, that 'in God we are, and live, and move.'"[62] Humans were created to live and move "in God" rather than "in themselves." Thus, humans are not only created good, but created for this purpose.

Yet, sin disrupts this communion—precisely by one's act of trusting and acting "in oneself" apart from God, rather than acting in God, in participation in God. What Calvin does in this move is to map the language of union with Christ and union with God in the Gospels and Paul onto his account of creation and sin. To be sinful is to be alienated from God—to act in "the old self" rather than trusting and acting "in God," "in Christ," and "in the Spirit." Thus, when the Spirit comes to effectually regenerate sinners, it is not a violent, coercive act, but God "renews a right spirit in their inner nature" to restore and fulfill the created goodness of humanity by bringing them back into an "in God," "in Christ," and "in the Spirit" reality.[63] As such, the Spirit enables a glad heart to embrace the gospel and enter into this identity. In the later confessional words of the Canons of Dort, God's "divine grace of regeneration does not act in people as if they were blocks and stones; nor does it abolish

---

60. See Jan Rohls, *Reformed Confessions: Theology from Zurich to Barmen* (Louisville: Westminster John Knox, 1998), 64–68.

61. See Calvin, *Institutes* 2.1.5; 2.2.1.

62. Calvin, Genesis 2:9, CTS; *CO* 23:38.

63. Calvin denies that God would "coerce anyone by violence." Instead, "so that he may have willing [*voluntarios*] servants who follow of their own accord and obey, he creates a new heart in them and renews a right spirit in their inner nature." See John Calvin, *The Bondage and Liberation of the Will*, ed. A. N. S. Lane, trans. G. I. Davies (Grand Rapids: Baker, 1996), 193–94, 232.

the will and its properties or coerce a reluctant will by force, but spiritually revives, heals, reforms, and—in a manner at once pleasing and powerful—bends it back."[64] Divine regeneration revives, renovates, and restores a bound will through the power of the Spirit.

In *Bondage and Liberation of the Will*, Calvin expresses this through an ad hoc use of the Aristotelian categories of "substance" and "accidents" to explain the implications of his biblically derived proposal. The good, created nature of human beings is the "substance" of human nature; yet the Fall adds the "accidental" characteristic of sin, which disrupts this primal communion with God and with neighbor in the creation.[65] In the fallen state, humans still bear traces of God's image—which Calvin appropriately calls "a participation in God."[66] Thus, when the Spirit regenerates a sinner, giving faith and uniting the sinner to Christ as an adopted child of the Father, this primal "participation" and union with God is *restored* in redemption. The primal "substance" of human nature is restored by the Spirit, for grace is given "to restore the nature that has fallen."[67] As the Spirit moves believers along the path of sanctification, they die to the "old self" in mortification—but that is *not* dying to the good, created nature, but to the sinful, dehumanizing self that trusts and acts in autonomy from God. In this way, the Spirit's effectual work in uniting believers more and more to Christ is a restoration of the "substance" of primal human nature, leading humans to an even higher union with God than the first Adam, since Christ, the second Adam, enjoys a more intimate union with God than the first Adam.[68] Nonetheless, Calvin is clear and emphatic: in creation and redemption, God and human creatures are *united* in a differentiated way; grace restores and fulfills nature; the ontological reality of this union provides ample ground for affirming the reality of Calvin's language when he speaks of union with Christ by the Spirit, union with God, over and against a metaphysical dualism that divides God from the creaturely realm.

---

64. The Canons of Dort, the Third and Fourth Main Points of the Doctrine, article 16, in *Our Faith*, 133.

65. Calvin, *The Bondage and Liberation of the Will*, 46–48.

66. Calvin, *Institutes* 1.2.1.

67. Calvin, *The Bondage and Liberation of the Will*, 99.

68. See Calvin, 1 Corinthians 15:46, CTS.

## The Reformed Tradition and
## the Ontological Status of the Sacraments

The theological clarification above provides crucial context for framing the ontological status of the sign and signified of God's action in the Supper. As noted in chapter 3, the Reformed confessions describe the sacraments as God's word, specifically God's covenantal promise, which are given as "signs and seals" of God's grace. The majority of the Reformed confessions affirm that the bread and wine are "instruments" of the Spirit that exhibit and offer Christ, and that the elements are not to be adored in themselves. The elements, in themselves, are instruments in this drama, not actors. In his biblical exegesis, Calvin repeatedly contrasts "the old self"—and creation seen "in itself"—and the restoration of creation "in Christ," "in the Spirit," and "in God." Because of the covenantal context related to union with Christ, Calvin uses this framework to explain the logic of the confessional account of the status of signs. The Supper does not offer "empty signs," but at the Supper believers feed upon Jesus Christ himself by the Spirit. Jesus Christ is the "substance," the signified, of the sacramental signs: he is given by the Spirit through the sacramental signs, and received in trust. Yet, to offer adoration to the bread and wine is to see these "in themselves" rather than as instruments "in Christ" and "by the Spirit." "What is idolatry if not this: to worship the gifts in place of the Giver himself?"[69] The signs "exhibit" Christ by the Spirit, but for Calvin adoration of the signs sinfully disorders God's purpose for creation: to participate in God, recognizing God alone as the source of all good, rather than creation "in itself." In concordance with this, both Calvin and the Reformed confessions seek a balance on the issue of sign and signified in the sacraments: the sacramental sign is never "empty" in holding forth God's grace to be received; yet, sign and signified cannot be so closely identified as to lead believers to trust in the sign "in itself," apart from its instrumental function "in Christ," "in the Spirit."

Thus, rather than make a general argument for "sacramental ontology" from the nature of the God-creation relation, as Milbank and Boersma do, the Reformed confessions follow cues from their biblical exegesis to present an ontology that is covenantal in character, shaped by the characteristics of a biblical theology of union with Christ. One of the most controversial features of this approach is also one of the most ecumenically fruitful: in addition to utilizing a covenantal account of union with Christ to shape an ontology of signs and signified, the Reformed confessions insist that two distinct yet insep-

---

69. Calvin, *Institutes* 4.17.36.

arable gifts received in union with Christ are justification and sanctification. This was explored in chapter 3 in the three articles of the Belgic Confession that expound union with Christ by faith, justification as forgiveness by God's forensic declaration, and sanctification as the inseparable gift of new life generated by the Spirit. Other major Reformed confessions concur.[70] This is incredibly significant for the promise of the gospel and the promise of the Supper: it is both forensic and transformational, it entails both forgiveness and new life by the Spirit. The promise of baptism and the Supper always involves both. The promise of the gospel always entails both.

The tendency in the circles of RO is to flatten the biblical witness on this point. Rather than affirm two gifts, retaining the power of both the forensic and the transformational images for union with Christ in Scripture, RO collapses the two into one. For RO, the tendency is to interpret the forensic language of justification as really "transformational" in the end, leading to the attacks upon a forensic doctrine of justification, noted above. In contrast, others react to this challenge to a Reformed doctrine of justification by clinging to God's forensic action in a way that strongly downplays a sense of mystical union with Christ by the Spirit.[71]

The tendency to reduce the benefits of the gospel to either forgiveness or transformation is not limited to scholars—it occurs frequently in congregations as well. As noted in chapter 1, for many congregations, the gospel is about "forgiveness" and entrance into heaven. Sometimes justification is seen as the whole of the gospel, connected to one's "conversion experience." Not surprisingly, the sacraments in these contexts usually relate mainly to remembering the benefits of God's forgiveness, since that is the primary benefit of salvation. In other congregational contexts, the gospel is approached more as a tool for transformation: as a tool for social and political transformation, for calling people to justice; or as a tool for transformation to "personal holiness"—a

70. See J. Todd Billings, "Union with Christ and the Double Grace: Calvin's Theology and Its Early Reception," in *Calvin's Theology and Its Reception: Disputes, Developments, and New Possibilities*, ed. J. Todd Billings and I. John Hesselink (Louisville: Westminster John Knox, 2012), 63–67.

71. See Bruce McCormack's critique of Calvin's language of mystical union with Christ, along with Calvin's appropriation of the church fathers on the point. See Bruce McCormack, "What's at Stake in Current Debates over Justification?," in *Justification: What's at Stake in the Current Debates?*, ed. Mark Husbands and Daniel J. Treier (Downers Grove: InterVarsity, 2004), 104–5. For a cogent response to McCormack on this point, see Michael Horton, "Union and Communion: Calvin's Theology of Word and Sacrament," *International Journal of Systematic Theology* 11, no. 4 (2009): 398–414.

way to move beyond the wayward ways of the world; or as a tool for more of a self-help transformation—for a positive self-image, an empowered life where one's goals can be accomplished.

On both sides of this fence—among theologians and congregations—there is a grain of truth. But both offer a reduction of God's gospel promise in Scripture, and an overly narrow view of the gifts received in baptism and the Lord's Supper.


## Moving beyond Reductions of the Gospel and the Supper

In light of these reductionisms of the gospel—which correspond to sacramental reductionisms—what is the way forward? As noted in chapter 1, these reductionisms of the gospel tend to correspond to reductionisms in the way congregations practice the Supper. When the Supper is celebrated solely in remembrance of the cross and forgiveness of sins, that tends to be that congregation's view of the "gospel." There is a different temptation for those who de-emphasize the cross and forgiveness—then the Supper can be reduced to an event simply about inclusion or transformation without a proper recognition of the tremendous gift of forgiveness through the cross to sinners at the table. Both reductionisms offer a conundrum about how to move forward to a fuller, more multifaceted taste and vision of the gospel and the Supper.

What is the way forward? It is for communities of Word and sacrament to return to God's word in Scripture to enliven our vision, our taste, our knowledge of the triune God made known to us in Christ. Key for this endeavor is directing our attention, our desires, our meditations toward God's word in Scripture, fulfilled in Christ. Methodologically, this means that our sacramental theology must have enough definition to direct us toward this Trinitarian, Christ-centered end. Yet, we always do theology as pilgrims—pilgrims who are hearing Scripture anew, being reshaped by God's Word until we encounter our Lord face-to-face on the final day. As we will see in the upcoming chapters, this approach provides enough determinacy to guide congregations in celebrating the Supper in remembrance, communion, and hope. Yet, it is also open to fresh insights from biblical exegesis that are flexible enough to enliven various worship practices. A Reformed account of union with Christ at the table is simple enough to be embraced by the young and mysterious enough to be contemplated by the old. But at its core, by embracing the table as a divine instrument through which Christ offers himself by the Spirit, received in faith, congregations enter onto a path that disrupts common ways of reducing the good news itself to less than what God promises in Scripture.

In *The King Jesus Gospel*, Scot McKnight rightly critiques accounts that reduce the gospel to "justification by faith" or a "plan of salvation" of how to receive forgiveness.[72] This "plan of salvation" is combined with a "method of persuasion"—of pressuring people to make a "decision" for Christ—in a way that actually obscures the central New Testament teaching that "because the Jesus Story completes the Israel Story, it saves."[73] Unfortunately, in the contemporary West, "the Plan of Salvation and the Method of Persuasion have been given so much weight they are crushing and have crushed the Story of Israel and the Story of Jesus. This has massive implications for the gospel itself."[74] The gospel is culminated in the story of Jesus, but that is only understandable as a fulfillment of the story of Israel. To reduce the gospel to a story about "how to get forgiveness" and the methods for persuading a personal decision is to distort the gospel message. In contrast, McKnight argues that there is an urgent need for congregations today to recover a multifaceted sense of the gospel by returning to the scriptural narrative of Israel, as fulfilled in Christ.

Although he does not give an extended historical argument, McKnight associates the origin of this decline with the Reformation, perhaps because he senses that some "new Calvinists" reduce the gospel to "justification." Yet, neither Calvin, nor Luther, nor the later Reformed or Lutheran confessional traditions reduce the gospel simply to "justification" and to pressuring toward a "decision" for Christ. An explanation with more power is the transition briefly chronicled in the nineteenth century with Charles Finney and the new measures; this approach has become characteristic of later American evangelicalism and revivalism in particular.[75] As seen in the decline of the holy fairs, there was a move away from attention to the triune God's action in union with Christ and toward, in the case of revivalism, pressure exercised through a "method of persuasion" for sinners to respond to the "plan of salvation." But McKnight's overall point stands: there is an urgent need for congregations today to recover a multifaceted sense of the gospel by returning to the scriptural narrative of Israel, as fulfilled in Christ.

---

72. See Scot McKnight, *The King Jesus Gospel: The Original Good News Revisited* (Grand Rapids: Zondervan, 2011), 26, 37.

73. McKnight, *The King Jesus Gospel*, 37.

74. McKnight, *The King Jesus Gospel*, 43.

75. For a historical account of the ways in which these features of Finney's approach became characteristic in American evangelicalism, see Randall Balmer, *The Making of Evangelicalism: From Revivalism to Politics and Beyond* (Waco: Baylor University Press, 2010), especially 20–27.

Thus, a healthy theology of union with Christ at the Supper needs only a Trinitarian and covenantal ontology, as this chapter has explored. It should be shaped by ongoing biblical exegesis on the pilgrim path of theology—seeking the mind of Christ for the church. It needs to draw upon the narrative of the whole of Scripture to show how, exactly, the story of creation, of Israel, of the covenant, of the temple is fulfilled in Christ, and thus the significance of union with this same Christ by the Spirit. Thus, for congregations, one cannot and should not simply focus on "union with Christ" passages in the New Testament in renewing the theology of union with Christ. One needs to read all of Scripture as *fulfilled* rather than *displaced* by Christ. As the risen Christ says to his disciples in Luke 24:44, "everything written about me in the law of Moses, the prophets, and the psalms must be fulfilled" (NRSV). Christ does not complete the Old Testament in a way that leads to its being set aside, but he *fulfills* it. As tempting as it is to settle for a one-sided gospel, or a one-sided Christ, we need to return again and again to the particularity of Scripture to discern how—in a nonreductionistic way—it is fulfilled in Christ Jesus, to whom we are united by the Spirit in the word of the gospel, both in preaching and in the sign-acts of the sacraments. To this task we will turn in the final three chapters of this book, as we explore the biblical, theological, and practical enactment of the Supper as an icon of the gospel—in remembrance, communion, and hope.

## PART 3

∾

# The Supper and the Gospel
# in Remembrance, Communion, and Hope

A central task for pastors and congregational leaders in the contemporary late modern context is how to move congregations from a static, nominal encounter with the gospel into a deeper, transformative embrace of the gospel of Jesus Christ. In this book, I have been making the case for how a renewed theology and practice of the Lord's Supper can be an instrument toward this larger goal. As an instrument, the Lord's Supper is God's chosen means for reshaping his adopted people into Christ's image by the power of the Spirit—an instrument that moves our affections, changes our perceptions, and sets forth a new identity for Christians to live into in the church and the world.

But how exactly does that happen? As congregational leaders, our tendency is often to look to "quick fix" approaches: learning to attract more people by adopting a different worship style, by adding new programs to nurture young families, or even by moving from infrequent celebrations of the Lord's Supper to frequent ones. All these are good, concrete ideas to consider—and for congregations that currently celebrate the Supper infrequently, I would strongly recommend more frequent celebration. But there is no "quick fix," or solve-all approach, to a deep and transformative embrace of the gospel. The gospel is not a natural human phenomenon. The gospel begins and ends with the God of Jesus Christ—the Alpha and the Omega, the Beginning and the End, the only source for any true life and communion that we experience. While we need to experience this gospel in our lives, it remains external to us in its origin: it is the good news of God—with a divine source, and a divinely enabled destination. If this is the case, then moving on a path of deep transformation always involves offering ourselves on a path of prayer and worship to "hear more" and "see more" of what God has for us in Christ. In these final three chapters, we explore how the Lord's Supper can be the divine instrument through which we take this journey, enabling us to have a multifaceted encounter with the good news that spans past, present, and future, experiencing the Supper in remembrance, communion, and hope.

As we begin exploring what participating in the Supper as remembrance, communion, and hope involves, we first need to see that this movement is not initiated or sourced through our own self-improving ambitions, but through the Lord Jesus's action in and through us by the Spirit.

## Remembrance, Communion, and Hope: An Expansive, Biblical Vision

If our identity is to be transformed in the triune drama of salvation, then we need a robust and multifaceted *remembrance* of God's promises. This will be inseparably connected with a present *communion* with our Lord Jesus Christ mediated by the Spirit. This will also involve a *hope* for the return of the same Christ, and the final consummation of creation giving way to the promised kingdom. Through all this, dwelling upon and receiving God's word in Scripture, we are given words of life that direct our path, reveal our script in the drama, and show us the identity to which the Spirit is conforming us in Christ.

Why is this threefold approach necessary? N. T. Wright claims that the story of Jesus is incomplete without the story of Israel in the past, and also without the story of God's future, which frames the church's present.[1] In parallel to this, Wright speaks about the Lord's Supper as a place where "past and present come together. Events from long ago are fused with the meal we are sharing here and now."[2] Moreover, "if the bread-breaking is one of the key moments when the thin partition between heaven and earth becomes transparent, it is also one of the key moments when God's future comes rushing into the present."[3] For "Jesus—the real Jesus, the living Jesus, the Jesus who dwells in heaven and rules over the earth as well, the Jesus who has brought God's future into the present—wants not just to influence us, but to rescue us; not just to inform us, but to heal us; not just to give us something to think about, but to feed us, and to feed us with himself. That's what this meal is

1. N. T. Wright, *How God Became King: The Forgotten Story of the Gospels* (New York: HarperOne, 2012), 113, 153.

2. N. T. Wright, *Simply Jesus: A New Vision of Who He Was, What He Did, and Why He Matters* (New York: HarperOne, 2011), 154.

3. Wright, *Simply Jesus*, 154.

all about."[4] The Supper—like the gospel itself—involves a convergence of God's mighty acts and promises in the past, the in-breaking and anticipation of God's future, and nourishment upon Christ in the present. Anything less is a reduction, something other than living before the face of the triune God.

This simple framework moves powerfully beyond myopic views of the gospel and the Supper, toward a more deeply biblical encounter of both. Both the gospel and the Supper hinge upon the biblical story—from creation, where God creates a people with whom to dwell; to the story of Israel, with its prophets, priests, and kings; to the story's culmination in Christ, the true prophet, priest, and king in his saving person and the saving work of his life, death, and resurrection. The gospel involves nothing less than the forgiveness of sins because of the cross of Christ and the gift of eternal life. But it involves more: the ascended Christ continues to exercise his Lordship in the church by the Spirit, giving new life that conforms his people to his image through God's Word. Believers remember the great narrative of God's mighty promises and acts culminated in Christ and continue to feed upon Christ by Word and sacrament as they abide in Christ's word in acts of love toward God, in loving service, and in witness to neighbor. All this is in the context of confessing Jesus Christ as the one true Lord, the true King, and participating in his reign until that day when the feast of the Supper will give way to the marriage feast of the Lamb of God with his bride, the church (Rev. 19:7–9). On that day, when heaven and earth come together, God's intent for creation, to make his home on the whole earth as a temple, will be fulfilled: "Look! God's dwelling place is now among the people, and he will dwell with them. They will be his people, and God himself will be with them and be their God" (Rev. 21:3). Indeed, the final city of God "does not need the sun or the moon to shine on it, for the glory of God gives it light, and the Lamb is its lamp" (Rev. 21:23). On that day, the face of the Lord will truly and completely shine on his people, as he dwells with them in loving fellowship.

### The Sacrament as Past, Present, and Future

How can we briefly state the catholic and Reformed connections between the Supper and the gospel, as remembrance, communion, and hope? A liturgical formulation from the Reformed Church in America, entitled "Meaning of the Sacrament," can assist in this articulation:

4. Wright, *Simply Jesus*, 154.

Beloved in the Lord Jesus Christ, the holy Supper which we are about to celebrate is a feast of remembrance, of communion, and of hope.

We come in remembrance that our Lord Jesus Christ was sent of the Father into the world to assume our flesh and blood and to fulfill for us all obedience to the divine law, even to the bitter and shameful death of the cross. By his death, resurrection, and ascension he established a new and eternal covenant of grace and reconciliation that we might be accepted of God and never be forsaken by him.

We come to have communion with this same Christ who has promised to be with us always, even to the end of the world. In the breaking of the bread he makes himself known to us as the true heavenly Bread that strengthens us unto life eternal. In the cup of blessing he comes to us as the Vine in whom we must abide if we are to bear fruit.

We come in hope, believing that this bread and this cup are a pledge and foretaste of the feast of love of which we shall partake when his kingdom has fully come, when with unveiled face we shall behold him, made like unto him in his glory.

Since by his death, resurrection, and ascension Christ has obtained for us the life-giving Spirit who unites us all in one body, so are we to receive this Supper in true love, mindful of the communion of saints.[5]

Statements like this have limitations as liturgical forms—they tend toward the verbose and didactic, rather than entering directly into the prayer and worship of the sign-act of the Supper.[6] But for our purposes, it provides a helpful summary of how Reformed and catholic themes—such that I developed in chapters 1–4—relate to this threefold approach to the gospel and the Supper. It highlights how the Lord's Supper is a site for divine action—one in which God's covenantal action in the past and his covenantal promise for the future

5. *Worship the Lord: The Liturgy of the Reformed Church in America* (Grand Rapids: Reformed Church Press, 2005), 11. This "meaning of the sacrament" adopted by the Reformed Church in America is frequently attributed to Howard Hageman (1921–1992), a Reformed liturgical scholar, professor, and pastor.

6. See the appreciative critique of Christopher Dorn regarding the didactic character of this Lord's Supper liturgy in his fine book *The Lord's Supper in the Reformed Church in America: Tradition in Transformation* (New York: Peter Lang, 2007), especially 185–91.

are apprehended and fed upon in covenantal communion in the present. The sign-action is done in remembrance of God's mighty acts and promises culminated in Christ ("Do this in remembrance of me" [Luke 22:19; 1 Cor. 11:24]). It involves a *koinōnia* and sharing in Christ's body and blood, and the ecclesial community gathered ("The cup of blessing that we bless, is it not a sharing in the blood of Christ? The bread that we break, is it not a sharing in the body of Christ? Because there is one bread, we who are many are one body, for we all partake of the one bread" [1 Cor. 10:16–17 NRSV]). As believers eat and drink in this fellowship, they also hope for final consummation of God's kingdom with the bodily return of Christ ("For as often as you eat this bread and drink the cup, you proclaim the Lord's death until he comes" [1 Cor. 11:26 NRSV]).

The importance of the convergence of past, present, and future at the Supper is not only emphasized by Anglican scholars such as Wright and my own Geneva strand of the Reformed tradition. It is a point of ecumenical overlap, thus a point in which a broadly catholic-Reformed tradition can provide an entryway. For example, Roman Catholic theologian Dom Anscar Vonier speaks of this dynamic elegantly in his highly regarded work *A Key to the Doctrine of the Eucharist*. For Vonier, the sacrament is a sign—indeed, a sign that makes a declaration—that is simultaneously pulling together the past, present, and future. "Every sacrament, then, has something to declare: it recalls the past, it is the voice of the present, it reveals the future," Vonier writes. "If the sacrament did not fulfill its function of sign proclaiming something which is not seen, it would not be a sacrament at all. It can embrace heaven and earth, time and eternity, because it is a sign."[7] For Vonier, the *sign* character of the sacrament connects it indelibly with the salvation history of creation and Israel, fulfilled in Jesus Christ. Precisely because of this canonically derived history, the *sign* character of the sacrament is not a vague "grace," but a specified one. "Were it only a grace it would be no more than the gift of the present hour; but being a sign the whole history of the spiritual world is reflected in it: 'For as often as you shall eat this bread and drink the chalice, you shall show the death of the Lord, until he comes.'"[8] The sign character of the sacrament flourishes, displaying its expansive biblical scope, when it is received as the convergence of past, present, and future in the triune God's economy of redemption. Rediscovering the sign-act of the Supper as remembrance, communion, and hope is part of an ecumenical Christian vision.

7. Dom Anscar Vonier, *A Key to the Doctrine of the Eucharist* (n.p.: Assumption Press, 2013), 14.

8. Vonier, *Key to the Doctrine*, 14.

However, these chapters do not simply seek to provide a Reformed entryway into a larger catholic space. They seek to give biblical and theological insight into the gospel and the Supper that can help congregations to move more deeply into their personal and corporate identity in Christ. While pastoral leaders frequently receive advice on how to "reinvent" and "revive" their congregations, their ultimate need is not a new mission statement or a strategic plan or a marketing strategy. It is to look to Jesus Christ for new life and their union to him as adopted children of the Father by the Spirit. Christ is the Alpha and Omega—we inhabit our true history in him, we enjoy the sweetness of present communion with him and others, and we hope for the coming kingdom feast with him as the crucified and risen Lamb. Rather than looking for "quick fix" strategies for congregations, we should look to the Spirit's own divinely given instrument: the Lord's Supper as a sign-act of the gospel itself—remembering, communing, and hoping with Jesus Christ, our only hope in life and death.

~

# CHAPTER 5

# Remembrance in Union with Christ

"Do this in remembrance of me." The Lord Jesus delivers this command at the Last Supper and at the instituting of the Lord's Supper. In many evangelical congregations, these words are the high point of the Supper's significance. This is engraved on the communion table; these words are repeated again and again to the congregation. The act of remembrance is seen as the center point of the Supper; the promise "this is my body" and the command to celebrate "until he comes again" find their places on the outer edge.

There is a profound value to this form of piety: it usually emphasizes a remembrance of Christ's cross as a once-for-all sacrifice for the forgiveness of sins. It frequently occurs amidst the music and song of solemnity, and it emphasizes personal repentance in preparation for the Supper. In all these ways, the practice cultivates a congregational perception of the gospel as the forgiveness of sins through the cross.

Pastors should not spurn these themes, but embrace them. It is a deep theological mistake to downplay the earthshaking significance of Christ's cross. We are sinners approaching a holy God—and as such we need to look to Christ and his cross for forgiveness. However, when this theme becomes singular rather than integrated with other themes, it provides a myopic vision of both the Supper and the gospel. As N. T. Wright and Scot McKnight both argue, it portrays a view of the gospel that fails not because of what it *includes*, but because of what it *displaces*: the broader biblical narrative of the triune God's work in and through creation and Israel, culminated in Jesus Christ—who is present now by the Spirit—as we anticipate and await the fullness of God's new creation. As an icon of the gospel, the Supper is a visible sign-action of the gospel itself. Thus, the Supper as "remembrance, communion, and hope" gives a multifaceted sense of what the Supper is, and of what the gospel is. Indeed, ultimately we underplay the significance of even "remembrance" when it is severed from communion and hope. If we desire to live into this larger vision, we need to move more deeply into discovering what remembrance in union with Christ really means.

## *Anamnesis* and Recovering Remembrance

Jesus commands that we *do this* (eat and drink at the Supper) in *remembrance* (*anamnesis*) of him. The term for "remembrance" at the Supper in Luke and 1 Corinthians 11, *anamnesis*, is richer than a contemporary English sense of "remember" or "memorial" can portray. Forms of the term are used in Paul's account of the words of institution in relation to the bread and the cup in 1 Corinthians 11:24–25 and in relation to the bread in Luke 22:19. As Anthony Thiselton convincingly argues, to "remember" in this sense is "not simply to call to mind" the mighty acts of God, but to "assign them an active role in one's 'world.'" Specifically, remembering God and his works is to "engage in worship, trust, and obedience"—a remembering that "transforms attitudes and action."[1] Using recent philosophical investigation to expound the implications of this biblical "remembrance" tradition,[2] Thiselton notes that for Eric Voegelin and Paul Ricoeur, "remembrance" is crucial for "the establishing and integration of identity."[3] For Ricoeur, it involves inserting oneself into "a meaningful 'plot' of narrative history" in which "past, present, and future" are brought together in a narrative in terms of "memory and hope."[4] Some "remembering" is trite—like remembering a shopping list; but other remembering is identity forming—opening up a new world, a new drama to inhabit.

The connections between the Lord's Supper and the Jewish Passover can illuminate the type of remembrance intended at the Supper. When the Israelites remembered their deliverance from Egypt, it was not a casual act but an identity-forming one. Jewish theologian and biblical scholar Jon Levenson gives a helpful portrayal of the Passover's formational impact, leading participants to inhabit a new drama.

1. Anthony C. Thiselton, *The First Epistle to the Corinthians* (Grand Rapids: Eerdmans, 2013), 879.
2. As Thiselton notes regarding the contribution of Voegelin and Ricoeur, "none of this deviates from what may be inferred from lexical research [on anamnesis], still less contradicts it." Thiselton, *First Epistle to the Corinthians*, 880.
3. Thiselton, *First Epistle to the Corinthians*, 879.
4. Thiselton, *First Epistle to the Corinthians*, 880.

Levenson notes the way in which the covenantal character of God's relation to Israel, displayed through the Passover, internalizes the history of God's acts in the past for the present, giving a view of the future. Levenson highlights the contemporaneous way in which covenant renewal takes place as the Lord speaks to a later generation of Israelites through Joshua at Shechem: "'You saw with your own eyes what I did to the Egyptians' (Josh. 24:7). History is telescoped into collective biography. What your ancestors saw is what *you* saw. God's rescue of them implicates *you*, obliges *you*, for *you*, by hearing this story and responding affirmatively, become Israel, and it was Israel whom he rescued. Telling the story brings it alive."[5] For, "in the words of the rabbinic Passover liturgy (Haggadah), 'Each man is obligated to see himself as if he came out of Egypt.'"[6] The great Passover festival, following the instructions in passages such as Exodus 12:1–27 and Deuteronomy 16:1–4, is established as "a day of remembrance for you. You shall celebrate it as a festival to the LORD" (Exod. 12:14 NRSV). With the sacrifice of the Passover lamb at the temple, and the celebratory meal of lamb, unleavened bread, and bitter herbs, the Israelites did not move into private introspection (like many contemporary Christians do in remembrance); instead, they inserted themselves into the public history of YHWH's saving action on behalf of his people. As a covenant people, Levenson argues, "they do not determine who they are by looking within, by plumbing the depths of the individual soul, by seeking a mystical light in the innermost reaches of the self. Rather, the direction is the opposite. What is public is made private. History is not only rendered contemporary; it is internalized. . . . One looks out from the self to find out who one is meant to be. . . . He *appropriates* an identity that is a matter of public knowledge. Israel affirms the given."[7]

It is in this powerful, identity-shaping covenantal context of Passover that Jesus's Last Supper command to feast in "remembrance" of him is placed. For in the Lord's Supper, the public event of God's mighty acts culminated in Jesus Christ is appropriated as one's own biography, one's own corporate history. "It is the event of Calvary, of the atoning death of Jesus as an event within the public domain, that is now appropriated in 'this is my body for you.'"[8] God's script for our drama does not originate from within, but in the history of Jesus Christ—his life, death, and resurrection. That is *our* history, as ones who belong to Christ.

---

5. Jon D. Levenson, *Sinai and Zion* (New York: HarperOne, 1985), 38.
6. Levenson, *Sinai and Zion*, 38.
7. Levenson, *Sinai and Zion*, 39.
8. Thiselton, *First Epistle to the Corinthians*, 877.

This history is not only made contemporary—believers are *incorporated* into it. It is "internalized," to use Levenson's term, so that they can become who they are—God's covenant people, one with Christ by the Spirit. Moreover, just as Jews are to see themselves as among those coming out of Egypt when they celebrate Passover, so Christians are to see themselves as among the disciples at the Last Supper. Like Passover and the Last Supper, believers celebrate a "covenant-meal, receiving afresh God's promise in Jesus."[9] For at both Passover and the Last Supper, the covenant Lord holds forth a promise to his people— indeed, the Lord makes a "pledge of the covenant itself."[10]

Because of the Lord's promise, the covenant history envelops the present lives and identity of God's people. Just as Israel can "become Israel" (in Levenson's terms) with the covenant renewal at Shechem, so also in remembrance of the Last Supper, those incorporated into the covenant through Christ find their identity and destiny in his history; they are members of Christ's body, united to him by the Spirit in his death and resurrection. The true identity for the Christian is beheld and tasted at the table—one that will be fully revealed in the eschaton. As Paul says in Colossians 3:3–4: "For you have died, and your life is hidden with Christ in God. When Christ who is your life is revealed, then you also will be revealed with him in glory" (NRSV). In the words of Augustine in a sermon on the table,

> So now, if you want to understand the body of Christ, listen to the Apostle Paul speaking to the faithful: "You are the body of Christ, member for member" [1 Cor. 12:27]. If you, therefore, are Christ's body and members, it is your own mystery that is placed on the Lord's table! It is your own mystery that you are receiving! You are saying "Amen" to what you are: your response is a personal signature, affirming your faith. When you hear "The body of Christ," you reply "Amen." Be a member of Christ's body, then, so that your "Amen" may ring true![11]

9. Alasdair I. C. Heron, *Table and Tradition: Toward an Ecumenical Understanding of the Eucharist* (Philadelphia: Westminster, 1983), 31.

10. Heron speaks of the Last Supper as a covenant pledge, though this can apply in its own way to the Passover as well. See Heron, *Table and Tradition*, 31.

11. Augustine, Sermon 272, Early Church Texts, http://www.earlychurchtexts.com/public /augustine_sermon_272_eucharist.htm.

## Remembrance: The Resurrection Meals and the Lord's Supper

Christ is revealed through the breaking of the bread not only at the Last Supper, but also in the resurrection appearances. In much congregational piety these are separated by a wide chasm. For some, the solemnity of the Supper is a space for the mental reenactment of the cross of Christ—perhaps a mental replay of various Hollywood productions of the cross that they have seen. But why should we think that it is just a coincidence that Christ offers bread in his self-disclosure in the Last Supper, and then makes himself known to the disciples on the road to Emmaus through "the breaking of the bread"? The Lord's Supper is a celebration. It is for good reason that the church ordinarily celebrates together on Sundays, the day of resurrection, and not on Fridays, the day of his crucifixion. The Lord's Supper inserts us not only into the meal with Jesus at the Last Supper, but also into the meal of the disciples with the risen Lord. The Lord's Supper should not be an attempt to "unthink" the resurrection and return to the Last Supper, untainted by this later experience. When we remember the cross, it is in light of his resurrection, and our incorporation into the life of the crucified, risen, and ascended Lord.

Indeed, we can go a step further. New Testament scholar Oscar Cullmann has puzzled about how the first believers were filled with such overwhelming joy in the "breaking of the bread" in Acts 2. Cullmann has also wondered how the church in Corinth had such enthusiasm at the Supper that it "seems to have degenerated into excess" (cf. "one person remains hungry and another gets drunk" [1 Cor. 11:21]).[12] Is it likely that such joy and enthusiasm would arise from a solemn remembrance of the Last Supper? (Put in contemporary terms, is it likely that a congregation where individuals closed their eyes, reflected on their sin, and viewed a "mental replay" of the crucifixion would have overwhelming joy at the table?)

Cullmann argues that "there is only one group of meals, the recollection of which could fully justify this overflowing joy"—namely, the meals "the eleven and their companions ate with the Risen One on the night of Easter Day."[13] For in Luke 24, after failing to be recognized by two disciples, Jesus sat with them at a meal: "When he was at the table with them, he took bread, gave thanks, broke it and began to give it to them. Then their eyes were opened and

---

12. Oscar Cullmann, "The Breaking of Bread and the Resurrection Appearances," in Oscar Cullmann and F. J. Leenhardt, *Essays on the Lord's Supper*, trans. J. G. Davies (Atlanta: John Knox, 1958), 16.

13. Cullmann, "The Breaking of Bread," 8.

they recognized him, and he disappeared from their sight" (Luke 24:30–31). They had been eating with the risen Christ, and, as they told their companions later, they recognized him "when he broke the bread" (Luke 24:35). Then again, the risen Christ appeared to a larger gathering of disciples, showing them his nail-scarred hands and feet. Then Christ himself invited them to eat with him: "While they still did not believe it because of joy and amazement, he asked them, 'Do you have anything here to eat?' They gave him a piece of broiled fish, and he took it and ate it in their presence" (Luke 24:41–43).

For Cullmann, the Gospel of John was reflecting a similar insight about the Lord's Supper. Rather than focus upon the Last Supper, the eucharistic discourse of John 6 calls readers to believe, abide, and feed upon Christ—themes reflecting joyful communion with the risen Christ.[14] The apostle Paul has similar elements, even as he connects the Last Supper with the Lord's Supper as well, in his words of institution in 1 Corinthians 11. Paul holds together a notion of the Lord's Supper as a celebration with the risen Christ with a proclamation of Christ's death, "until he comes" (1 Cor. 11:26).[15] For, "faced with the excesses at Corinth, he was forced to remind the faithful that it is not only the Risen One who, at the Lord's Supper, manifests himself to the community but the Crucified One."[16] The risen Christ invites us to break bread with him, but, as in Luke 24, it is the risen Christ with nail scars in his hands.

Readers may or may not be fully convinced by the historical work that Cullmann has done in situating the Synoptic Gospels, John, and Paul's writings. But he illuminates a key feature of the biblical texts about the Supper that most congregations miss today: their central assumption is that we eat and drink *with* the resurrected Lord. We remember Christ, yes. Just as the Jews remembered God's mighty acts in the Passover, we remember the mighty acts of God in the life, death, and resurrection of Jesus Christ. This remembrance, however, is simultaneous with a fellowship with the living Lord, and a living into the reality accomplished by Christ's cross and resurrection.

Indeed, when we hold the cross and resurrection together, we can see how "remembrance" fits within a larger sign-action context of enacting a God-given identity at the Supper. While Christ's cross is essential in Paul's account of the words of institution, a whole series of actions are commanded— included in the command "to do" are taking the bread and cup, giving thanks,

14. Cullmann, "The Lord's Supper and the Death of Christ," in Cullmann and Leenhardt, *Essays on the Lord's Supper*, 8, 22.
15. Cullmann, "The Lord's Supper," 22.
16. Cullmann, "The Lord's Supper," 18.

sharing it, and declaring the words of Christ. In the words of Max Thurian, "'To do this' is therefore to execute a eucharistic *action*, a *giving* of thanks, a liturgical *celebration*, by word and deed."[17] Thus, when Jesus commands "do this," it is the whole sign-action of the Supper itself that is commanded.

Thus, the sign-action of "remembrance" commanded by Christ opens up a Trinitarian drama for believers to inhabit—one that encompasses and brings together past, present, and future. As Joseph Fitzmyer notes about 1 Corinthians 11:24–25, "the sharing in the Lord's Supper not only looks back with *anamnesis* to the death of Jesus on Calvary and proclaims it at present, but it also looks forward to his eschatological coming."[18] This takes place as the "body of Christ" (1 Cor. 12:27) is "made to drink of one Spirit" (1 Cor. 12:13)—all of whom are children of "the Father, from whom all things came and for whom we live" (1 Cor. 8:6).

### Zwinglianism, Remembrance, and the Sacred

Congregations that focus exclusively on "remembrance"—and center their practice on individual recollection of Christ's cross—often self-identify as "Zwinglian." Certainly, particular questions from the debates among Zwinglian, Genevan, and Lutheran accounts of the Supper have relevance on this point. For example, are the sacraments instruments of divine grace or reminders of grace received in the past? Moreover, are human beings the main actors in the sacramental acts or is the triune God the main actor? Zwingli denied that the Lord's Supper is an instrument or means of grace, and claimed that the central actors at the Supper are the worshipers themselves.[19] As indicated

---

17. Max Thurian, *The Eucharistic Memorial*, part 2, *The New Testament*, trans. J. G. Davies (Richmond, VA: John Knox, 1959), 35.

18. Joseph A. Fitzmyer, *First Corinthians* (New Haven: Yale University Press, 2008), 445.

19. As Gottfried Locher notes in his careful study, for Zwingli, "as opposed to Luther (and Calvin), the actor of the celebration is not Christ, but the congregation. It is not the 'This is . . .' but rather the 'Do this . . .' which is emphasized. This difference could well be much more significant than the whole controversy about the elements" (Gottfried W. Locher, *Zwingli's Thought: New Perspectives* [Leiden: Brill Academic, 1997], 177). Jacques Courvoisier claims that Calvin, Luther, and most modern interpreters have misunderstood Zwingli, who (in his view) believed that through the Supper the congregation itself was "transubstantiated," in a certain sense, into the body of Christ. "Transubstantiation no longer concerns the bread, but the whole congregation, and it is this 'body of Christ' which the congregation offers in oblation to its Lord. The body, then, is not localized in the bread but in the Church gathered about the bread. Precisely here is the doctrine of the real presence in Zwingli's theology" (Jacques Courvoisier, *Zwingli: A*

earlier, I disagree with Zwingli's position on these two points; I affirm the sacraments as *instruments* of the Spirit that hold forth Christ, and I affirm that the *triune God* is the central actor in and through the sign-actions of the sacraments. (In this regard, I stand well within the Reformed confessional tradition, as chapter 3 has shown.)

Why are many congregations today exclusively "memorialist" in their eucharistic theology and practice? It would be tempting to draw a straight line from Zurich and Zwingli to these congregations—saying that the "Zwinglian" tradition is at the root of these churches with "Zwinglian" practices. But such an approach is misleading. It fails to recognize the extraordinary influence of modernity—the rise of rationalism, downplaying the role of the affections and the body, etc., as chronicled in chapter 2. In actual fact, today's "Zwinglians" usually have a sub-Zwinglian practice. As leading liturgical historians such as James White note:

> Today, it is common to consider purely symbolic interpretation of the eucharistic bread and wine as the legacy of Zwingli. Such an approach to the eucharist prevails in much of American Protestantism and is often labeled as "Zwinglian." But that is far too simplistic an interpretation. Zwingli worked within a sacralized universe. He certainly believed in the presence and activity of God in that world, but the universe of many modern Protestants is that of the eighteenth-century Enlightenment, a universe completely desacralized. To call the Enlightenment position Zwinglian is to miss an important shift that occurred in the eighteenth century. The desacralized worldview of many modern Protestants makes sacraments or any other divine intrusions in the world questionable. The world of Zwingli saw God, far from being absent, as *intervening* in the midst of the worshiping congregation.[20]

Thus, contemporary "Zwinglian" theology and practice are ultimately a product of the modern Enlightenment, not of the Reformation. As long as

---

*Reformed Theologian* [Eugene, OR: Wipf and Stock, 2016], 76). Courvoisier is right to stress the ecclesial dimension of Zwingli's thought, and his suggestion is intriguing. However, there is weak historical and textual evidence for this interpretation of Zwingli. See B. A. Gerrish, *Continuing the Reformation: Essays on Modern Religious Thought* (Chicago: University of Chicago Press, 1994), chap. 3, especially pp. 67–69.

20. James F. White, *Protestant Worship: Traditions in Transition* (Louisville: Westminster John Knox, 1989), 60.

we look at the "purely symbolic" accounts of the Supper today and say "that's Zwinglian," we are projecting an inaccurate portrait on the past and buying into a false genealogy. We have not truly confronted the challenge of major strands in modernity, with its suspicion of the body and affections, its dualism between spiritual and earthly realities, and its prioritizing of reason and thinking over action and habit.

In diagnosing the contemporary tendency toward a narrow memorialism, however, one point in White's analysis should give us pause. Is it the case that "modern Protestants" have a "desacralized worldview"? Certainly some do, but I sense that the reality in our late modern times is more complex. As James K. A. Smith has argued, contemporary culture is filled with "secular liturgies," such as a trip to the shopping mall, that shape our affections and perceptions as well as our actions in the world.[21] Dell deChant has made the case that contemporary consumer culture, in particular, traffics in the sacred: it has its own liturgical calendar (including Mother's Day as a "Feast Day," Valentine's Day as a "Major Holy Day," and Super Bowl Sunday as a "Secondary Holy Day").[22] It includes sacred sites (e.g., department stores), sacred rituals and exchanges (the acquisition of products) through priestly exchanges (purchasing from a cashier), and a concluding priestly utterance or blessing ("Thank you," "Have a nice day").[23] Both Smith and deChant remind us of an important reality about contemporary Western culture: rather than simply being "desacralized," often our culture reflects a misplaced sense of the sacred. The market, with its promise of a new identity through consumption, becomes the sacred idol for many in late modernity. Rather than entering into the drama of the triune God's action, we act in a script reflected to us by promises of the commercial for the hot new car, or by the confident and sexy figures facing us through the department store window. As we continue to explore the path opened up through entering into the way of discipleship, in Christ through the Spirit, we need to be attentive to the ways in which—as individuals and as communities—we are shaped by idols. Consumerism and other idols not only *reduce* our sense of the sacred in Christian worship, they also *misplace* it by locating our heart's delight in the ritual of consumption rather than in fellowship with the triune God.

21. James K. A. Smith, *Desiring the Kingdom: Worship, Worldview, and Cultural Formation* (Grand Rapids: Baker Academic, 2009), 99–100.
22. Dell deChant, *The Sacred Santa: Religious Dimensions of Consumer Culture* (Eugene, OR: Wipf and Stock, 2008), 142–43.
23. See deChant, *The Sacred Santa*, chap. 5, especially pp. 81–82.

## Out of Balance? Examining Historic Struggles on
## Remembrance in the Reformed Tradition

At this point, some readers may experience cognitive dissonance. Many times I have received a set of questions from seminary students from a charismatic or Pentecostal background. Through weekly celebration of the Lord's Supper at Western Theological Seminary chapel and studying Calvin's theology, they have become attracted to the beauty and dynamism of Reformed sacramental theology. But then they attend worship services at other churches in the Reformed and Presbyterian tradition, and they are disappointed and confused. How did worship get so lifeless and heady? Why is the Lord's Supper celebrated so infrequently? If the Reformed confessions are not deductively Zwinglian, how did we get here? How did many congregations in the Reformed tradition come to emphasize "remembrance" in a one-sided way?

A central piece of my response to this relates to the modern prioritizing of reason over affections, mind over body, as displayed by the nineteenth-century critique of the holy fairs in chapter 2. But, in addition, a neo-Zwinglian Reformed movement in the nineteenth century located the Supper's significance in a mental act of recollection rather than in the presence of Christ in remembrance, communion, and hope at the Supper. We can gain a clearer understanding of this neo-Zwinglian movement by examining a critical debate between two theologians of that day: John Williamson Nevin, who sought to defend Calvin's eucharistic theology, and Charles Hodge, who defended a more Zwinglian understanding of the Supper.

On the one hand, Nevin and Hodge held much in common as they envisioned the church's response to the challenges of their age. Both opposed the "new measures" and semi-Pelagian revivalism discussed in chapter 2. Both sought to work from the Reformed confessional tradition. Hodge had been Nevin's professor at Princeton Seminary. But in 1846, Nevin published a scholarly and trenchant treatise, entitled *The Mystical Presence: A Vindication of the Reformed or Calvinistic Doctrine of the Holy Eucharist*, that claimed that Reformed sacramental theology and practice had declined from the higher standard of the Reformers and the Reformed confessions. "The view of the Eucharist now generally predominant in the *Reformed* Church," he wrote, is a "departure" from "its proper and original creed, as exhibited in its symbolical [confessional] books. An unchurchly, rationalistic tendency, has been allowed to carry the Church gradually more and more off from the ground it occupied in the beginning."[24]

24. John Williamson Nevin, *The Mystical Presence: A Vindication of the Reformed or Calvin-*

Nevin felt that the Reformed tradition had become deeply disoriented, and had lost its sense of the implications of the incarnation, the church, and most of all, union with Christ. For Nevin, union with Christ was the core ontological reality underlying the sacraments and salvation itself.

> The sacramental doctrine of the primitive Reformed Church stands inseparably connected with the idea of an inward living union between believers and Christ, in virtue of which they are incorporated into his very nature, and made to subsist with him by the power of a common life. In full correspondence with this conception of Christian salvation, as a process by which the believer is mystically inserted more and more into the person of Christ, till he becomes thus at last fully transformed into his image, it was held that nothing less than such a real participation of his living person is involved always in the right use of the Lord's Supper. (50–51)

Thus, in a way similar to considering the Supper as the "icon" of the gospel, Nevin wrote that the "mystery of the Holy Eucharist" is the "epitome" of "the mystery of Christian salvation itself" (233). From a historical perspective, Nevin tended to be one-sided in his interpretation of the Reformed confessions in a Genevan direction (with a particular emphasis on Calvin). Nevertheless, he presented an insightful and detailed account of how a vital theology of union with Christ was key for Calvin and the Reformed confessions in the Lord's Supper, ecclesiology, and salvation more generally.

In contrast, Nevin declares that the "modern Puritans" betrayed the Reformed inheritance with a rationalism that turns the Supper into a mental act of remembrance, not an instrument of grace in union with Christ. While Nevin is more sympathetic with earlier Puritans such as John Owen (93–98) other Puritans such as Jonathan Edwards and Timothy Dwight fall under a harsh critique (111–19). In Nevin's view, modern Puritans assert that with Christ's body "we can have no communion at all, except in the way of remembering what was endured in it for our salvation" (118). He continues, noting that the "modern Puritan view" "will allow no real participation of Christ's person in the Lord's Supper"—thus all one is left with is a remembrance, with Christ's words of institution being received as a "mere figure" (118). In evaluation, Nevin claims

---

*istic Doctrine of the Holy Eucharist*, ed. J. Philip Horne (n.p.: CreateSpace Independent Publishing Platform, 2012), 48. Hereafter, page references from this work will be given in parentheses in the text.

that the "modern Puritan theory of the Lord's Supper" not only involves "a falling away from the general faith of the Reformation," but it also "finds at the same time no sanction whatever in the faith of the primitive Church" (131). In Nevin's view, mid-nineteenth-century American Puritanism was neither Reformed nor catholic.

On the one hand, I think there are reasons to question the adequacy of Nevin's interpretation of Puritans such as Jonathan Edwards.[25] Yet, *The Mystical Presence* succeeds in highlighting the forces in revivalist American Christianity that undermined a robust theology of union with Christ and forced memorialism into a narrow, rationalistic mold. In particular, the reclaiming of Zwingli's assertion that the Supper is *not* an instrument of grace had a different effect in the nineteenth century than in the sixteenth century. It was accompanied by an exaltation of the "man of reason" over affections, the body, and the material senses as an avenue for divine action. Ironically, American revivalism did and still does emphasize the importance of emotions and the body in its own way. What historian David Bebbington observes about British evangelicalism is true of American evangelicalism as well: from the eighteenth century until recent decades, a constitutive feature of Puritan and more broadly evangelical practice is the emphasis on the internal assurance of salvation in a memorable conversion experience. This was true among Calvinists as well as Wesleyan Protestants, though more muted among Anglicans.[26] This was a new twist on an old theme. As Bebbington notes, "Assurance had been an important theme of pre-Evangelical Protestant spirituality, but the experience had never been regarded as the standard possession of all believers."[27] In contrast, as we have explored in this book, assurance of forgiveness is connected by Calvin and the Reformed confessions with both justification and sanctification; this assurance is nourished preeminently through receiving the preached Word and the sacraments. Indeed, the sacraments are the "clearest promises of God" to material, embodied creatures like ourselves, and in looking for assurance Calvin insists that we look to Jesus Christ in the sacrament, for "the Supper is given us as a mirror in which we

---

25. For a more charitable account of Edwards's eucharistic theology in relation to Calvin and the Reformed confessional tradition, see Timothy Hessel-Robinson, "Calvin's Doctrine of the Lord's Supper: Modern Reception and Contemporary Possibilities," in *Calvin's Theology and Its Reception: Disputes, Developments, and New Possibilities*, ed. J. Todd Billings and I. John Hesselink (Louisville: Westminster John Knox, 2012), 166–72.

26. David W. Bebbington, *Evangelicalism in Modern Britain: A History from the 1730s to the 1980s*, rev. ed. (London: Routledge, 2003), 6–7.

27. Bebbington, *Evangelicalism in Modern Britain*, 7.

may contemplate Jesus Christ."[28] Yet, in eighteenth- and nineteenth-century Puritanism and most streams of more recent evangelicalism, assurance was no longer tied to receiving the material means of grace in Word and sacrament. It was internalized and people were encouraged to share their testimonies, to tell their conversion stories as a means of assurance. The means of grace moved from external to internal. This transformed the doctrine of assurance in a powerful way. In the words of Bebbington:

> The fulcrum of change was the doctrine of assurance. Those who knew their sins forgiven were freed from debilitating anxieties for Christian mission. Typical was Abigail Hutchinson, a young girl whose experience of conversion Edwards related. "She felt a strong inclination immediately to go forth to warn sinners," according to Edwards; "and proposed it the next day to her brother to assist her in going from house to house. . . ." The activism of the Evangelical movement sprang from its strong teaching on assurance. That, in turn, was a product of the confidence of the new age about the validity of experience. The Evangelical version of Protestantism was created by the Enlightenment.[29]

The *internalization* of the mark of assurance served as a catalyst to emphasize personal experience. In comparison to earlier evangelical Protestantism, it involved a *movement* of the sacred from an external, bodily sign of the gospel (in the sacraments) to the sign and mark *as* the internal experience itself. This self-referential ground for assurance led to debates about when conversion should happen and whether it could ever be gradual or unconscious. Anglican evangelicals, in contrast, held the notion that conversion could be gradual.[30] This, paired with a built-in liturgical stability, fit with their ongoing emphasis upon the external, sacramental means of grace. In contrast, for Presbyterian Christians in this era, deeply affective worship experiences continued, but the Supper lost its position as the centerpiece, not being celebrated at all in the multiday festivals.[31] Like many other evangelicals, the external means of grace in the Supper were replaced with the internal marks of conversion and "new

28. Calvin, *Institutes* 4.14.5; Calvin, "Short Treatise on the Lord's Supper," Section 10, CTS.

29. Bebbington, *Evangelicalism in Modern Britain*, 74.

30. Bebbington, *Evangelicalism in Modern Britain*, 7–8.

31. Leigh Eric Schmidt, *Holy Fairs: Scotland and the Making of American Revivalism*, 2nd ed. (Grand Rapids: Eerdmans, 2001), 208–12.

measures" such as the anxious bench. The Supper was left to the place of rationalistic act of memory, not a deeply affective yet externally enacted means
of God's grace.

Nevin attacked this development head-on with extensive references to
Reformers and the Reformed confessions to make his case for decline, but the
response to *The Mystical Presence* was largely apathetic. In spite of its Reformed
pedigree, denominational publications of Reformed churches condemned
Nevin's approach as too close to Roman Catholicism.[32] In a particularly revealing example, Elbert Porter, editor of the *Christian Intelligencer*, "the leading
paper of Dutch Reformed circles," condemned Nevin and his colleague Philip
Schaff "for stressing the Church and sacraments at the expense of personal
conversion and individual piety."[33]

One response to *The Mystical Presence* was anything but apathetic:
Charles Hodge published a fifty-two-page book review.[34] In his scathing essay,
Hodge gives his "reasons for thinking that Dr. Nevin is tenfold further from the
doctrines of our common fathers, than those he commiserates and condemns"
(227). Hodge notes some common ground with Nevin: the union that believers have with Christ and with one another is a "mystical union"—it is a "great
mystery" and not "merely moral, arising from agreement and sympathy, [for]
there would be no mystery about it." Instead, as the Scriptures teach, "it is a
vital union, we are partakers of his life" (228). This union takes place by the
Holy Spirit, and "this union relates to the bodies as well as the souls of believers" (228). In these affirmations, as well as with Nevin's condemnation of the
"new measures" of Finney and the Second Great Awakening, Hodge stands
with Nevin over and against a human-oriented, decisionist gospel—against the
reduction of the "gospel" to a "plan of salvation," to utilize the terminology of
Scot McKnight. Both Hodge and Nevin engaged Reformers and the Reformed
confessions extensively, making their case in terms of both Scripture and these
later Reformed authorities.

Yet, the differences were stark. Hodge surveys the language of Zwingli,
Bullinger, and Calvin along with key confessions, but gives priority to confes-
sions emerging from Zwingli and Bullinger's Zurich. He considers Bullinger's
Second Helvetic Confession of Zurich perhaps "the most authoritative of all

32. See Christopher Dorn, *The Lord's Supper in the Reformed Church in America: Tradition
in Transformation* (New York: Peter Lang, 2007), 52–53.

33. Dorn, *The Lord's Supper*, 52.

34. Charles Hodge, "Review of *The Mystical Presence*," *Biblical Repertory and Princeton
Review* 20 (Philadelphia: Mitchell, April 1848): 227–78. Hereafter, page references from this
work will be given in parentheses in the text.

the symbols [confessions] of the Reformed church," and interprets Calvin's theology in light of the Consensus of Zurich, even though that consensus was a compromise statement for Calvin (251, and see 241, 238–39). In addition, where differences remain between his Zwinglian view and the Geneva tradition of Calvin, he asserts that "the private authority of Calvin" and "the dubious expression" of Reformed confessions reflecting Calvin's view have less authority than the confessions emerging from Zurich, and that the higher Reformed sacramental tradition is not theologically coherent (251–52). Thus, Hodge either explains away or dismisses as "dubious" key features of the sacramental theology that Nevin highlights in the Reformed confessions. Hodge agrees with Nevin that the Reformed confessions teach a "spiritual" yet not local presence of Christ at the table. But for Hodge this means "the presence is to the mind, the object is not presented to the senses, but apprehended by faith" (245).

In making these moves, Hodge showed how the Zurich-based strand of Reformed sacramental language can be both intellectualized and internalized. Nevin agreed that the partaking is "spiritual" and by "faith," for the sacramental gift is "all by the Spirit; and for the communicant himself, all hangs upon the condition of faith." But this is all in the context of God's *external* offer to us in the material means of grace. For "the grace exhibited, the action of the Spirit is here present, belongs to the sacrament in its own nature." And that nature is that "Christ communicates himself to us . . . under the form of the sacramental mystery as such."[35] There is a distinction, but still a union, between the "outward and visible" and the "inward and invisible."[36] Reformed and evangelical Christians of his day severed these two: the Supper became an outward rite of recollection, rather than a gift *through the instrument* of bread and wine. "It is not as the object of thought simply or lively recollection, that he is made present in the ordinance. Nor is it by the activity of our faith merely, that he is brought nigh. His [Christ's] presence is identified objectively with the sacrament itself; and we receive him in the sacrament as the bearer of his very life itself."[37] In Nevin's view, the power of the sacrament as *gift* had been undermined by the forces of his day reducing it to *recollection*—replacing the external means of grace with internal experiences of conversion as an experiential sign and mark of God's work.

Although in most regards Hodge was a stalwart defender of Reformed orthodoxy, most historians would agree that Nevin was closer to Calvin

35. Nevin, *The Mystical Presence*, 171.
36. Nevin, *The Mystical Presence*, 172.
37. Nevin, *The Mystical Presence*, 171.

than Hodge was on the Lord's Supper.[38] I concur. Hodge gives an unpersuasive account of the Reformed confessions, particularly in making Calvin's consensus statement with Bullinger the central creed for Reformed Christians.[39] However, the much more serious theological and pastoral problem with both Hodge and the neo-Zwinglian strands of the Reformed tradition in the nineteenth century is the reduction even of what it retains: remembrance of the cross itself is weakened to become mental recollection. The Lord's Supper, far from filling a central place as the icon of the gospel, becomes an occasion to recall a moment in the history of salvation. In its place, a dubious theology of "conversion" becomes a sign and mark of assurance of God's pardon.

If a reduction of "remembrance" to mental recollection is central to the problem with modern Reformed and much broader evangelical theology of the Supper, what is a better way forward? Some of the solution, as noted in the introduction to part 3, is moving toward a multifaceted account of the Supper in terms of remembrance, communion, and hope. Another part of the solution is retrieving the Supper as an identity-forming action of incorporation into God's drama in Christ, particularly highlighting the connections between the Supper and the Passover, as well as between the Supper and the resurrection meals. But for this serious theological and pastoral problem, a multipronged response is necessary. For the remainder of this chapter, I discuss two further ways to deepen the Supper as "remembrance": with a renewed theology of the cross, and with a renewed theology of God's kingship. This "remembrance" goes far beyond mental recollection; it is a remembrance in union with Christ, a participation in the dying and rising of Christ; believers receive and inhabit a new identity in God's drama, living in lament and hope as children of the ascended and returning King.

---

38. See Douglas Sweeney's assessment of the historians in Douglas A. Sweeney, "'Falling Away from the General Faith of the Reformation'? The Contest over Calvinism in Nineteenth-Century America," in *John Calvin's American Legacy*, ed. Thomas J. Davis (New York: Oxford University Press, 2010), 125.

39. Nevin rightly points to this in his response to Hodge's review: "It is arbitrary, in the extreme, to exalt the *Consensus Tigurinus* to the rank of a supreme law for the entire creed of the church," particularly since Calvin himself insisted that the document did not express his eucharistic theology in fullness. Sweeney, "Falling Away," 122.

## Labor Pains and New Birth: Cross and Resurrection

In Jesus's farewell discourse in John's Gospel, Jesus's teaching involves both an abiding union with Christ (John 15: vine and the branches) and discourse about his exaltation to the Father and sending of the Spirit. But in John 16:16–22, he also speaks of the cross and resurrection with a powerful analogy:

> Jesus went on to say, "In a little while you will see me no more, and then after a little while you will see me." At this, some of his disciples said to one another, "What does he mean by saying, 'In a little while you will see me no more, and then after a little while you will see me,' and 'Because I am going to the Father'?" They kept asking, "What does he mean by 'a little while'? We don't understand what he is saying." Jesus saw that they wanted to ask him about this, so he said to them, "Are you asking one another what I meant when I said, 'In a little while you will see me no more, and then after a little while you will see me'? Very truly I tell you, you will weep and mourn while the world rejoices. You will grieve, but your grief will turn to joy. A woman giving birth to a child has pain because her time has come; but when her baby is born she forgets the anguish because of her joy that a child is born into the world. So with you: Now is your time of grief, but I will see you again and you will rejoice, and no one will take away your joy." (John 16:16–22)

Jesus's analogy does not present a comprehensive theology of the cross, but it does give a glimpse of what it means to participate in Christ in his death and resurrection. The reference to childbirth as a gateway to redemption is filled with Old Testament precedence. Isaiah repeatedly speaks of a woman's labor pains as an image for "the travail and pain that precedes the deliverance of God's people."[40] Moreover, Jesus's phrase that "her hour has come" also has prophetic echoes pointing to the coming deliverance of God.[41] A woman, as an image for God's people, bears the pain of labor and comes to the promised hour of the Lord's salvation.

In the Gospel's analogy, it is Jesus himself who suffers labor pains on the cross. Yet, it is impossible to approach the cross apart from the resurrection:

---

40. Marianne Meye Thompson, *John: A Commentary* (Louisville: Westminster John Knox, 2015), 342. In particular, see Isa. 26:16–21; 66:7–19.

41. See George R. Beasley-Murray, *John* (Waco: Word, 1987), 285–86.

the seemingly pointless suffering, pain, and disgrace of the cross are fundamentally productive and fruitful. What appears to be defeat (the false conviction and torturous death of Jesus, the disciples' innocent teacher) is in fact fruitful in unfolding a triumph. As John's Gospel elsewhere teaches, when Jesus is "lifted up" to the cross, it is not a defeat; despite what it seems, it is a victory. Indeed, the cross is a glorification and exaltation: "'And I, when I am lifted up from the earth, will draw all people to myself.' He said this to show the kind of death he was going to die" (John 12:32–33).

Moreover, Jesus applies the analogy not only to himself but also to his disciples. "Now is your time of grief, but I will see you again and you will rejoice, and no one will take away your joy" (John 16:22). Here, Jesus's words take on a double sense. On the one hand, they refer to the experience of the disciples after the cross: the disciples "will weep and mourn while the world rejoices" (John 16:20). But the context of John 16 suggests that this passage also refers to the return of the Son to the Father in the ascension. For "now I am going to him who sent me," Jesus says; for "I am going to the Father, where you can see me no longer" (John 16:5, 10). His disciples ask what this means, and Jesus's response with the labor pains and new birth analogy is twofold: Jesus's impending departure to the cross followed by his presence in the resurrection appearances *and* his ascension to the Father and the sending of the Spirit.

Thus, in John's Gospel, Jesus is addressing not just the ancient disciples but also the present ones with the promise of the parousia ("I will see you again . . . no one will take your joy from you").[42] The life of the Christian in the twenty-first century involves weeping and mourning and pain, awaiting the final appearance of the risen Lord. As Christians remember the cross at the Supper, they experience both pain and victory—being incorporated into a story of both dying and rising. Martin Luther expounds this image in John's Gospel with a vivid reminder of both the pains and the dangers of childbirth, particularly in the ancient world: "For her the hour of endurance is now and no one can say whether she will recover or die. All is anguish and anxiety, with no foreseeable end. But everything is concentrated on the moment when the child is born into the world. In that moment the anguish is immediately forgotten because of the happy sight of the newborn child."[43]

42. On this connection to the parousia, see C. Kingsley Barrett, *The Gospel according to St. John: An Introduction with Commentary and Notes on the Greek Text*, 2nd ed. (Philadelphia: Westminster John Knox, 1978), 491–92.

43. Martin Luther, *Sermons on the Gospel of St. John, Chapters 14–16*, in *Luther's Works*, vol. 24, ed. Jaroslav Jan Pelikan, trans. Martin H. Bertram (Saint Louis: Concordia, 2007), 382.

The pain of Christ's disciples today is both sharp and dull—"anguish and anxiety"—without clarity about whether new life will come. But in Jesus's analogy, it is ultimately a productive pain that brings the new creation to birth. We remember Christ's cross *with* the crucified and risen Lord, and in him. At the Supper when we feast "in remembrance of [Christ]," we taste both the bitterness and the sweetness of the sacrifice that shows God's astonishing love on our behalf. Rather than a conversion experience, it is only in tasting the bitterness at the Supper—as an icon of bitterness in the Christian life under the cross—that we also taste the sweet fruit of pardon and new life. Experiences, even conversion experiences, can be generated, manipulated, and ultimately called into question. In stark contrast, the bitter yet sweet fruit of the cross and resurrection comes from *outside* the believer's subjective experience. Thus, parallel to Nevin rather than Hodge, at the Supper believers are incorporated into an external drama that they did not create, ingesting it in their bodies to make it their own. Just as Jews are incorporated into the external story of the Passover, so also believers are incorporated into the story of dying and rising with Christ.

In this sense, "remembrance" of Christ's cross is always remembrance in light of its fruitfulness in new life. Christians should not try to "unthink the resurrection" when they remember the cross. The pains and disgrace of the cross are great, but they are labor pains for the new creation. This tying together of the resurrection with the cross is not triumphalism. Rightly interpreted, the passage in John does not imply that Christians should experience *only* joy now, but that they taste joy even as they continue suffering with Christ, in union with his dying. As long as suffering, unbelief, and injustice disorder this world, Christians will lament in the Spirit, longing for the new creation. But even this is penetrated with joy. John Calvin helpfully warns against triumphalism when he comments on this passage in John: "But as we have received nothing more than the first-fruits, and these in very small measure, we scarcely taste a few drops of that spiritual gladness, to soothe our grief and alleviate its bitterness. And yet that small portion clearly shows that they who contemplate Christ by faith are so far from being at any time overwhelmed by grief, that, amidst their heaviest sufferings, they rejoice with exceeding great joy."[44]

Christians taste great sweetness and joy in remembering that Christ's cross is made fruitful in new creation. In light of union with Christ, Calvin suggests, our "sorrow" can produce "joy." Yet this is not an automatic result of

44. Calvin, Commentary on John 16:21, CTS.

our pain and sorrow. It is because Christ—in a once-for-all manner—bore the suffering of the cross, giving birth to the new creation.

What Calvin hints at in his John commentary he makes explicit elsewhere: that in light of union with Christ, our fellowship and union with Christ's dying and rising have a double sense. In one sense, only Jesus Christ bears the sacrifice for sin—for only Jesus Christ is the true High Priest. Christ alone offers a sufficient sacrifice for sin on the cross. Christ's cross and the cross of his disciples are fundamentally distinct. Unlike the sacrifices of Israel's priests, offered again and again, Jesus Christ the priest "offered for all time one sacrifice for sins" (Heb. 10:12). In light of this theme in Hebrews, and the connection between the cross of Christ and forgiveness in justification, Calvin indicates that this sacrifice of atonement is something that we *cannot* participate in. Rather, we receive its benefit: forgiveness of sins.

Yet the gift of justification is inseparable from the second gift of the double grace, sanctification. Calvin says this is expressed in a "sacrifice of praise"—a eucharistic expression of Paul's vision to present oneself as "a living sacrifice, holy and pleasing to God—this is your true and proper worship" (Rom. 12:1). This is a self-offering of gratitude, overflowing generosity to others. "This kind of sacrifice has nothing to do with appeasing God's wrath, with obtaining forgiveness of sins, or with meriting righteousness; but is concerned solely with magnifying and exalting God." It expresses itself in "all the duties of love."[45] Thus, we participate in the crucified and risen Lord asymmetrically—in remembrance of Christ's cross and the sacrifice that we could never offer for ourselves. And yet, we also remember as ones who participate in his death and resurrection—as ones who have died to sin and taste the new life of the Spirit, expressed in grateful love of God and neighbor. Christ's dying and rising is unique, and yet it is echoed in our lives as his people, as we join him on a path that involves both "weeping" and "joy" (cf. John 16) as we anticipate the culmination of our union with him.

What does it look like for a congregation to enter into a multifaceted remembrance of Christ at the Supper? There is no single answer. A celebration in a congregation of fifty will differ from one in a congregation of five hundred; a celebration on Good Friday will differ from one on Easter Sunday; a celebration in Nairobi will differ from one in Nebraska. But for the sake of rejuvenating our imagination, I will offer a congregational "snapshot" of what remembrance at the Supper can involve.

45. Calvin, *Institutes* 4.18.16.

## Congregational Snapshot

It is 9:55 a.m. on Sunday, and on a bustling Boston-area street corner with restaurants and shops, a stream of people break off from the busy sidewalks to gather at a stone church building offset from the street. Some who hurry in are single and married graduate students from the nearby research universities. Several families with children and teenagers enter through the doors wearing brightly colored traditional African dress. A few homeless men and women, familiar to the neighborhood, come in from the street to the sanctuary (seating about one hundred) as well. Other families move toward the church after finding parking places on the street—having lived in the Boston area for a long time, but now traveling from other parts of the city. Graduate students; immigrant families from Cameroon, Nigeria, and Ghana; homeless people; "locals" who have moved to a different part of the city—sojourners all.

They gather in the sanctuary while the volunteer organist, in her late seventies, plays the prelude. Greetings, hugs, smiles fill the space as the service begins. This week's bulletin lists the sequence for the upcoming worship: "Gathering, The Word, The Lord's Supper, Sending."

A voice at the front of the sanctuary rises above the noise to beckon the congregation to say a psalm together:

> May God be gracious to us and bless us
>     and make his face shine on us—
> so that your ways may be known on earth,
>     your salvation among all nations.
> May the peoples praise you, God;
>     may all the peoples praise you. (Ps. 67:1–3)

As the congregation prays and moves to a hymn, phrases from the psalm reverberate in their hearts: "Your salvation among all nations"? Even in "post-Christian" New England? Let all the peoples praise—our parents and brothers and sisters, even if they live on another continent. How long, O Lord? But let all the people praise him—even as I struggle with addiction? Even as my faith is scoffed at in my graduate program? Let all the people praise him.

A woman from Cameroon with an authoritative voice and a deep purple dress invites the congregation to confess their sins. What sins do they have in common—from different locations, social and economic classes, ethnicities? They belong to Jesus Christ, and alike fall short of his way. "We confess that we have not loved you with our whole heart, soul, and mind. We confess that we have not loved our neighbor as ourselves." The congregation moves from sitting to standing, as the worship leader declares that we look to Christ again, for he is the ground for assuring of pardon. "Who is in a place to condemn? Only Christ, and Christ died for us, Christ rose for us, Christ reigns in power for us, Christ prays for us."

The worship leader instructs the congregation to pass the peace, but the words are almost drowned out by the roar that accompanies the hugs and handshaking. From pew to pew, the peace is passed—from grad student to homeless, from third-generation local to immigrant.

After calling the congregation back to their seats, the pastor prays for the Spirit to bless the hearing of Scripture. A boy in the youth group walks to the pulpit and reads Psalm 4, and a middle-aged woman follows him to read from the Gospel about Jesus and the sisters of Lazarus. The people look in the bulletin as the pastor pauses and see the sermon title, "Being Seen by the Lord."

The pastor notes that the psalms sometimes call us to seek the face of the Lord, but Psalm 4 appears to be more passive:

> "O that we might see some good!
>    Let the light of your face shine on us, O LORD!" (Ps. 4:6)

They seek to *see* good, and seek the Lord, but the center of the drama in the passage is about being *seen*: let the face of the Lord *shine* on us. In the Aaronic blessing, "The LORD make his face to shine upon you, and be gracious to you; the LORD lift up his countenance upon you, and give you peace," the writer speaks not just of a vision of the Lord. The passage is about being taken in *by* the Lord—a shining of the Lord's face upon us. God is the actor here, and we are acted upon.

Yet, the pastor continues, being *seen* by the Lord in this way does not leave us passive. It does not leave us anxious, like when we are "seen" in social media, hoping that others will be impressed by what we share. This "being seen" is actually more powerful and formative than anything we could have initiated. We seek God—as we should—but God cannot be found. Mary and Martha sought the Lord, Jesus Christ, as they should have, for their brother, but they were helpless to bring life to their brother or to make the Lord act at the time and in the way that they wanted. Mary speaks the truth when she says to Jesus, "Lord, if you had been here, my brother would not have died" (John 11:32). Her raw plea is our raw plea as we see violence in our world, violence in our own hearts, bitterness rather than healing, unbelief rather than trust. We plead and we should cry out to the Lord.

But the central actor is not us, even as the ones who pray, but the Lord. In prayer we ask to be "seen" by the true King, and thus enter into his royal court. "Being seen" connotes a desperate people with an exalted, covenantal identity, that of citizens of the one true kingdom. As children of the King, when we are seen, we enter into a drama we did not create, follow a script we did not develop, and act as adopted children in a family we did not choose.

At times, we may say of self-deluded persons, "they see what they want to see." Of course, that is the constant danger for all of us. That is a danger for our faith as well: we serve an idol formed in our own image. But that is why we gather together as a people to *be seen* by the Lord—in prayer, in confession, in praise. We are seen by the Lord as he speaks through his word in Scripture. And we are seen by the Lord as he is the host who welcomes us to his table. Friends, let us come to the feast, in *remembrance* of our Lord, who was crucified, died, and was buried—and is risen and present with us for the meal of our new family. Let's bring our cries, our worries, our petitions. But let's also rest in the fact that "you alone, LORD, make [us] dwell in safety," as Psalm 4:8 says—our hope and rest and life are in being seen, welcomed, and incorporated by the Lord into his people, his way of dying to self and living to God, his forgiveness and new life.

The pastor moves to the communion table and begins the invitation: "Friends, this is the joyful feast of the people of God! They will come from east and west, and from north and south, and sit at table in the kingdom of God."[46] Indeed, those gathered have already traveled from across the ocean, from the homeless shelter, from graduate student housing to feast together. The congregation continues with the Prayer of Great Thanksgiving, then bongo drums start a beat as the congregation sings, "Holy, holy, holy Lord, God of power and might, heaven and earth are full of your glory. Hosanna in the highest." The prayer continues, and there is silence. The pastor picks up a loaf of bread. "Take, eat. This is my body, given for you. Do this in remembrance of me." As the pastor distributes the bread to the elders on silver plates, the music revives and the congregation joins together singing several West African songs of praise, accompanied by the bongo and a guitar. Anticipating the bread, some of the congregation swing to the beat in confident hope that they belong to King Jesus, and are being seen by him as host at the table. After everyone is served a cube of bread, all partake together; the music begins again for another song of thanksgiving, followed by the pause: "Drink now, in remembrance of the

---

46. Presbyterian Church (USA), *The Service for the Lord's Day: The Worship of God*, Supplemental Liturgical Resource 1 (Philadelphia: Westminster, 1984), 87.

one who brings us into our new identity and has been crucified and raised for our sake." The organist begins a final hymn as the elders return to their seats, greeting parishioners along the way.

After verse 4 of the hymn, visitors are invited to stay for further feasting—a potluck in the basement. Those who make their way down the stairs find several West African dishes, a Filipino noodle entree, fried chicken, and several homemade vegan dishes. They have gathered from their sojourns, and continue with a loud roar of fellowship and food in the church basement for the next hour. It is a eucharistic gospel—bringing many peoples into one.

In sum, we have seen how Jesus's call to "do this in remembrance of me" is not to a mere mental recollection of the cross. The gathered are called to inhabit the story of God's mighty acts of deliverance, the God of the exodus. Thus, at the table believers not only join in the Last Supper meal as they hear the words of Jesus instituting the meal, they also join the disciples in the Easter meal, with the Lord as host. In this sign-act at the table, remembrance with Christ occurs with the new household of God, a covenantal fellowship with people of different ages, races, and genders. All are incorporated into the drama of the triune God. As sharers in Christ, they embrace Christ's death and resurrection as their own history, their own identity-forming events. Indeed, believers experience both pain and joy as they come to inhabit the story of Christ's dying and rising as their own. Truly, Christ alone atones for sin and brings new life through his cross and resurrection. But until the final day of the Lord, the church tastes both sweetness and bitterness in presenting a self-offering of praise. There is pain and grief in living as ones who long for the kingdom in the midst of injustice and unbelief. Yet, even this grief can be made into a fruitful labor pain for the new creation; for in receiving nourishment at the table, believers receive the sweetness of being seen by the King, being received by the Lord, entering into the drama of dying and rising with Christ. The children of the King can do this with confidence, trusting that this season of tears will not be the final act, but that the resurrection feast is yet to come.

# CHAPTER 6

༄

# Communion in Union with Christ

At the feast of remembrance, communion, and hope, the Spirit enables the church to enact its true identity as a people constituted by the life, death, and resurrection of Jesus Christ. In their remembrance, dying and rising with Christ become a present experience of the community. In communion at the Supper, the Lord Jesus Christ offers his own person, his very presence, to his people, those who are hopelessly incomplete without him. In hope, God's people enjoy a foretaste of heavenly manna, a taste that deepens our hunger and focuses our desires on the kingdom that only Jesus Christ can bring.

In this chapter, we focus upon the middle term, "communion." As we commune, Jesus Christ offers himself to his people at the Supper by the Spirit, even as he exercises his Lordship over the church as head of the body. As such, the church is not a voluntary association like the PTA, nor is it a collection of self-made individuals seeking to fully actualize their potential. The church is a people gathered by and around the Word, Jesus Christ. We are utterly dependent creatures who look for life outside of ourselves. For "your life is now hidden with Christ in God" until "Christ, who is your life, appears" (Col. 3:3, 4). Instead of championing the individual's right to define oneself on one's own terms, Christ declares, "Apart from me you can do nothing" (John 15:5b).

Communion at the Lord's Supper is other focused, entailing a dual encounter with Christ and with others around the table. "Is not the cup of thanksgiving for which we give thanks a participation in the blood of Christ? And is not the bread that we break a participation in the body of Christ? Because there is one loaf, we, who are many, are one body, for we all share the one loaf" (1 Cor. 10:16–17). For Paul, communion with Christ leads believers to seek fellowship with other flesh-and-blood persons who have been adopted into God's household. This accords with Jesus's teaching in John's Gospel, that union with Christ bears fruit in other-centered actions: "I am the vine; you are the branches. If you remain in me and I in you, you will bear much fruit" (John 15:5a). This fruit of obedience is characterized by self-sacrificial love. "My command is this: Love each other as I have loved you" (John 15:12).

Thus, as congregations cultivate a growing desire for the table, it should not simply be a desire for the bread and wine as consecrated elements. The bread and wine find their place as instruments in a much larger drama. On the most fundamental level, through the sign-act of the Lord's Supper, the almighty God of the universe fulfills his pledge to come and dwell among his creatures—to find a home with them as he dwelt in the temple, to be married to them in covenantal love as he promised to Israel. In Jesus Christ, the culmination of creation and covenant, God made his temple dwelling-place among humans: "The Word became flesh and made his dwelling among us. We have seen his glory, the glory of the one and only Son, who came from the Father, full of grace and truth" (John 1:14). The Word became flesh; the King of the kingdom invites us as the host to a banquet. This is a king's banquet, but that of a crucified and risen King: Christ takes the bread and cup, gives thanks, and shares them as one who displays the self-offering love of the triune God.

As mind-bending as it may seem, when the Spirit incorporates us into the loving communion of Jesus the Son, we are incorporated into a durable, eternal love that is older than creation itself. This is a love that does not move to and fro like the updating of one's "relationship status" on Facebook; it is not a product of Valentine's Day swooning. This eternal love echoes through the ages in the praise the creation itself sings to the Creator.

> Let the heavens rejoice, let the earth be glad;
>     let the sea resound, and all that is in it.
> Let the fields be jubilant, and everything in them;
>     let all the trees of the forest sing for joy. (Ps. 96:11–12)

In the sign-act of the Supper, God gives an instrument to his people to participate in his steady, eternal love. Through the Supper, the Spirit joins God's people into the life and mission of the Son sent by the Father to show the triune God's love to the world. The triune God's love is not a spigot or even a fountain, but a raging waterfall that carries along his people as they are moved and sent into a world parched for life. Indeed, as believers come to the table, they always bring their own parched lives, in need of renewal and refreshment. For the eternal love of God, made known in Jesus, gives water that will "become in them a spring of water gushing up to eternal life" (John 4:14 NRSV).

## A Grand Yet Gritty Drama

The Lord's Supper incorporates believers into a great drama; it is a grand vision, but also a gritty one. On the one hand, union with Christ restores, rather than annihilates, our created identity. Our bodies, as we eat and drink in time and space, are good; communion with God and one another in Christ is the end toward which we were created, and we participate in this true life at the Supper. And yet we are not idealized, angelic beings, acting like we "have it all together." The Supper is celebrated in a gritty place, east of Eden, before the descent of the new Jerusalem. We have lost our way, acting in scripts that lead us to enmity with God and others. In order for our alienation toward God and neighbor to be overcome, we need to die and find life in Christ. Thus, our path of healing through union with Christ is also deeply threatening. The temple and dwelling place of God has no place for wickedness, self-assertion, enmity, and injustice. Incorporated into Christ, the true temple, believers are called to die to their ways of alienation and to live by the Spirit into Christ, their righteousness. As God prepares to restore the whole creation to be a temple of the Lord, he separates and purifies. Followers of the crucified and risen Lord receive the Lord's personal and corporate discipline on the path of discipleship.

Moreover, when Christ beckons us to become one with him, it is to a marriage with him that involves a daily, conjugal commitment. Intimacy with Christ is both joyful and searing. Christ is the proper end for all our delights, all our affections. And yet, this love also leads us where we may not want to go. We are called to separate ourselves from the loves that compete with the primacy of Christ our spouse, and yet, Christ also woos us into fellowship with others: the pimpled, dysfunctional, argumentative people who gather with us around the table on Sunday morning. Some Christians "shop" for churches, moving from one to another until they find a people who share their political convictions, their sense of propriety, their taste in music, or the finer points of theology. Indeed, many of us desire a church that matches our "tribe" of political leanings, cultural background, life stage, etc. But the Host for the feast of love does not just invite hipsters or squares, conservatives or liberals, whites or blacks; the Host invites people we would rather not see there. For we are not masters or owners of this table; it is "the Lord's table" (1 Cor. 10:21). It would be easy to return to the privacy of a smartphone and generate some outrage on social media about the "unenlightened" Christians in our midst. It would be tempting to "feed upon Christ" but to spurn the actual flesh and blood of Christians who surround us. But the Host invites not only us into God's household fellowship, but also others in our congregations, in our denominations, and in the worldwide body of Christ. As the church lives into her identity as the temple, the bodies owned by her spouse, Jesus Christ, she enters into the messy and open-ended task of loving those she did not choose as adopted brothers and sisters in the Lord.

Thus, while many Christians today prefer to love Jesus but not his church, a scripturally rooted celebration of the Lord's Supper does not leave that option open. To be in communion with the beautiful, alluring Christ is impossible without communion with his broken and sinful—yet cleansed and redeemed—bride, the church. In the words of Calvin, "We cannot love Christ without loving him in the brethren."[1]

Even more, union with Christ at the Supper not only means communion with brothers and sisters at the table, it also leads to loving encounters that seek communion with wounded neighbors among us: the poor, the naked, the prisoners. "I needed clothes and you clothed me, I was sick and you looked after me, I was in prison and you came to visit me" (Matt. 25:36). In the second century, Justin Martyr recommended that the practice of almsgiving be joined to the celebration of the Lord's Supper, and Bucer and Calvin commended the practice as well.[2] For Calvin, the Supper is inextricably connected to the "sacrifice of praise" that leads to a loving concern for neighbor, far and near. Specifically, this self-offering is expressed in a concern for justice (*ius*) and equity (*aequitas*) for those outside of the church in society at large.[3] Feeding upon Christ at the Supper empowers believers to act in the world by the Spirit—acting with love for the other and advocating justice and equity, even for those who have harmed us.[4] The fruit of the Supper includes love of neighbor both locally and globally, and love of neighbor involves both compassion for individuals in need and, on a larger scale, advocacy for justice and equity to be reflected in the structures of society. Indeed, not only do the implications of the Supper relate to Christian involvement in society, but there are also cosmic implications. As Christ renews the whole creation, the church of Word and

1. Calvin, *Institutes* 4.17.38.

2. For more on Justin Martyr and Bucer on this point, see Nicholas Thompson, *Eucharistic Sacrifice and Patristic Tradition in the Theology of Martin Bucer: 1534–1546* (Leiden: Brill, 2005), 197. For Calvin's connection of the Lord's Supper to almsgiving, see *Institutes* 4.17.44.

3. See J. Todd Billings, *Calvin, Participation, and the Gift: The Activity of Believers in Union with Christ* (Oxford: Oxford University Press, 2008), 165.

4. For an account of the way in which Calvin's view of the Lord's Supper involves the renewal of social ties with implications not only for fellowship in the church but also for society at large, see Andre Bieler, *Calvin's Economic and Social Thought*, ed. Edward Dommen, trans. James Greig (Geneva: World Alliance of Reformed Churches, 2005), 236–42.

sacrament offers a foretaste of the new creation to a world wracked with corruption, abuse, and environmental degradation. "I am making all things new," Jesus tells us in Revelation 21:5 (NRSV). The church is not the Savior, but in feeding upon Christ at the Supper and bearing witness to him in the world, the church acts as John the Baptist, prophetically crying out in the wilderness that there is one who is making all things new: Jesus Christ.

In light of the expansive vision of communion with Christ that I have just sketched, we need to modify the leading questions that are often posed in sacramental theology. Often the first question that arises in eucharistic discussions is this: Do you believe in the real presence of Christ? In response to that question, my answer is yes, though with Calvin I would prefer to use the language of true participation in Christ at the Supper. But when we truly consider the stakes, I sense that the question should be different. It is not simply a question of object—whether an object is present or absent at the Supper; it is a question about the way in which we partake in the life-giving yet disruptive *person* of Jesus Christ. Do we really want to be united to Christ, to enter into loving fellowship with others in our congregations, in our denominations, in the church as a whole? We may be attracted to the ideal of loving communion with others, but do we really desire to be members of Christ's body with imperfect, sometimes uncool believers in our midst? Do we really desire an intimacy with Christ—the Christ who properly *owns* our bodies, their actions, and their loves? Do we really desire to enter into the new life of a sacrifice of praise that calls us to repent of our injustice and alienation, moving in love toward those who appear unlovable? Entering into "communion with Christ" is much more earth-shattering and earthy, more beckoning and threatening, more welcoming and fear inducing than we usually realize.

## "You Are Not Your Own": The Body and Union with Christ in 1 Corinthians 5–6

The Heidelberg Catechism opens with an answer that is both simple and astonishing: "I am not my own, but belong—body and soul, in life and in death—to my faithful Savior, Jesus Christ."[5] It draws from an even more astonishing section of 1 Corinthians in which Paul argues that believers are united to Christ in a marriage-like union, for "anyone united to the Lord becomes one spirit with him" (1 Cor. 6:17 NRSV), and that Christians are not

---

5. Heidelberg Catechism, question and answer 1, in *Our Faith*, 69.

free to do whatever they please with their bodies because "you are not your own" (6:19). If a religious leader today told his people, "Your bodies belong to me," those gathered would (rightly!) be alarmed. Indeed, few principles in modern legal thought are more fundamental than this: the autonomy and self-determination of the individual. Before going into the hospital for a serious surgery, patients are asked to assign someone as a "power of attorney" to make medical and financial decisions for them if they are unable to do so after the surgery, or if they would die from the procedure. The government, or even a family member, needs to bow to the will of the patient while she is able to make a decision: it's her body, after all. What does it mean for Paul to claim that the bodies of Christians are not their own? In addressing this question in terms of Paul's thought in 1 Corinthians, we will see how communion with Christ in salvation undergirds Paul's view of the church and her life, and ultimately extends into the imperatives and warnings he gives about the Lord's Supper in 1 Corinthians 10 and 11.

Paul's declaration "you are not your own" occurs in a section of chapters 5 and 6 that weaves together themes related to union with Christ, disciplinary judgment, and the body. In chapter 5, Paul responds to a report of incest in the congregation in Corinth. The persons involved have not repented and indeed are apparently proud of their ongoing relationship as a demonstration of Christian freedom from the law. Paul's response reflects an aspect of union with Christ that may surprise many Christians today: because of their union with Christ, believers are to separate themselves from those living in unrepentant immorality. In 1 Corinthians 5:5, Paul uses the challenging language that "you are to hand this man over to Satan for the destruction of the flesh, so that his spirit may be saved in the day of the Lord." But, as Anthony Thiselton argues, "flesh" here does not refer to the body but the old self, seeking autonomy from God.[6] Handing over "to Satan" is not a way to speak about the final judgment, but the disciplining judgment of temporary exclusion from the church fellowship. The exclusion takes place to encourage repentance "so that his spirit may be saved in the day of the Lord" (1 Cor. 5:5).[7] The temporary exclusion that Paul commands is a form of what Protestants call "discipline" in the church;

6. Anthony C. Thiselton, *The First Epistle to the Corinthians* (Grand Rapids: Eerdmans, 2013), 395–400.

7. Thus, Paul is not requiring perfection from believers. Rather, as Richard Hays points out, Paul "thinks of the Corinthian church, composed primarily of Gentile converts, as belonging to God's covenant community," thus bearing "the same moral responsibilities given to Israel in scripture." Richard B. Hays, *First Corinthians: A Bible Commentary for Teaching and Preaching*, Interpretation (Louisville: Westminster John Knox, 2011), 80.

it is not an attempt to eliminate or even regulate all sin in the church. Instead, discipline relates to the healthy functioning of the covenant community and its distinctive witness in a world of moral confusion.

Paul continues by discussing the ways in which believers should reflect their new identity in Christ, rather than one involving dissension, greed, and sexual immorality (6:1–10). Instead of reflecting these sinful identities, Paul declares to those in the church, "you were washed, you were sanctified, you were justified in the name of the Lord Jesus Christ and by the Spirit of our God" (6:11). The gifts of forgiveness and new life in union with Christ give the church her true identity and show her true calling. Specifically, Paul argues, the bodies of believers *belong* to Christ, just as a husband's body belongs to his wife, and the wife's body belongs to her husband (7:3–4). Believers are one with Christ in a way that parallels marital and sexual union. The bodies of believers are "for the Lord" (6:13); indeed, Christ and the believer enter into a one-flesh union similar to, yet even more intimate than, the union of husband and wife, as he quotes Genesis 2:24: "The two shall be one flesh" (NRSV).

This one-flesh union with Christ has profound consequences for the communal and personal action of believers in Corinth. When believers offer their bodies to other lovers (whether sexual or other loves manifested by "thieves, the greedy, drunkards, revilers, robbers" [1 Cor. 6:10 NRSV]), they betray their true identity as one with Christ, their true lover and spouse. "Do you not know that your bodies are members of Christ? Should I therefore take the members of Christ and make them members of a prostitute? Never! Do you not know that whoever is united to a prostitute becomes one body with her?" (6:15–16 NRSV). It's in this context that Paul reminds the Corinthians of the resurrection of the body (6:14) and that "It is said, 'The two shall be one flesh.' But anyone united to the Lord becomes one spirit with him" (6:16–17 NRSV).[8] Union with Christ is at the center of Paul's vision not only of the

---

8. While Paul changes from "one flesh" in marriage to speaking of "one spirit" (*hen pneuma*) in union with Christ, this contrast does not undermine the significance of union with Christ, but accentuates it. As Joseph Fitzmyer points out, this "spiritual union of the Christian with 'the Lord' has a marital connotation" here—yet "whoever thus joins himself to the Lord transcends human bodily existence and acquires a new identity, as one becomes 'one spirit' with Christ" (Joseph A. Fitzmyer, *First Corinthians* [New Haven: Yale University Press, 2008], 268). This new, marriage-like identity in Christ does not displace the significance of somatic, bodily action, but gives it a new orientation, to "glorify God in your body" (1 Cor. 6:20 NRSV). For an extended analysis of 1 Cor. 5–7 that shows the close connection between the marriage-like state of the believer with Christ and the physical body of the believer and its actions, see Alistair May, *The Body for the Lord: Sex and Identity in 1 Corinthians 5–7* (London: Bloomsbury T. & T. Clark, 2004), especially 110–43.

church, but also of how Christians offer their bodies to Jesus Christ, their spouse. As Ciampa and Rosner point out, Paul's language of dividing Christ through uniting oneself to a prostitute points back to a rhetorical question of chapter 1: "Has Christ been divided?" (1:13 NRSV). Surely not! For "quite literally, at the heart of Paul's world stands Christ the risen Lord, for whom all believers live and in whom they find their purpose and identity."[9]

In light of this profound union, Paul says, remember that you are not your own. For the body, which belongs to Jesus Christ as spouse, is also the temple of the Holy Spirit. "Shun fornication! Every sin that a person commits is outside the body; but the fornicator sins against the body itself. Or do you not know that your body is a temple of the Holy Spirit within you, which you have from God, and that you are not your own? For you were bought with a price; therefore glorify God in your body" (6:18–20 NRSV). Paul's reference to believers as the temple for the indwelling Spirit harkens back to 1 Corinthians 3:16: "Don't you know that you yourselves are God's temple and that God's Spirit dwells in your midst?" The temple is the dwelling place of God—displaying the Lord's glory and purity to the world. When the body is united to another in fornication, the temple's purity is contaminated and the body's ownership by Jesus Christ the spouse is betrayed. Far from any contemporary ideas of "casual sex," Paul paints a clear contrast: a believer can either unite to a prostitute, thus denying God's ownership of the body and the final participation in Christ's resurrection, or unite to Christ and his body, the church.[10] Moreover, this unholy union of a member of the church with the prostitute "creates an unholy bond between the Lord's members and the sinful world," Hays notes. "The result is both defilement and confusion" for the whole community.[11] The bond with the Lord Jesus is relational, unitive, like with a spouse, and also asymmetrical: for as believers have received forgiveness of sins in this union through no merit of their own, they should remember Paul's words: "You were bought with a price; therefore glorify God in your body."

Thus, Paul holds several realities of union with Christ together at once: a marriage of believers with Christ by the Spirit (often called "spiritual marriage" by the later Christian tradition; cf. 1 Cor. 6:16–17); the indwelling of the Holy Spirit in the body as temple; and a reorientation of Christian desires and actions to conform to a new identity in Christ and the covenantal responsibilities

9. Roy E. Ciampa and Brian S. Rosner, *The First Letter to the Corinthians* (Grand Rapids: Eerdmans, 2010), 257.

10. See Ciampa and Rosner, *First Letter to the Corinthians*, 258–59; May, *Body for the Lord*, 138–40.

11. Hays, *First Corinthians*, 105.

of Christian fellowship. A key point of connection throughout his discourse is a focus upon *the body*. Paul's discourse on the body moves against the instincts of modern, individualist assumptions about our use of our bodies. Our *bodies* are not our own. Our *actions* should reflect the reality that we are not our own. And the church—in its unity, its mutual responsibility, its witness—should reflect the reality that she is not her own, but belongs to Jesus Christ. As the church, the persons and community are called to offer our bodies and whole selves to Christ in love and obedience and to one another in fellowship, but with a self-control that reflects the faithfulness to Christ the spouse, and the sacred character of the bodies of believers as the dwelling place of God, the temple of the Holy Spirit.

### The Body and Union with Christ in 1 Corinthians 10 and 11

How does all this relate to the Lord's Supper? After speaking about the use of the body in sexual relations in chapter 7, Paul examines another bodily and communal practice within the covenant community of the church in chapters 8 and 9: the practice of eating meat sacrificed to idols, the possibility that this may cause weaker brothers and sisters to stumble, and the nature of true Christian freedom. In chapters 10 and 11, then, Paul continues his discourse on these temptations of the church to idolatry and unfaithfulness by contrasting idolatry with a different feast: the Lord's Supper. The church is bound together in Christ, who enables communion with Christ and others, entailing covenantal responsibilities. As in chapters 5 and 6, action that treats our bodies as "our own" rather than as Christ's is subject to judgment: those who commit such acts "eat and drink judgment against themselves"—though this is not the final judgment, but a discipline: "when we are judged by the Lord, we are disciplined so that we may not be condemned along with the world" (1 Cor. 11:29, 32 NRSV). Union with Christ leads to nourishment and life and involves mutual fellowship in Christ, but, as in 1 Corinthians 5–6, a misuse of the body leads to disciplinary judgment.

Paul continues to apply key aspects of Israel's story to the Corinthians in chapters 10 and 11. In chapter 10 he evokes the language of the temple that he used in chapters 3 and 6: the temple was the place of sacrifice for Israel and also the place where God disclosed his presence, his glory. Idolatry violates the purity of the temple.[12] In addition, Paul sees Israel's time with the Lord in

---

12. Thiselton, *First Epistle to the Corinthians*, 316.

REMEMBRANCE, COMMUNION, AND HOPE

the wilderness as the prefiguration of the church's life and temptations. The Israelites "all passed through the sea, and all were baptized into Moses" (10:1–2 NRSV). Like the Corinthian Christians, the Israelites received a type of baptism, and they also received a meal as a covenant people. For they "all ate the same spiritual food, and all drank the same spiritual drink"—referring to manna (Exod. 16:1–36) and the water from the rock (Exod. 17:1–7). Moreover, "the rock was Christ" (1 Cor. 10:4 NRSV); thus, like the Corinthians, they enjoyed the material signs of God's covenant grace and fellowship.[13]

But rather than enjoying the proper fellowship with God—the "spiritual food" and "spiritual drink" of the Lord's Supper—the church in Corinth is tempted to idolatry, like the Israelites in the wilderness. Thus, Paul admonishes them to "flee from idolatry" (10:14). Taking a path far different from some today who imply that only the God of the Old Testament judges idolatry (in contrast to a "permissive" God of the New Testament), Paul insists that the God of Israel made known in Jesus Christ requires sole allegiance. This is "the God of Israel," as Hays says, "a jealous God who sternly condemns idol-worship and punishes all who dare dabble in it."[14] Because they offered their bodies in worship to idols rather than the true Lord, "God was not pleased with most of them, and they were struck down in the wilderness," Paul says (10:5 NRSV). This did not forfeit Israel's election as God's covenant people, but they nevertheless received a judgment for responding to the "baptism of Moses" and the "spiritual food" and "spiritual drink" with ingratitude, giving themselves over to their sins and to gods other than the Lord.

In the context of this contrast between receiving gifts in idolatry and receiving them in self-offering worship to God, Paul points to the power of the *koinōnia* (fellowship, participation) at the Supper: "Therefore, my dear friends, flee from the worship of idols. I speak as to sensible people; judge for yourselves what I say. The cup of blessing that we bless, is it not a sharing (*koinōnia*) in the blood of Christ? The bread that we break, is it not a sharing (*koinōnia*) in the body of Christ? Because there is one bread, we who are many are one body, for we all partake of the one bread" (10:14–17 NRSV). Lest the Corinthians miss his contrast, Paul declares that self-offering to other gods and offering to the Lord at the Supper are mutually exclusive: "I do not want you to be partners (*koinōnous*) with demons. You cannot drink the cup of the Lord and the cup of demons. You cannot partake of the table of the Lord and

---

13. Hays, *First Corinthians*, 160.
14. Hays, *First Corinthians*, 159.

the table of demons. Or are we provoking the Lord to jealousy?" (10:20–22 NRSV). The parallel with 1 Corinthians 6 is striking: union with Christ—like marital love—requires exclusive allegiance, a self-offering in worship to the Lord rather than to other gods. One becomes united "with demons" and idols *or* with the body and blood of Christ and all who partake of the body and blood of Christ.

Thus, when Paul moves to his more specific address of the Lord's Supper and its abuses in chapter 11, all these dynamics from chapters 5, 6, and 10 are in play. Paul is not just concerned about literal idol worship; he is also concerned about greed, divisions, sexual immorality, and other sins with corporate, covenantal implications, as I suggested in my earlier analysis. Like Israel, the Corinthians have turned away from God's self-offering, the love of their true spouse, and toward other loves instead. Specifically, they have turned from the spiritual manna and drink offered in the body and blood of Christ and acted against their true identity as a covenant people united in Christ. "Indeed, there have to be factions among you. . . . When you come together, it is not really to eat the Lord's supper" (11:19–20 NRSV). Rather than receiving the *koinōnia* of Christ and offering themselves in *koinōnia* to one another, the rich celebrate separately from the poor; those with status eat while those without status go hungry. Just as mistreatment of the poor was characteristic of Israel's departure from fidelity to their spouse, YHWH, so also the Corinthians neglected the poor and spurned the reconciliation and communion that he has brought. This is *not* "the Lord's Supper." The Lord's Supper requires a participation in Christ that is inseparably connected with fellowship in the body of Christ. The Corinthians have rejected the *koinōnia* offered in the bread and cup in 10:16–17. As Calvin movingly asserts:

> We shall benefit very much from the Sacrament if this thought is impressed and engraved upon our minds: that none of the brethren can be injured, despised, rejected, abused, or in any way offended by us, without at the same time, injuring, despising, and abusing Christ by the wrongs we do; . . . that we ought to take the same care of our brethren's bodies as we take of our own; for they are members of our body; and that, as no part of our body is touched by any feeling of pain which is not spread among all the rest, so we ought not to allow a brother to be affected by any evil, without being touched with compassion for him.[15]

15. Calvin, *Institutes* 4.17.38.

Just as Israel was called to covenantal obedience, living into its identity as the chosen people of God and spurning the worship of other gods, so the church is called to exclusive obedience to the Lord in mutual fellowship, compassion for the poor, reconciliation, and unity. The church cannot offer this exclusive obedience on her own—she needs the life-giving fellowship given by the Spirit. Thus, the covenantal obligations of God—as a way of living into the gift of belonging to Christ's body, the church—are emphasized by Paul in 1 Corinthians 10.

Paul's teaching in 1 Corinthians 11 also builds upon his earlier emphasis on the *body*—in terms of both individual bodies and the corporate body of Christ—the way it should be offered in self-giving worship to the Lord, the way it is owned by Christ the spouse, and the way it requires nourishment through Christ, the true manna in the wilderness. The Corinthians have acted as if their bodies were their own; instead, Christ, the spouse and the manna, offered his own body by the Spirit as an instrument of grace—an instrument for experiencing communion with Christ *and* communal unity in Christ's body. Indeed, the bodies of the Corinthians are properly oriented only when they look to Christ as the true source of their nourishment, the true center for their personal and communal identity. Feeding upon Christ comes first, and this leads to and enables communion with others in Christ, and an expression of the Spirit's new life in the world. In the words of Calvin, communion with the body and blood of Christ is primary, yet it calls believers to "purity and holiness of life, and to love, peace, and concord." "For the Lord so communicates his body to us there that he is made completely one with us and we with him. Now, since he has only one body, of which he makes us all partakers, it is necessary that all of us also be made one body by such participation."[16] Communal reconciliation and oneness are made possible only through union with Christ. Thus, when the corporate body of Christ turns away from her spouse, a disciplining judgment should take steps to renew corporate faithfulness to Christ.

This judgment about the Supper is, strikingly, framed in terms of the body as well: "Whoever, therefore, eats the bread or drinks the cup of the Lord in an unworthy manner will be answerable for the body and blood of the Lord. Examine yourselves, and only then eat of the bread and drink of the cup. For all who eat and drink without discerning the body, eat and drink judgment against themselves. For this reason many of you are weak and ill, and some have died" (1 Cor. 11:27–30 NRSV). In the history of Christian theology, this passage has often been read as a relatively isolated set of teachings about

16. Calvin, *Institutes* 4.17.38.

the Supper. But considering these words in light of Paul's earlier chapters, we can see that Paul's words fit a clear pattern. Our bodies belong to Jesus Christ, our spouse, who offers his own body as food and drink. Our bodies are thus temples of Christ's presence by the Spirit, and our lives should be given in self-offering worship to the Lord and in fellowship with his people, acting as witnesses to Christ in a sinful world. The body, as the Spirit's temple, can be contaminated with idolatry; the body can be united to Christ's body, or united to a prostitute's body in betrayal of the Christian's true spouse. Both bodily actions involve spurning the life-giving self-offering of the Lord Jesus Christ, just as the Israelites spurned the "spiritual food" and "spiritual drink" offered by the covenant Lord (10:3–4).

Thus, for Paul writing to the Corinthians, partaking in an "unworthy manner" is not mainly about partaking without proper catechetical preparation (as beneficial as that is!); nor does worthy partaking require that participants be "perfected" Christians who can find no sin in their lives. Instead, this "unworthy manner" without "discerning the body" involves a personal and corporate double-discernment: discerning that Christ offers his body as one who owns our bodies and has incorporated ours into his; and discerning that we have been incorporated into the communal body of Christ, which joins together rich and poor to taste the glorious presence of the Lord. Indeed, supplemented with the themes elsewhere in Paul, we can suggest that properly "discerning" the body of Christ in the church involves discerning that in Christ we should not use ethnicity, race, or gender as grounds for excluding membership in the covenant people. "So in Christ Jesus you are all children of God through faith, for all of you who were baptized into Christ have clothed yourselves with Christ. There is neither Jew nor Gentile, neither slave nor free, nor is there male and female, for you are all one in Christ Jesus. If you belong to Christ, then you are Abraham's seed, and heirs according to the promise" (Gal. 3:26–29). We properly "discern" the body when we embrace the unity and holiness of the bonds of covenant fellowship. The gift of the body of Christ thus comes with this warning: Christ's personal presence is offered at the Supper, but it is not a "comfortable" presence; instead, it is intimate and even invasive. If we decide in advance that we will partner with idols or prostitutes rather than with Christ and his people, then the Supper becomes a mockery and we are "answerable for the body and blood of the Lord" (1 Cor. 11:27 NRSV).

## Who Is Invited to the Table?

Having explored the biblical context for Paul's theology of union with Christ in 1 Corinthians 5–6 and 10–11, we are able to face the question that vexes many congregations and denominations today: Who should be invited to the table? Should the table be "open," "closed," or perhaps "fenced" from sinners for discipline? (Hint: those are not the only options, as we shall see!) These sections in 1 Corinthians provide us with the most direct response to that question, but there is a very wide range of responses in both official church positions and practice.

On the one hand, official Roman Catholic and Eastern Orthodox doctrine teaches a form of "closed" or "close" communion. As noted in chapter 3, under ordinary circumstances, Roman Catholics do not permit Protestants to partake in the Mass. Orthodox churches do not open communion to those outside their membership.[17] Pope John Paul II gives a key part of the Roman Catholic rationale for not further "opening" the table to Protestants in his encyclical *Ecclesia de Eucharistia*: "Precisely because the Church's unity, which the Eucharist brings about through the Lord's sacrifice and by communion in his body and blood, absolutely requires full communion in the bonds of the profession of faith, the sacraments and ecclesiastical governance, it is not possible to celebrate together the same Eucharistic liturgy until those bonds are fully re-established."[18] Thus, from this standpoint, an "open table" would reflect a kind of pseudo-unity, not the kind of unity required by full communion. Indeed, it may be *"an obstacle to the attainment of full communion,* by weakening the sense of how far we remain from this goal."[19] Thus, according to official Roman Catholic and Orthodox teaching, an "open table" would be a weakened table—one that does not display genuine unity of doctrine and ecclesial order—a table without the accountability that comes from full, shared communion.

In stark contrast to this side of the ecumenical conversation, others today advocate an "open table." The phrase itself is used in a variety of ways, but for the purposes of clarity in this book, an "open table" is an invitation to the Supper to those who are not baptized and who do not profess faith in Jesus Christ. This means that all who are gathered are invited to eucharistic

---

17. See discussion on p. 66 of chap. 3.

18. John Paul II, *Ecclesia de Eucharistia*, April 17, 2003, paragraph 44, http://w2.vatican.va/content/john-paul-ii/en/encyclicals/documents/hf_jp-ii_enc_20030417_eccl-de-euch.html.

19. John Paul II, *Ecclesia de Eucharistia*, paragraph 44.

sharing—including agnostics, seekers, and persons who adhere to a religion other than Christianity.

Why would one advocate an "open table" invitation? Significant cultural forces in the late modern West push against any kind of "separation" or even specificity in inviting people to the Supper. If someone is interested enough in the Christian faith to come to the table, who are we to say that he or she should not? Shouldn't the table be a sign of welcome to all? Popular personal narratives of receiving the Supper as a stepping-stone to faith contribute to this trend; the Supper, thus, can be a strategy for evangelism.[20] In light of such experiences, some muse that perhaps we should abandon the historic Christian requirement of at least baptism before entry to the table.[21] Indeed, perhaps this "reform" is necessary to align the church's practice with the gospel: the good news that we are all included, no one is excluded. As Renee House eloquently puts it, we should not be "concerned to protect Jesus from the world any more than he was concerned to protect himself. And we are not concerned to protect our neighbors from Jesus."[22] Just as Jesus had table fellowship with tax collectors and sinners, shouldn't congregations welcome the unbaptized and others without trust in Christ to the table?

I take a middle position between the two approaches above: that baptized Christians should be invited to the table regardless of denomination. On the one hand, I do not share Roman Catholic or Orthodox ecclesiology or sacramental theology that would require the table to be closed. But on the other hand, in light of the most sustained biblical treatment of this issue (in 1 Corinthians), a completely "open" table—with an invitation to those with no baptismal or faith connection to Christ, and the spurning of any possibility of discipline—is simply unsustainable if we are to take Paul at his word.

For Paul, the Lord's Supper is a meal of covenantal fellowship (1 Cor. 10:16–17), always involving our real, concrete bodies—and an intimate union with Christ, and family fellowship with others who have received the sign of adoption into God's household (baptism). There is no doubt that the apostle Paul thinks that unworthiness is a possibility, and that it is a betrayal of this

---

20. See Sara Miles, *Take This Bread: A Radical Conversion* (New York: Ballantine Books, 2008), as a widely publicized example.

21. The question of whether to continue requiring baptism as a prerequisite for communion has been widely discussed in recent years in mainline Protestant denominations. For an overview of the issues involved in those discussions, see Ronald P. Byars, *The Sacraments in Biblical Perspective* (Louisville: Westminster John Knox, 2011), 225–29.

22. Renee House, "Going Public," *Perspectives: A Journal of Reformed Thought*, November/December 2016, 7.

fundamental intimacy (11:27–34). Indeed, Paul repeatedly uses the language of marital, sexual union in speaking about this covenantal fellowship with Christ: the point is not to "protect Jesus from the world," but to protect the marriage of believers to Jesus Christ. Believers are "members of Christ" fulfilling the marital covenant that "the two will become one flesh." Because of this marriage, believers are called to give their bodies to their lover in Christ, and not to other lovers (6:15–20). Openness and welcome are a good thing. All are invited to embrace faith in Christ; no one is barred from receiving baptism, a sign of covenantal entry. But as we have seen, for Paul the Lord's table is a table of union with Christ, and he describes this union as parallel to the marital fidelity required by the covenant of marriage. If this is the case, then the table should not be completely "open," any more than an "open marriage" (with multiple partners) would be a faithful way to uphold the covenantal commitment of marriage.

Thus, while I think a Protestant congregation should welcome baptized believers to the table, we should not give a generic invitation for anyone to partake. In addition, related to the concern of Paul in 1 Corinthians 11:27–34, I think congregations need to be open to the possibility of temporarily "fencing" members from the table as an act of discipline. I realize that many readers have seen the distortion of church discipline firsthand. A "fencing" from the table can be used to settle personal scores, or as a power play by a pastor. Some have been so wounded by the misuse of church discipline, and the fencing of the table as a part of that, that they become alienated from the church community itself—which is the opposite of the true goal of church discipline.

However, in light of 1 Corinthians, it is clear that we must seek to uphold proper discipline in relation to the sacrament, unless we want to move away from Paul toward a Marcionite view of the church that marginalizes the significance of the Old Testament. It would be tempting to assume that God only disciplined his people for acts of idolatry, sexual immorality, and callous greed in the Old Testament, and not in the New. But Paul's discussion of the Lord's Supper proclaims the contrary—that just as God disciplined Israel's idolatry in the wilderness (10:10), so the Christians in Corinth are already at risk of this discipline (10:11–22), and in some ways have already received it through their corruption of the Supper celebration (11:30–32).

Yet, a critic could counter that perhaps partaking in an "unworthy manner" (11:24–27) is *simply* the act of exclusion itself. These interpreters rightly point out that Paul's word of judgment is for those in Corinth who celebrated the Supper in factions—apparently with the rich celebrating apart from the poor and others without status (11:18–21). This view is right in what it affirms but wrong in what it denies; it disregards the overall context of the preceding chapters in 1 Corinthians and Paul's connection of the church's story with the story of Israel. The Corinthians are not admonished for the sin of exclusion in 1 Corinthians 5, 6, and 10, but for the sin of betrayed allegiance to Jesus Christ, their spouse and their life; believers are declared to be the temples of the Holy Spirit, both communally (3:16–17) and as individual members (6:19). Sins such as sexual immorality and the exclusion of the poor are not "private" sins, as our late modern context considers them, but communal sins.[23] For Paul, the church's identity as God's temple involves a corporate responsibility to display holiness, and thus to take responsibility for discipline when necessary.[24] Christ's Lordship extends to all areas of life. Thus, Paul insists that some should be temporarily excluded from Christian fellowship (and from the table)—a penultimate separation in hopes that they would repent before the final separation in the day of the Lord (5:5; 11:32). Although "exclusion" can seem like the ultimate punishment in a late modern context, in this case its intent is restorative: exclusion is for the sake of the community and the excluded themselves—providing the latter an opportunity to repent and thus avoid the final separation on the day of judgment. The church temporarily excludes in order to restore true communion with Christ and other believers.[25]

A contemporary example can illustrate this need for (temporary) exclusion for the sake of faithfulness to Christ and covenantal fellowship. In 1982, a large ecumenical group of Reformed churches, the World Alliance of Reformed Churches (WARC), declared racial apartheid to be a heresy. The word "heresy" is significant. For years, many Reformed Christians around the globe had condemned both apartheid in South Africa and the Dutch Reformed Church's (DRC) advocacy of that political policy. But talk alone can

23. As Thiselton notes about the case of sexual immorality in 1 Cor. 5, Paul attacks both "the immoral act of the individual person" and the "corporate sin of the community in condoning, accepting, and tolerating the situation, with no overt sign of concern." Thiselton, *First Epistle to the Corinthians*, 390.

24. On this point, Lyle Vander Brook is right to see parallels between the sin of incest and the corporate failure to address it with discipline in 1 Cor. 5, and the danger of sinning "against the body and blood of the Lord" in 1 Cor. 11:27. In both, the holiness of the body of Christ is violated. See Lyle Vander Brook, "Discipline and Community: Another Look at 1 Corinthians 5," *Reformed Review* 48 (1994): 7.

25. For a concrete example of how this can function on a congregational level in the United States to supplement the example from South Africa below, see Brad Harper and Paul Louis Metzger, *Exploring Ecclesiology: An Evangelical and Ecumenical Introduction* (Grand Rapids: Baker, 2009), 175–82.

be cheap. With this 1982 declaration, the DRC was excluded from membership in WARC, and from the table at WARC events, until they repented. This act of discipline meant that WARC was serious about its declaration of heresy. An unconditional "welcome" of the DRC to the table, in light of their ongoing advocacy of apartheid, would have been a sham—a contamination of communion with Christ and his body, the church. It is no accident that within several years of this exclusion, the DRC began making clear moves away from their long-standing advocacy of apartheid.

Why was this exclusion necessary, particularly for an issue that may appear to be "political" rather than "ecclesial"? On this point, history is key. In a far-reaching 1857 decision, the DRC in South Africa made changes in their Reformed polity in order to permit white church members to exclude black members from their celebration of the Lord's Supper. Specific references were made to the principles of the apostle Paul: that the whites who did not want to celebrate the Supper with black members were "weaker brethren"; thus, the 1857 decision sought to offer pastoral accommodation. Eventually, this decision led to denominational separations based on race. Indeed, historians have pointed to this action as a decisive move toward the eventual advocacy of racial apartheid by the DRC.[26]

This 1857 "pastoral accommodation" was in fact a choice to bow to the idolatry of racism rather than the Lordship of Christ, a choice for one's members to join with the prostitute of racial superiority rather than to live as "you are not your own" (1 Cor. 6:19). It was a denial of Christ's reconciling work that created "one new humanity" in Christ (Eph. 2:15). As such, since single-race membership and racial prejudice were written into the very life of the DRC, an act of discipline (indeed, temporary exclusion) was appropriate. In this context, the DRC was invited to find her life once again in Jesus Christ and to enter into the task of living into this unity and covenantal fellowship in Christ. Indeed, in the words of the Belhar Confession, written shortly after the WARC excommunication, "unity is, therefore, both a gift and an obligation for the church of Jesus Christ; that through the working of God's Spirit it is a binding force, yet simultaneously a reality which must be earnestly pursued and sought." In contrast to the exclusion based upon race, God's people in Christ "have one God and Father, are filled with one Spirit, are baptized with one baptism, eat of one bread and drink of one cup, confess one name, are

26. For an account of this genealogy of apartheid theology, see Dirkie Smit, "South Africa," in *Essays in Public Theology: Collected Essays 1*, ed. Ernst Conradie (Stellenbosch, South Africa: Sun Press, 2007), 11–27.

obedient to one Lord, work for one cause, and share one hope."[27] Indeed, for the sake of witness to the world, "this unity must become visible so that the world may believe that separation, enmity and hatred between people and groups is sin which Christ has already conquered."[28]

Thus, while it may sound "progressive" to have a communion policy completely "open" to anyone—believer and nonbeliever, never fencing the table for discipline—it's profoundly naïve concerning the power of human sin and the all-encompassing allegiance those who are in Christ are called to offer. Celebrating this feast of feeding upon Christ's body while denying the poor and persons of other races and ethnicities a place at the table is a sin against "the body and blood of the Lord" (1 Cor. 11:27). A temporary fencing of the table, in this context, is not to protect the status and privilege of the congregation, but to testify to the unity and reconciliation accomplished in Christ. All persons are invited to enter into this spousal relationship with Christ and communion with God's people, the church, through faith and baptism. But precisely because it is a covenantal relationship—in which Christ is Lord, Christ is the one true spouse, and the church is the new, adopted family—the table is reserved for those who have entered into the gift and responsibility of that covenantal relationship.

### Faith and Self-Examination: The Cases of Baptized Children and Unbelieving Adults

Even if one grants my case that restorative discipline may be a necessary component for "discerning the body" in table fellowship, we still face questions. What kind of "faith" does the Supper require? And what does it mean to "examine" oneself before eating of the bread and drinking of the cup (1 Cor. 11:28)? First, let us explore these questions through examining whether baptized children (in Christian households) should be invited to the table. Does Paul teach that self-examination is a prerequisite for the table? Do young, baptized children have the "faith" to come to the table?

My own view is that baptized children in the covenant fellowship of the church should be welcomed to the table when they display age-appropriate faith in Jesus Christ. This is not paedocommunion in a strict sense of the term—in which infants receive the Supper by virtue of their baptism alone

27. Belhar Confession, in *Our Faith*, 147.
28. Belhar Confession, in *Our Faith*, 146.

(as in Eastern Orthodoxy).[29] On the other hand, I do not think there are strong reasons for asking children to wait for the table until they are teenagers or young adults (by making a formal "profession of faith" before the elders, for example). This also has implications for members with intellectual disabilities: they should be welcomed to the table when they display ability-appropriate faith, even when the disability is profound.[30] Both young children and persons with intellectual disabilities can trust in Christ without having a thorough knowledge of the ins and outs of eucharistic theology. Through faith, they are members of Christ and belong to him. They should be welcomed to the table to feed upon him.

But, we might ask, doesn't one need the intellectual ability to examine oneself (1 Cor. 11:28) and to discern the body (11:29) before coming to the table? To require that would be to misunderstand Paul's admonition to the community in Corinth. In many churches, self-examination becomes the focal point of the Lord's Supper—with participants engaging in introspection about whether their sins are great enough that they should refuse the Supper. But Paul's admonition is not so much for introspection about one's own worthiness as it is for outward examination of the social dimension of covenantal fellowship. As a community, we need to act in accord with the covenantal fellowship that God has initiated. Just as the Lord judged Israel for neglecting the covenant after eating "spiritual food" and drinking "spiritual drink" in the wilderness (10:3–4), so also can a neglect of the covenant at the table bring judgment. Specifically, do not celebrate the Supper in a way that treats brothers and sisters in Christ with indifference, failing to recognize that they also are united to Christ and to oneself in covenantal fellowship.[31] Do not celebrate in a self-serving way that neglects the poor (11:21) and divides the people the Lord has united into factions (11:18). This self-examination and discernment, then, are not a high-level cognitive task. In the words of Richard Hays, discerning the body "means recognizing the community of believers for what it really is: the one body of Christ."[32] Both require

---

29. For an Orthodox account of the reception of infants to Holy Communion, see Kallistos Ware, *The Orthodox Way* (Crestwood, NY: St. Vladimir's Seminary Press, 1979), 108–9.

30. For an accessible account presenting a biblical and pastoral case for this approach, applying the case to persons with disabilities as well, see the Christian Reformed Church in North America document of 2011, "Children at the Table: Toward a Guiding Principle for Biblically Faithful Celebrations of the Lord's Supper, Revised Edition." My thanks to Randy Blacketer for pointing me to this document and the writings of Musculus on children at the table below.

31. See David E. Garland, *1 Corinthians* (Grand Rapids: Baker Academic, 2003), 551–52; Ciampa and Rosner, *First Letter to the Corinthians*, 555–56.

32. Hays, *First Corinthians*, 200.

an age- and ability-appropriate tending of the bonds of covenantal fellowship in light of what Christ has done in incorporating the baptized into one body.

While recent New Testament scholarship offers reasons for interpreting "discerning the body" as recognizing and treating the gathered fellowship as the corporate body of Christ, there is a long Protestant pedigree for another version of this position, albeit a minority report in Protestant circles.[33] Sixteenth-century Reformed theologian Wolfgang Musculus makes this case. His argument is similar to one given in chapter 5 of this book regarding the Passover: "The little children of Jews" took the Passover, Musculus observes, so why should our children not partake of the "new Passover," the Lord's Supper? Moreover, he questions whether Paul is listing *qualifications* for receiving the Supper in 1 Corinthians 11:27–29, arguing that they are communal warnings. Rather than Paul seeking to exclude young children in his admonitions about unworthy partaking, Musculus feels that "none of this [is] to be feared in the little children of them that do believe." Instead of listing qualifications to participate in the Supper, Paul is warning against the abuse of "the sacrament of grace." Indeed, the unity that Paul champions in 1 Corinthians 11 can be an important reason to invite children to the table. For when they are excluded, young children already partake of the "signified" (union with Christ) even though the "sign" (bread and cup) is denied them. For Musculus, central to the case for including children is the truth "that Christ is the Saviour of the whole body, that is to say the church, and that the infants also do belong unto the integrity and wholeness of the ecclesial body."[34]

Whether or not one accepts my case for inviting baptized children with age-appropriate faith to the table, it is vital to recognize that the catechetical process should be held in high esteem, even if a full catechetical process is not a "prerequisite" to table fellowship. The third-century document the *Apostolic Tradition* describes a beautiful (and elaborate) process of baptism for adults. Edward Yarnold draws upon fourth- and fifth-century sources to show how adults who desired baptism entered into a catechetical process that included doctrinal, liturgical, and ethical dimensions.[35] The Roman Catholic

33. For a survey of the literature on "discerning the body," see Thiselton, *First Epistle to the Corinthians*, 890–94.

34. Wolfgang Musculus, *Common Places of Christian Religion*, trans. John Man (London: Reginalde Wolfe, 1578). This paragraph draws upon Todd Billings, "The Sacraments," in *Christian Dogmatics: Reformed Theology for the Church Catholic*, ed. Michael Allen and Scott R. Swain (Grand Rapids: Baker Academic, 2016), 359–60.

35. Edward Yarnold, SJ, *The Awe-Inspiring Rites of Initiation: The Origins of the RCIA*, 2nd ed. (Collegeville, MN: Liturgical Press, 1994), 3–49.

Church has drawn from this tradition in the rite for Christian initiation of adults (RCIA). The Reformed tradition has a rich heritage in this regard, with the Heidelberg Catechism fulfilling a key role in catechetical instruction. Its main elements—expositions of the Apostles' Creed, the Ten Commandments, and the Lord's Prayer—are shared with other catechisms of the age, such as the Catechism of the Council of Trent. Yet, the Heidelberg Catechism gives a distinctively Protestant entryway to those catholic waters of catechesis. Not just children or youth, but adults as well, can benefit from the Heidelberg Catechism's instruction. Whether or not children are welcomed to the table, congregations should provide age- and ability-appropriate catechesis for baptized members to deepen the pilgrimage in their life in Christ, including their celebration of Holy Communion.

If baptized children can be welcomed to the table on the grounds I've described, what about unbelievers? As noted in chapter 3, for a catholic and Reformed approach to the Supper, faith is not an "achievement" but a gift; yet, faith is still an *instrument* for receiving the benefits of union with Christ in salvation, as well as at the table itself. So, apart from age-appropriate and ability-appropriate faith, the table offers no benefits. Moreover, Paul's dire warning in 1 Corinthians 11:27–30 should give us pause. Just as the Supper is life-giving when received rightly, it can carry a penultimate judgment—like the judgment in 1 Corinthians 5–6 and 10—when received in an "unworthy manner." Indeed, retrospectively Paul suggests that this "is why many among you are weak and sick, and a number of you have fallen asleep" (11:30). This "judgment" is not administered by the church, but mercifully by God himself. For "when we are judged in this way by the Lord, we are being disciplined so that we will not be finally condemned with the world" (11:32).

Thus, inviting only the covenant community to the table is not about claiming that they are "worthy" while unbelievers are "unworthy." It is a table of covenant fellowship, and the congregation itself has not properly "discerned the body" if they act as if no connection to Christ is necessary in order to feed upon him at the Supper. Moreover, the community disrespects the unbelievers when they invite them to the family table, by acting as if they hold convictions they do not.

A much better approach is to find ways to welcome unbelievers to worship that honor their own journey and welcome them to Christ—and hold forth table fellowship as a possibility once the proper steps are taken. For example, some congregations invite baptized Christians to the table, and then encourage those not receiving communion to meditate on one of the following prayers:

"Lord Jesus, you claimed to be the way, the truth, and the life. As I search for spiritual truth, please guide me, teach me, and open to me the life that you promise. Amen."

*Prayer of Belief*

"Lord Jesus, Son of God, have mercy on me, a sinner. Trusting in God's love and in your death and resurrection on my behalf, I ask you to forgive me, most merciful Lord, and fill me with your Holy Spirit. Relying on your grace, I promise to confess you publicly before others, to serve you daily, and to walk in your way. Amen."

*Prayer of Commitment*

"Lord Jesus, you have called us to follow you in baptism and in a life of committed discipleship in your church. Grant that I may take the necessary steps to be one with your people, and live in the fullness of your Spirit. Amen."[36]

In this way, unbelievers are invited to faith, and they can join the family table if and when they take steps to join the Lord's family, through confessing the faith and baptism. God issues a universal invitation for sinners to become adopted members of his family. But precisely because this adoption and cleavage to Christ and his body, the church, are such a watershed for human identity, we should avoid the "disordering" of this process and reserve the table for the baptized community of God's covenant.

## Sweet Communion: Intimacy, Longing, and the Spiritual Marriage

What is the nature of our *koinōnia*—our communion and participation—in the body of Christ at the table (1 Cor. 10:16–17)? In earlier sections I have explored its scope: both communion with Christ and communion with the body of Christ, the church. In this Supper, believers are given life and incorporated

---

36. While similar prayers are used in a variety of congregations, the wording here is from the bulletin of Pillar Church, Holland, Michigan, on January 1, 2017, http://pillarchurch.com/.

into the drama of the triune God—united to Jesus Christ by the Spirit, as sons and daughters of the Father, members of one new household of God. This gift of union includes both the forgiveness of sins and new life by the Spirit—overflowing in lives of love of God and neighbor in the world, heralding the Lord of the present and coming King, Jesus Christ.

But now we come to a more intimate question. In light of Paul's arguments in 1 Corinthians about our bodies belonging to Jesus Christ as spouse, what does it mean to enjoy a participation (*koinōnia*) in his body and his blood? Here we need to piece together various parts of Paul's portrait and see how it fits with a larger theme in the biblical canon: Christ's marriage to his covenant people by the Spirit, or, in shorthand, "spiritual marriage."

First, we should recognize that in the broader grammar of Paul's theology of union with Christ, believers are both married to Christ and also not yet married. Marriage to Christ functions in a similar way to union with Christ in baptism. For Paul, the baptized "have been united with him [Christ]," and thus can "count [themselves] dead to sin" (Rom. 6:5, 11). These are statements of fact about the Christian's new identity, the indicative. But they lead toward the imperative: "Therefore do not let sin reign in your mortal body so that you obey its evil desires. Do not offer any part of yourself to sin as an instrument of wickedness, but rather offer yourselves to God as those who have been brought from death to life; and offer every part of yourself to him as an instrument of righteousness" (Rom. 6:12–13). So, are the baptized united to Christ or not? If they are united to Christ and dead to sin, why do they have to keep sin from "reigning" in their bodies? Here we encounter the mystery and dynamism of the "already" and "not yet" of the kingdom in Paul's grammar. Believers are "in Christ," but they are also admonished to "put on Christ," to live into their new, conferred identity. As Joseph Fitzmyer observes about Paul's argument about the body belonging to Christ in 1 Corinthians 6, "Paul is contrasting the indicative and the imperative." As a Christian, you "belong" to Christ, not to yourself; so now go *live* as if you belong to Christ as Lord rather than yourself.[37] Paul speaks of this with the temple imagery in a communal sense in 1 Corinthians 3, and in an individual sense in 1 Corinthians 6: given the fact that "whoever is united with the Lord is one with him in spirit" (indicative), Paul admonishes believers to flee immorality and idolatry (imperative), since "he who unites himself with a prostitute is one with her in body" (1 Cor. 6:17, 16). The clinching argument is that Christ *owns* our bodies; we are the bride, Christ is the husband. Therefore, since we

---

37. Joseph A. Fitzmyer, *First Corinthians* (New Haven: Yale University Press, 2008), 270.

are not our own, we are to offer our bodies to Christ, our true spouse, rather than to false lovers.

Thus, the "spiritual marriage" is both a present reality and a future hope. In this context, "communion" is not just "spending time" with Christ in Sunday morning worship, or even entering into the presence of Christ. Experiencing communion with Christ's own self-giving in his body and the self-offering of one's own body connects the Lord's Supper to some of the deepest human desires: to know and to become known; to become one with a lover—in both body and soul—in a covenantal relationship. The oneness in this spiritual marriage does not annihilate the difference between Christ and his people; yet, it threatens any sense that the church may have of "autonomy" from Christ, of owning her life and actions apart from Christ. Paul's admonition for the married applies to the bride of Christ as well: "The wife does not have authority over her own body but yields it to her husband. In the same way, the husband does not have authority over his own body but yields it to his wife" (1 Cor. 7:4). This "yielding" and mutual self-offering take place in the communion, when Christ offers his body as food, and we offer our bodies as sacrifices of praise to our loving spouse, Jesus Christ.

In communion, Christ and his people experience mutual fellowship; it is reciprocal, but it is also asymmetrical. Christ is Lord; the church is not. He initiates the loving communion, as the Word sent from the Father, and the Spirit enables this fellowship. But Christ has deigned to make himself one body with the church, and to give himself for her in love, calling forth our self-offering in response. Christ's embracing love, rooted in the triune God's astonishing love for creation, brings the church into covenantal fellowship. Christ is Lord of the covenant, but he willingly condescends to be a covenant partner as well in intimate fellowship with his people. A hint of this marital intimacy is reflected in a wedding vow from the 1559 Book of Common Prayer: "With this ring I thee wed: with my body I thee worship: and with all my worldly goodes, I thee endow."[38] The self-offering of the body goes hand in hand with marital intimacy.

But the church is not only Christ's spouse . . . she is also "not yet" fully united to her lover. In response to some in Corinth who apparently assumed that they had *already* been resurrected with him, Paul insists in 1 Corinthians 15 that those who are in Christ still need to *wait* for the consummation.[39] As

38. The Book of Common Prayer—1559, accessed May 4, 2017, http://justus.anglican .org/resources/bcp/1559/Marriage_1559.htm.

39. See Thiselton, *The First Epistle to the Corinthians*, 1173–74.

Paul makes clear again and again, baptized believers are still sinners who need both to put sin to death and to put on the Lord Jesus Christ. In terms of the Supper, this means that our present communion with Christ is as ones who belong to him—it is an experience of oneness with Christ; but this oneness with Christ is a foretaste, one that deepens our longing for the coming wedding feast of the Lamb. "Blessed are those who are invited to the wedding Supper of the Lamb!" (Rev. 19:9). Now, our bodies are temples for fellowship and participation in Christ rather than other lovers; these bodies feed upon the bread and the wine, making the food and drink one with them. We taste this intimate, bodily fellowship with Christ. But as we will explore further in the next chapter, Christians hope for the day in which union with God in Christ will be such that our loving fellowship with God and others will reach its full consummation. "Now I know in part; then I shall know fully, even as I am fully known" (1 Cor. 13:12). In our present age, sacraments mediate this oneness and communion with Christ through the Spirit; in the age to come, the communion will still be embodied (in resurrected bodies), but direct, face-to-face; the marriage will be fully consummated.

As chapter 2 displayed in some detail, there is a long history of connecting the Lord's Supper with the spiritual marriage in Reformed circles: the Song of Solomon was frequently preached upon at celebrations of holy fairs, evoking desires of both longing and delight. Other parts of the Reformed tradition championed this bride of Christ imagery as well, such as the "further Reformation" in the Dutch Reformed tradition, in which seventeenth- and eighteenth-century preachers and theologians appropriated the spiritual marriage tradition, drawing upon Catholic giants such as Bernard of Clairvaux (1090–1153) and his lengthy commentary on the Song of Solomon. The Supper, as a site for communion and union with Christ and a foretaste of the wedding feast, also became the site for overwhelming joy and gladness. Communion with Christ was not simply a mental exercise. It was an experience of sweetness, along with aching for further union and communion with Christ, and communion with others. In many of these Reformed celebrations, the Lord's Supper was not only a foretaste of the wedding feast; framed in terms of the Song of Solomon, it was also a foretaste of the wedding bed, coming to know and be known by Christ the lover in an intimate act of self-offering with body and soul.

How can this biblical connection between the Lord's Supper and spiritual marriage be retrieved today? To answer this we must consider, on the one hand, a theology and practice of the body and discipleship—one that seeks fidelity to Christ the spouse, for "you are not your own," but belong to Christ.

On the other hand, this marriage to Christ, which will come to fullness at the wedding banquet and an intimate "face-to-face" communion, brings a sweetness to the present practice of communion. For Paul, many of the practices already discussed in this chapter present a vision of discipleship in light of spiritual marriage: a consecration of the body as an instrument of service to God, not to idols, prostitutes, money, or other lovers; a communal "discerning the body" that lives into the new humanity in Christ—living into faithful fellowship with one another, both as a communal witness to the world and at the table, in particular; and yet, there is more to the sweetness.

That "more" is hard to put into words. Even attempting to do so might make some of us squirm: the Supper is a foretaste of not only the wedding feast, but also the mutual self-offering of body and soul in the wedding bed, in covenantal, sexual love. If we inhabit an "intellectualist" approach to the Supper, as described in part 1, this sweetness of the Supper may be out of reach. Embracing this sweetness involves a submission—a release of the mind's constant attempt to "master" its objects of perception. But this experience of sweetness also emerges from and reflects theological reasoning that we need to examine. If believers belong to Jesus Christ and desire union with him at the Supper—and if that desire is analogous to the sexual desire that husband and wife have for union with one another—then we have to face a fundamental question about the analogy: What is more basic: sexual desire for union, or desire for union with God?

Sarah Coakley notes that while Freud sought to ultimately reduce all religious desires to sexual ones, for ancient Christian authors such as Dionysius, "Freud is turned on his head." For, "Instead of 'God' language 'really' being about sex, sex is really about God—the potent reminder woven into our earthly existence of the divine 'unity,' 'alliance,' and 'commingling' that we seek. This in turn has profound ascetical implications, of course; for no one can move simply from earthly, physical love (tainted as it so often is by sin and misdirection of desire) to divine love—unless it is via a Christo-logical transformation."[40] If our desire for God is ultimately more basic than our sexual desires, then rightly ordered love of God means recovering Christ as our first love, the proper end for our body's desires for oneness, for delight, for fruitfulness. This means that all Christians—whether single or married—are called to testify to Jesus Christ as their true spouse, even as they live as desiring creatures in these present days. As I have argued elsewhere, single Christians have a

---

40. Sarah Coakley, *God, Sexuality, and the Self: An Essay "On the Trinity"* (Cambridge: Cambridge University Press, 2013), 318.

special calling to testify to the way in which all Christians should relate to the world: with chastity and with passion directed to Jesus Christ their spouse.[41] In this way, because marriage to Christ is even more basic than sexual intimacy, single Christians have an indispensable witness to the meaning of marriage to Christ in a world with many competing lovers.[42] Likewise, married Christians testify to a spiritual marriage that is *even more fundamental* to their identity than their earthly marital fellowship. As Paul argues, the coming together of male and female in marriage points to "a great mystery" at the heart of union with Christ: that just as God is bringing together heaven and earth in his new creation, the Lord unites male and female in a covenantal relation of oneness to testify to the oneness and fidelity of Christ with the church (Eph. 5:32).[43]

What does this "sweetness" mean for the celebration of the Supper? It might mean the sweetness of song and dance during the Supper's communal celebration. Since the Supper is a bodily communion, it might involve finding a way to make it a celebration that does not ignore the senses but engages them: through large rather than meager portions of bread; through a use of sanctuary space such that members of Christ's body see one another during the celebration; through finding practices that recover the joy of mutual "table fellowship" in the midst of the meal.

The expectation for this "sweetness" also implicates how we prepare for the Supper. At times, the Reformed tradition has so heavily emphasized penitence before the Supper that guilt and inwardness become a kind of "prerequisite." As noted above, a healthy appropriation of the Reformed tradition recognizes that Paul's admonition to "examine yourselves" is not a command

---

41. J. Todd Billings, "More Than an Empty Bed," *Regeneration Quarterly*, vol. 8 no. 2 (Winter 2002): 12–13. In this article I offer a meditation on Gregory of Nyssa's *On Virginity*.

42. While at first glance the retrieval of "spiritual marriage" in a late modern context might seem to speak deeply only to married Christians, I think that the opposite is the case. When marriage to Christ is the most fundamental relation in human identity, then both singleness and marriage are covenantal callings to reflect this spousal love for Christ.

43. In this reading of Ephesians, I am following N. T. Wright's suggestion that Paul's discourse of the coming together of male and female in marriage (Eph. 5) fulfills a purpose to "bring unity to all things in heaven and on earth under Christ" (Eph. 1:10). Thus, "this is realized in advance in Ephesians 2.11–21 in the coming together of Jew and Gentile within the single new Temple, the new body; and then in Ephesians 4 in the many gifts which contribute not to the fragmentation of the church but to its unity and maturity. This is then worked out in Ephesians 5 in the differentiated unity of male and female in monogamous marriage." See Wright, "Mind, Spirit, Soul and Body: All for One and One for All Reflections on Paul's Anthropology in His Complex Contexts," *NTWrightPage* (blog), March 18, 2011, http://ntwrightpage .com/2016/07/12/mind-spirit-soul-and-body/.

to confess all your unconfessed sin in order to make you "worthy" of participation. Instead, it is a call, in an age- and ability-appropriate way, to "discern
the body"—to seek reconciliation and covenantal fellowship with brothers
and sisters in Christ. In light of 1 Corinthians 5–6 with its focus on sexual
immorality, greed, etc., there is also a call to repent of "personal" sins more
broadly, but that call is not to make ourselves worthy—it is to prepare for the
sweetness of meeting our betrothed at the table. Our bodies belong to our
covenantal spouse and lover.

In fact, a cycle of bodily fasting and feasting is especially appropriate for
the Supper: fasting for a period of time from food, from television, from social
media, or from other "goods" that are not the "ultimate good" and thus have
the danger of becoming idols that hold us under their control. On Sundays,
particularly when the Supper is celebrated, it is time for a communal feasting,
a foretaste of the wedding banquet of the Lamb and of the Sabbath rest of the
new creation. Submitting ourselves to habits such as these provides a fitting
context for a preparation and celebration of the Supper that rediscover the
sweetness of communion with Christ.

While a wide variety of worship styles and formats express the sweetness
of communion, two in particular have special relevance in rediscovering the
spiritual marriage at the Supper: silent, contemplative prayer and charismatic,
ecstatic prayer. While these may appear to be opposites, Coakley rightly points
out that they can simply be different ways of praying through the "wordless
groans" of the Spirit: "We do not know what we ought to pray for, but the
Spirit himself intercedes for us through wordless groans" (Rom. 8:26). Just
as the mutual giving of bodies in the wedding bed moves to a place beyond
simply "rational" control, so also contemplative and charismatic prayer experiences unite us in communion with God in Christ that goes beyond "rational" control.[44] In 1 Corinthians, along with the spiritual marriage theme, Paul
expresses his approval of ecstatic utterances in prayer ("I thank God that I
speak in tongues more than all of you" [1 Cor. 14:18]). Yet, this taste of sweetness needs to be communally intelligible and edifying in corporate worship
("But in the church I would rather speak five intelligible words to instruct
others than ten thousand words in a tongue" [1 Cor. 14:19]). In contemplative
prayer, believers come into Christ's presence and are still, sitting and listening
at the feet of the Lord (Luke 10:39). Rather than running in many directions
in busyness and distraction, they focus on the one thing that matters: being in
the presence of their beloved. As Jesus says to Mary's distracted sister Martha,

---

44. On this point, see Coakley, *God, Sexuality, and the Self,* chaps. 3–4.

"You are worried and upset about many things, but few things are needed—or indeed only one. Mary has chosen what is better, and it will not be taken away from her" (Luke 10:41–42). In contemplative prayer, Christians choose one thing—to become present and open to the Lord; they just taste the sweetness of being present with their lover. Even in times when God seems absent, in contemplative prayer believers are attentive to their beloved.

And yet, both contemplative and charismatic prayer can go awry apart from trust in God's covenantal means of grace—the way in which Christ has promised to present himself by the Spirit in Word and sacrament. Apart from the orientation of the concrete, external acts of the preaching of the gospel and the sign-acts of the sacraments, worshipers can become focused on themselves or their own experience as self-validating grounds for the presence of Christ. (We saw this tendency in the emphasis on the experience of "conversion," discussed in chapter 3.) But embraced along with a theology of Word and sacrament, these modes of prayer can be avenues for entering into the fullness of what the Word has disclosed: that we are given sweet tastes of Christ's presence, gifts of love from our lover, even as we long and ache for a "face-to-face" encounter with him at the end of days.

## Congregational Snapshot: Communion with Christ

What might it look like for a congregation to recover the gift of communion with Christ and one another at the table and in the gospel? There are many possibilities. I do not give this example to advocate a particular polity (Presbyterian) or mode (intinction) as the only way for a congregation to live into a catholic and Reformed celebration of communion with Christ, but I do hope that this snapshot can fuel our imaginations and help a wide range of congregations to consider the power of rediscovering communion with Christ.

North Presbyterian is located in Kalamazoo, Michigan, and has recently begun celebrating the Lord's Supper weekly. At first there was resistance: "Isn't it too Catholic?" "Won't it take too long?" However, after a season of discernment, the congregation has come to long for the weekly celebration. When my family and I visited, we were greeted warmly by an usher and with smiles from others in the pews. When my children squirmed and squealed early in the service, several gave long looks, but not to silence the disruption. They were simply observing the new kids in their presence and were happy to give them the space they needed.

The service opened with a call to feed upon Jesus Christ, the Word of God, and proceeded with hymns, songs, and several readings from Scripture. Some readers from the congregation had trouble pronouncing the words, but they occupied the space of the pulpit with dignity and honor, and the congregation followed the text in extra-large print in the bulletin. In the sermon, the pastor focused on the story of Mary and Martha. He admitted that at times he was busy and distracted, rather than being truly present to Christ and to those in his congregation. He assured the congregation that God has shown us his hospitality in becoming present to us, and that we are called to be present with Christ and to make the space for being present to one another in hospitable fellowship.

After the sermon, the congregation sang a hymn and loudly confessed together the Apostles' Creed. Then the pastor came to the prayers of the people. After praying for needs in the world, in the nation, and in the global church, the pastor moved toward the congregation, saying, "What can we pray for in our community?"

Immediately hands were raised. Some offered a prayer request and the community resounded with "Lord, hear our prayer." Others gave praises, which drew the response "Thanks be to God." But here the liturgy gave space for spontaneity, for sharing, for brokenness. One member listed about six prayer requests ("Lord, hear our prayer"). Some interrupted, anxious to get a word in. Another thought of more requests as the time went on—offering requests about griefs and losses ("I miss my old doctor"), prayers for the homeless, prayers for an acquaintance down the hall with a special need. Some members were highly educated and spoke concisely. Others struggled with disabilities or with mental illness. Loss, anger, confusion—they were brought before the Lord as a community. Over half of the congregation spoke up during this time, bringing prayers to God; the pastor gave a hospitable space for this fellowship, always pointing to Christ, bringing these petitions to the Lord.

After this concluded, the congregation moved into the structure of the liturgy—a structure particularly appreciated by persons with disabilities because it enabled their participation in this Scripture-soaked drama. As the liturgy moved toward the Lord's Supper, the congregation was invited to "pass the peace." Members of the congregation shot out of their seats and moved around the sanctuary. Some gave introductions and shook hands, others embraced fellow parishioners with smiles and hugs, and others still wept and shared from their hearts. Once again, a holy chaos filled the sanctuary. Eventually, the pastor was able to speak above the noise to gather all followers of Christ to feed upon our Lord at the table. The responsive sections of the Lord's

Supper liturgy were loudly proclaimed and at times sung to the melodies of spirituals. Then the congregation was welcomed to the table. From the first words of the service, the congregation had been invited to feed upon the Word for nourishment. This feeding had already been taking place, in communion with one another—with all the ticks and quirks that each person brings. With open eyes—attentive not only to the bread and cup but also to the needs, burdens, and joys of those gathered—rich and poor, black and white, "abled" and "disabled" shared in the Supper together. In this case, the congregation lined up to proceed to the front of the sanctuary. "The body of Christ," an elder said, pulling off a huge chunk of bread and placing it in my hands. "The blood of Christ," another elder said as she thrust a huge chalice forward for me to dip the bread. As we walked back down the aisle, it was clear that we were not partaking as strangers, but as brothers and sisters, grateful to feed upon the Word and to enter into communion with each other.

Communion with Christ and the gathered covenant community around the pulpit and the table—it is messy, sometimes chaotic, but ordered around Christ and his self-offering love, his threatening and comforting presence at the table. Communion with Christ at the table orients the communion with Christ and others in all areas of the Christian life. To whom do we offer our bodies? With whom do we share our lives? Where do we direct our affections? As the temple of the Lord, the spouse of the Holy One, the church, both individuals and community, orients her heart and body, her mind and action, to the Lord Jesus Christ. Because of the triune God's action in giving the church this identity—and these gifts at the Supper—strangers are turned into siblings, trials are turned into opportunities for caring fellowship, and a diverse people are gathered as witnesses to the searing and freeing love of God in Christ.

CHAPTER 7

 ∾

# Hope in Union with Christ

The Christian faith without hope for the future is not the Christian faith. Hope animates the celebration of the Supper. It penetrates the whole of the Christian life. As we consider this chapter's focus in relation to chapters 5–6, we should note that hope is not one discrete, separable aspect of the Lord's Supper. Remembrance is grounded upon hope for the Lord to incorporate us into the divine drama of the covenant. Communion is rooted in hope that the present sweet fellowship will culminate in spousal intimacy. And in hope we feast upon and long for the heavenly manna, a taste of the triune God's glorious reign. The glorious age finds its center in the embodied worship of Jesus Christ, the Lamb of God who is upon the throne, just as our celebration of the Supper now finds its heart in the worship of the ascended Christ and the offering of the baptized to one another in covenantal love.

All Christians and all congregations live in relation to hope for the future, whether they realize it or not. Sometimes congregations hope for a this-worldly reality: that Christians can bring in the "revolution" of Jesus's kingdom. At other times, congregations hope for escape to a disembodied "heaven"—a land of personal bliss, free from the social and bodily concerns of their life now. While these metaphors can orient Christian hope toward the future, I fear that both fall short of the earthy yet glorious promise of God that is our Christian hope.

In this chapter I explore the way in which the Lord's Supper nurtures and testifies to a genuine Christian hope—a trust-filled ache and joyful anticipation of the return of the ascended Lord who promises to come again, establishing a reign in which "righteousness and peace kiss each other" (Ps. 85:10). We can no more "establish" the coming of Christ's kingdom in fullness than the disciples could have caused or even hastened the resurrection on the Saturday that Jesus's body lay in the tomb. Our hope is not to ignite a "revolution," but to be part of the resistance to the present order of death and sin, entering into the "struggle" against "the powers of this dark world" (Eph. 6:12). Positively, we bring our bodies and our social relationships to the table, enjoying a foretaste of a harmonious kingdom in which all knees bow to Jesus Christ the King. We feed upon Christ, who brings life, and whose life in us by the Spirit bears fruit in acts of witness and love in the world; and yet, this feeding ultimately makes us more and more hungry. It is a foretaste that brings delight and also lament, a crying out for the future feast.

The Supper is not the eschaton. Jesus Christ has ascended; he has not yet returned in the second coming to set all things right. Yet, the Supper is not an empty token for a distant future either. The Lord's Supper is a visible sign-act and icon of the gospel, and as such, it has a unique power to orient Christians to a gospel-centered hope. The Supper is a gift, though it is not the final gift. In the words of Jean-Jacques von Allmen, the Supper is a "gift in anticipation of the final fulfillment," a "prefiguration of the Parousia," the final bodily return of Christ.[1] As such, it gives a taste of resurrection. For, in a mysterious way, the Lord's Supper "lifts the Church up into the Coming Kingdom . . . setting her in the resurrection world."[2]

The Lord who gives the gift of manna has prepared a great feast in heaven. The Lord's Supper is always a penultimate act, a foretaste, and all the more significant for it. It simultaneously exposes the reality that the Lord's heavenly reign has *not* yet come—our world of injustice and unbelief is not the kingdom. Yet, in the Word of God received in the gospel—in preaching, baptism, and the Supper—we hear, taste, and see the heavenly reign that is to come. This coming end is not a "human projection of perfection," as Christoph Schwobel claims. The coming age is both continuous and discontinuous with the present, and "only the death and resurrection of Jesus can point to an appropriate pattern of discontinuity and continuity." The gospel, as divine promise, provides a basis for hope in an unseen future "because we can already hear it, feel it, and taste it in the promise of the gospel and the celebration of the sacraments."[3] The Lord's Supper rightly orients Christian hope, testifying to neither a humanly initiated reign nor a disembodied escape from earthly realities. The coming future will be initiated by the triune God, constituted by union with Christ and a uniting communion with

1. Jean-Jacques von Allmen, *The Lord's Supper* (Cambridge: James Clarke, 2003), 103.

2. Allmen, *The Lord's Supper*, 105.

3. Christoph Schwobel, "Last Things First? The Century of Eschatology in Retrospect," in *Future as God's Gift: Explorations in Christian Eschatology*, ed. David Fergusson and Marcel Sarot (Edinburgh: Bloomsbury T. & T. Clark, 2005), 240.

other embodied persons. This coming future will not be oriented toward our personal wish fulfillment; instead, persons of many nations, with many skin colors and many cultures, shall unite in song with "every creature in heaven and on earth and under the earth and on the sea" to sing praise to the one at the center of the coming kingdom: the Lamb who was slain, the crucified and risen Lord (Rev. 5:12–13).

### Hoping in Heaven? Common Views of Heaven and Jesus Christ

How are congregations in the late modern West being shaped to desire heaven? Studies in the United States, in particular, show that belief in heaven is widespread. Around seven in ten Americans say they "believe in heaven—defined as a place 'where people who have led good lives are eternally rewarded.'"[4] But believing in heaven, in this sense, can be quite different from believing that unworthy sinners receive final vindication in Christ; it can be very different from trusting in God's promise in Christ for the coming kingdom. Embracing genuine Christian hope is deeply countercultural.

While a belief in heaven is widespread, the cultural expressions of this hope often approach it as poetic justice for those who live "good lives." Thus, not surprisingly, popular cultural expressions of heaven often involve extending current pleasures into the future: "Sex, golf, shopping, dinner, meeting famous people and not feeling bad," as a character in a Julian Barnes novel speculates. But in this heaven, as Scot McKnight notes, "there is a strange absence: there is no God in heaven."[5] In contrast, a biblical Christian hope for heaven is rooted directly and wholly in the crucified and risen Lord, Jesus Christ. Christians do not hope for heaven because it is "poetic justice" to provide appropriate endings to reward the goodness of human lives. Instead, Christians believe in Jesus Christ, whose resurrection is the firstfruits of the coming age that has entered into our age. For "Christ has indeed been raised from the dead, the firstfruits of those who have fallen asleep" (1 Cor. 15:20). God's new creation has entered into human history in the resurrection of Jesus Christ. Thus, our hope for heaven emerges from our

---

4. According to the Pew Research Center's "2014 Religious Landscape Study," 72 percent of Americans believe in heaven (in the sense defined). See Caryle Murphy, "Most Americans Believe in Heaven . . . and Hell," Pew Research Center, November 10, 2015, http://www.pew research.org/fact-tank/2015/11/10/most-americans-believe-in-heaven-and-hell/.

5. Scot McKnight, *The Heaven Promise: Engaging the Bible's Truth about Life to Come* (New York: WaterBrook, 2016), 4; Barnes in McKnight, 4–5.

trust in this resurrected Christ. What is the biblical answer to the common question, Who will be in heaven? McKnight's answer is right: "My answer is simple: Jesus." For "Jesus is the One who lived and died *and was raised into the presence of God and who will be the center of the kingdom forever and ever.*" Only after emphasizing this primary answer does McKnight move to the second part of who will be in heaven: "those who are in Christ."[6] Heaven is the dwelling place of God, where Jesus Christ has been exalted, and where this resurrected Lord will bring those who belong to him. Heaven is not first and foremost for us, but it is the dwelling place of God. The Word made flesh, Jesus Christ, has brought his flesh into heaven, preparing a place for his people ( John 14:1–4). The ordering of Paul's logic is unmistakable; each in turn: "Christ, the firstfruits; then, when he comes, those who belong to him" (1 Cor. 15:23).

Moreover, terminology about heaven can sometimes lead to confusion of Christian convictions about the age to come. Best-seller lists feature books like *90 Minutes in Heaven* by Don Piper, which refer to alleged "out-of-body experiences" as "heaven." No matter how one assesses such experiences, we have to be absolutely clear about terminology at this point: a biblical portrait of heaven is always *embodied*, not out of body—and it occurs in a coming age, following the second coming of Jesus Christ. To avoid this confusion, when I refer to "heaven," I am not referring to a place or state of Christians who have died and await the resurrection. When I refer to "heaven," I am referring to "the final heaven"—when the dead are resurrected, Christ the judge sets things right, the evils of Babylon are fully overcome, and the holy city, the new Jerusalem, becomes the dwelling place for God and his people. This is the object of Christian hope. Yes, I do affirm that those who have died in Christ are in his presence—I will refer to this disembodied state as "paradise"—as Jesus does in Luke 23:43. They wait in a blessed, but intermediate, state—in the conscious presence of Christ. They wait with the rest of creation for the coming "heaven" when Jesus Christ sets all things right, creation is restored, and the people of God receive new bodies that share in God's incorruptible life (Rev. 21:2).

The living and the dead are waiting for the second advent of Christ, the second appearing, to join Christ in his resurrection. Until then, Paul instructs the church in Corinth to celebrate the Supper in expectation, in hope, "until he comes" (1 Cor. 11:26). This fits with Paul's overall outlook in 1 Corinthians where he looks toward the coming "day of the Lord" (1:8; 5:5) and breaks into

6. McKnight, *The Heaven Promise*, 155–56.

prayer in Aramaic, *Marana tha,* "Come, Lord!" (16:22).[7] His hope looks to the return of Christ because only Christ can initiate this glorious resurrection world—the definitive answering of the Lord's Prayer that God's will be done on earth as it is in heaven. This makes common understandings of "heaven" in the modern West all the more problematic. A statement such as "I want heaven without Jesus" seems reasonable in a context in which religious persons seek tolerance by avoiding the particulars of their faith. The apostle Paul, however, will have none of it. If Christ is not raised, then there is no Christian hope for an "afterlife"; without this final hope, the Christian faith should not be kept. Apart from this very specific hope in the resurrection, the Christian faith as a whole is a cruel joke. For "if Christ has not been raised, your faith is futile; you are still in your sins. Then those also who have fallen asleep in Christ are lost. If only for this life we have hope in Christ, we are of all people most to be pitied" (15:17–19). Stated differently, if our lives of forgiving our enemies, worshiping Jesus Christ, and serving those in need *are not* lived in hope of the risen Lord, it is a false hope. We would have been testifying to a kingdom without a king, to new life that was simply the sum of our efforts rather than the resurrection hope of Jesus Christ, who will make all things new (Rev. 21:5).

Paul's words here are difficult. One of the most widespread projects of the West has been the framing of religious faith as worthwhile only because of the benefits it brings here and now. For Immanuel Kant (1724–1804), it meant "religion within the limits of reason alone"—religion shorn of its particular truth claims in history. Thus, while Kant indicated that having a moral exemplar is key, it need not be Jesus or any other particular person from history. If Jesus is the exemplar, then it reflects a "lack of faith in virtue" to ask for belief in Christ's miracles and resurrection, since Christ is a moral exemplar without these supernatural addenda.[8] Religion becomes fundamentally reducible to ethics; thus, neither the particularity of Jesus nor his resurrection is necessary. Yet, the apostle Paul's reasoning could hardly be more distant from Kant's. Yes, the Christian faith makes a difference in the here and now, but it does so *because of* the particular way in which God acts in and through Jesus Christ.

To the dismay of many in the modern age, genuine Christian hope for the future cannot be empirically verified. Even scientifically studied "near-death experiences" cannot ground genuine Christian hope—for the heart

---

7. Joseph A. Fitzmyer, *First Corinthians: A New Translation with Introduction and Commentary* (New Haven, CT: Yale University Press, 2008), 445.

8. Immanuel Kant, *Religion within the Limits of Reason Alone,* trans. Theodore M. Greene and Hoyt H. Hudson (Princeton: HarperOne, 2008), 56.

of the Christian claim is about the coming age, not simply sixty or ninety minutes after death.[9] The kingdom is coming, but its fullness will only come in the future. The kingdom has only one King, one who is the Lord and the prototype of the new creation that will come to be: the crucified and risen Lord, Jesus Christ.

The memorial acclamation puts this insight concisely: "Christ has died, Christ is risen, Christ will come again." This is the central key to the past, the present, and the future. Rather than acknowledging this, the late modern West does its best to control and colonize the future. We try to predict every election, every storm, each terrorist attack, each up and down of the market; but our failures are stunning. When a terrorist attack occurs, journalists pressure politicians for reassurance of how this will be prevented in the future. Only the most honest political leaders admit the reality: they cannot predict or prevent all future attacks. Nevertheless, our self-made identities claim the future as if it is a commodity to be exploited.

In contrast, when we approach the future in hope of God's promise, we have to release control, admitting that we are not masters of "data" about what is to come. In the words of Hebrews 11:1, "Faith is the assurance of things hoped for, the conviction of things not seen" (NRSV). Faith hopes in God's promise, but its fulfillment has not yet been seen—that is to come. As Anthony Thiselton notes, "If the future were the product of human imagination or of projection, it would remain sheer speculation." But Christian hope is different: "We may look beyond the present only on the basis of *promise*."[10] This is why the Lord's Supper is so central for reorienting the hope of Christian congregations today: it focuses our attention, our affections, our communities, upon being nourished by God's promise in Jesus Christ. Who is in heaven? Jesus Christ and those who belong to him. What is the central reality signified and enacted through the divine instrument of the Supper? Jesus Christ and union with him by the Holy Spirit. Indeed, the Supper provides us a holistic way to feed upon heaven—with our hearts, bodies, and minds, as individuals and as communities. We don't simply say "heaven is now" or "heaven is in the future." We feed upon Jesus Christ, who is our foretaste of heaven, and will be the heavenly bridegroom in the age to come.

9. For a brief but cogent theological assessment of the recent interest in near-death experiences, see McKnight, *The Heaven Promise*, chap. 16.

10. Anthony C. Thiselton, *Life after Death: A New Approach to the Last Things* (Grand Rapids: Eerdmans, 2011), 20.

## Do We Desire for Jesus to Come?

In some Christian circles it has become fashionable to look down on those who ache for either heaven or the Lord's return; indeed, for some, any talk of "heaven" is suspect. Does not a focus on heaven mean a turn away from life here and now with the world's injustices and problems calling for response? Shouldn't we avoid Christian spirituality that tries to "escape" our most trenchant societal problems by talking about the return of Christ or heaven?

I am sympathetic to these concerns. In the last century or so, many Christians have adopted a theology of "the rapture" and the consequent destruction of the earth that is problematic on biblical, theological, and ecological grounds. But for those of us who are not reading Hal Lindsey's best-selling *Late Great Planet Earth* or Tim LaHaye and Jerry Jenkins's Left Behind novels, are we to desire and long for the coming of the Lord? Should we really join Revelation in crying out, "Come, Lord Jesus" (Rev. 22:20)?

Some of the most substantial responses to this question come from biblical theologians such as N. T. Wright, Richard Bauckham, and Scot McKnight. They seek to counter a dispensationalist theology of the "rapture" by showing how God comes to renew, not destroy, creation. They also counter the common view that Christians die and just "go to heaven" by seeking to recover the two stages of historic Christianity: that the dead don't simply "go to heaven," but instead enjoy the conscious presence of Christ as they *wait* for the culmination, the coming day of the Lord. On that day the dead will be raised with new bodies, Christ will come as the judge to make things right, and God will dwell with his people, and his people with God and one another. On these points I concur. But I also think that in celebrating the Lord's Supper in hope we can concretely embrace these insights, *and* that there is something missing here that reprioritizing the Lord's Supper can help us recover.

At the Supper, the gifts of creation—and of human production in making bread and wine—are taken up into the larger kingdom drama. As many communions express in some form in their eucharistic prayers, "And as this grain has been gathered from many fields into one loaf, and these grapes from many hills into one cup, grant, O Lord, that your whole Church may soon be gathered from the ends of the earth into your kingdom."[11] The foretaste of the kingdom does not annihilate creation, but lifts it up as an instrument used by the Spirit. Even more significant is the *sharing* of the bread and cup at

---

11. *Worship the Lord: The Liturgy of the Reformed Church in America* (Grand Rapids: Reformed Church Press, 2005), 13.

the covenant meal. For the Reformed tradition in particular, the resistance to "local presence" goes along with a desire to hold together union with Christ at the table with communion with the concrete, embodied congregation at the covenant table.[12] In Reformed theologies of the Supper, particularly those in the tradition of Calvin, believers ascend to heaven at the Supper, enjoying a foretaste of heaven. If this is the case, we can extend the implications of this to the significance of "sharing" the bread and cup, typically the climax of the sign-act of the Supper for the Reformed. Participants should not close their eyes to imagine a disembodied, immaterial heaven; communicants should not ignore those in their midst to fixate upon the bread and cup. If Jesus Christ is the one in heaven, and heaven will be an embodied feast and fellowship of love of those who belong to him, then the Supper as a foretaste should be embodied as well—involving touch and taste, the embodied fellowship of brothers and sisters in Christ.

Therefore, in contrast to popular-level dispensationalist approaches, heaven's promise is for creation to be restored and glorified, not displaced and destroyed. A foretaste of heaven is nothing like the rapture—an escape from a hopeless planet of plants, animals, and human bodies. Instead, in the Supper we celebrate that these creatures will be taken up into the final new creation, the uncontested reign of God when sin, death, and the devil have gasped their last. Human bodies, even human acts of production (as in bread and wine), are taken up into the new creation, into a drama in which the Son is uniting himself to his people through the Spirit. While the biblical theologians listed above do not make these connections to the Supper, approaching the Lord's Supper as an icon of the gospel can be a way to embrace these insights on a congregational level.

And yet, these recent eschatological visions can fall short in two ways. One is helpfully identified by an advocate of those visions, Scot McKnight—it is the tendency to emphasize a "kingdom-centric" rather than a "theocentric" view of heaven. In the words of McKnight, some kingdom-centric visions are "so ordinary, they make me wonder if heaven might be a grand but endless celebration with news networks covering developments as they occur."[13] Indeed, in more directly theological terms, some scholars turn heaven simply into a "this-worldly" restoration of creation, or restoration of Eden. The glory and worship of the triune God in this model seem marginal rather than central, even though

12. For more on the Reformed objection to the "local presence" of Christ at the table, see chap. 4 above, pp. 78–81.
13. McKnight, *The Heaven Promise*, 12.

the worship of the Lamb of God is central to biblical visions of the eschaton. "We need to drop pious ideas of a perpetual worship service as our ultimate purpose in the eschaton," Richard Middleton says.[14] While Middleton makes valuable points about the restoration (rather than destruction) of creation, he does this in a way that downplays the theocentric and doxological face-to-face encounter with the Holy God in the coming age. Matthew Levering expresses a similar concern about N. T. Wright's highly influential book, *Surprised by Hope*. While full of insight, Wright's book emphasizes the continuity between the current order and the coming kingdom such that he speaks of resurrected persons going on "adventures" and doing "ministry" in the new creation. Levering points out that this makes it very difficult for Wright to account for Paul's lofty heavenly hope: that "this slight momentary affliction is preparing for us an eternal weight of glory beyond all comparison, because we look not to the things that are seen but to the things that are unseen; for the things that are seen are transient, but the things that are unseen are eternal" (2 Cor. 4:17–18 RSV). Is Wright's vision of the final glory "beyond all comparison" with the present order? It does not seem so. As Levering cautiously claims, "If Paul is right that our glory is to be 'beyond all comparison,' it may be that Wright overemphasizes the horizontal dimension of glory and underestimates its transcendent dimension."[15] While Paul's admonition to look to things that are "unseen" is a reference to the future, coming order (rather than a higher, Platonic realm), Paul's point is still stark: for all the continuity between the present order and the coming order, there is a fundamental difference that is not of degrees but of type. The new creation is paradigm-shaking; it is ultimately incommensurate with our experience of the present order, "beyond comparison." The Supper gives a foretaste of this mystery, utilizing the biblical images of temple, marital union, and face-to-face communion. We need to push beyond any conception of heaven that simply extends our current life of work and adventures into the future, and the Lord's Supper can help us do just that. The gifts of creation and our embodied fellowship are "taken up" into a foretaste of a heavenly com-

14. J. Richard Middleton, *A New Heaven and a New Earth: Reclaiming Biblical Eschatology* (Grand Rapids: Baker Academic, 2014), 174. For an extended account that shows the way that Middleton downplays biblical images of worship and face-to-face encounter in his eschatology, see Isaac Augustine Morales, "'With My Body I Thee Worship': New Creation, Beatific Vision, and the Liturgical Consummation of All Things," *Pro Ecclesia* 25, no. 3 (2016): 337–56, and Michael Allen, *Grounded in Heaven: Recentering Christian Hope and Life in God* (forthcoming from Eerdmans), chap. 1.

15. Matthew Levering, *Jesus and the Demise of Death: Resurrection, Afterlife, and the Fate of the Christian* (Waco: Baylor University Press, 2012), 10.

munion that both fulfills God's promises and reflects a glory that cannot be captured by our conventional categories for the present earthly order.

The second way in which the Lord's Supper can help congregations embrace a more well-rounded eschatology is indicated by Paul's simple phrase "until he comes" (1 Cor. 11:26). This is not only an emphasis in Paul; the Synoptic accounts add context as well. At the table of the Last Supper, Jesus gives the cup and proclaims: "I will never again drink of this fruit of the vine until that day when I drink it new with you in my Father's kingdom" (Matt. 26:29; cf. similar wording in Mark 14:25; Luke 22:15–16). "Until he comes." "Until that day" in "my Father's kingdom." The Supper orients the hearts and minds of believers to the return of Christ, the coming culmination of the kingdom of God.

While I disagree with dispensationalist eschatology overall, it does rightly emphasize a longing and expectation for Christ's return, enabling Christians to pivot from the spectacle of the present to ready themselves for the Lord's return. Dispensationalists teach that we should be like the virgins in Jesus's parable who were prepared and ready for the bridegroom's return: "Therefore keep watch, because you do not know the day or the hour" (Matt. 25:13). We should long for it, as John the Revelator longs for it, saying, "Come, Lord Jesus." This cry has been expressed at the Lord's Supper from the earliest days of the church. As the *Didache*, one of the earliest noncanonical Christian documents, expressed in its prayer at the eucharistic celebration: *Marana tha*, "Lord, Come."[16]

While longing for "the rapture" is not a biblical desire, longing for the visible return of the Lord Jesus is. Somehow, with many congregations focusing on the "kingdom of God here and now" along with a "this-worldly" view of the final heavenly redemption, many have lost the ability to pivot, to see the present as a passing order in light of eternity. A pastor whose church is focused on reaching millennials told me that in several years of pastoring, he could not recall any moments of preaching or services (such as funerals) that expressed longing for Jesus's return or for the coming culmination of the kingdom in heaven. "We just focus upon how we can participate in the Kingdom in our practices here and now," he said. But as he said it, he realized that there was something hollow about this. Is our action, our work, at the center of the cosmos? Or is God inviting us to participate in a new creation that bends our imagination and sheds light upon our present? For in the end, it is "heaven," even more than the present, that is truly real. In the words of C. S. Lewis, "Heaven is reality itself. All that is fully real is Heavenly. For all that can

---

16. See Geoffrey Wainwright, *Eucharist and Eschatology* (Akron, OH: Order of Saint Luke, 2002), 85–86.

be shaken will be shaken and only the unshakeable remains."[17] The day of the Lord is coming—Christ's return, judgment, and heavenly exaltation of the resurrection in union with Christ. Get ready. Long for it. It's coming.

With its orientation toward this coming heavenly kingdom, the Lord's Supper gives us a pivot point to care not only about the present world, but also about the world as it will be, reshaped under the Lordship of Christ. Reclaiming the Lord's Supper as an icon of the gospel will help congregations to experience both the "now" and the "not yet" of the kingdom in a way that leaves us longing for Christ's return. As such, the Lord's Supper should not satiate, but should deepen, our hunger for Christ and his coming reign in fullness.

### Hungry for Heaven: Feeding upon Jesus Christ

When the Gospel of John testifies to the Passover before Jesus's death and resurrection, the author portrays Jesus as a new Moses, nourishing his people for a new exodus into the promised land; Jesus himself is the bread, the food for "eternal life." Whether one understands John 6 as a sign-discourse about the Eucharist, or like Calvin, as signifying union with Christ by faith occurring at all times, its implications for the Lord's Supper are manifold. In Calvin's words, "I acknowledge that there is nothing said here that is not figuratively represented, and actually bestowed, on believers in the Lord's Supper."[18] In this section, I suggest a reading of John 6 that reflects this conviction of Calvin to show how the Lord's Supper emerges as a divinely given instrument for cultivating a pattern of feeding upon Christ for Christians who are hungry for heaven, longing for the final age.

At the beginning of John 6, John indicates that "the Jewish Passover Festival was near," and he records a "sign" performed by Jesus (John 6:4, 14): the feeding of the five thousand. As in the Last Supper in the Synoptics, "Jesus then took the loaves, gave thanks, and distributed" the bread (6:11). Foreshadowing the resurrection meal at the Sea of Tiberias (6:1), Jesus gives fish and bread to his disciples.[19] Both the Last Supper and the resurrection meals are evoked by John's Gospel, setting up the feeding of Jesus in John 6 to evoke the Lord's Supper for his readers. Moreover, his actions evoke those of Moses feeding the

---

17. C. S. Lewis, *The Great Divorce*, in *The Complete C. S. Lewis Signature Classics* (San Francisco: HarperOne, 2002), 388.

18. Calvin, John 6:54, CTS.

19. Marianne Meye Thompson, *John: A Commentary* (Louisville: Westminster John Knox, 2015), 140–41.

Israelites in the wilderness, causing his Jewish hearers to associate him with Moses as a "prophet" and anointed "king" in Jewish tradition.[20]

But these symbolically rich actions lead to the first of several false starts in response to Jesus. While the people rightly testify that "this is the Prophet who is to come into the world" (6:14), the gathered want to "make him king by force." Jesus is truly the new Moses, the true prophet and king. However, his pathway to kingship will not come about through seizing authority in Jerusalem or Rome, but through being "lifted up" by the Father—lifted up as the king who is crucified, is raised again, and ascends to the Father (20:17). Likewise, those who follow the new Moses should not expect the Christian life to be lived in "the promised land" under a temporal king, but should feed upon Christ, who himself is the promised land.

Given this context, when Jesus speaks to the crowd again the next day (6:22), the stage is set for the crowd to see Jesus's ministry as a new Moses who brings food for his people. From the outset in this discourse, Jesus puts these expectations into a lofty, eschatological context: "Do not work for food that spoils, but for food that endures to eternal life, which the Son of Man will give you" (6:27). Jesus is not just Moses, he is the "Son of Man"—a divine figure that Israel expected in the coming age (Dan. 7–8). Thus, in his person as the "Son of Man," he inaugurates the final days. Jesus's admonition to "work" for food that "endures" to eternal life provokes the question: "What must we do to perform the works of God?" (John 6:28 NRSV). Jesus responds by turning the "works" into one single "work" that squarely focuses upon himself.[21] "Jesus answered them, 'This is the work of God, that you believe in him whom he has sent'" (6:29 NRSV). Thus begins the scandal of 6:22–59: Jesus presents himself as the One from heaven, sent by the Father, who brings eternal life in himself.

The crowd asks for a "sign" that they may fulfill this work of God and believe. They quote Exodus 16:4 as a possible context for Jesus's work: "What sign are you going to give us then, so that we may see it and believe you? What work are you performing? Our ancestors ate the manna in the wilderness; as it is written, 'He gave them bread from heaven to eat'" (John 6:30–31 NRSV). The crowd may have realized that even for the first Moses, manna was not just sustenance but an eschatological sign. It was no accident that manna "tasted like wafers made with honey" (Exod. 16:31). Manna pointed beyond itself; it was a *foretaste of the promised land*—'the land flowing with milk and honey'

20. Thompson, *John*, 141–42.
21. Thompson, *John*, 147.

(Exod. 3:8)."[22] Manna was not the promised land, but a material sign and pledge that nourished God's covenant people as they journeyed to the promised land. The crowd, which raises the topic of manna, is right to think that the new, messianic Moses would bring a new manna, but that makes Jesus's response all the more astonishing: "Very truly I tell you, it is not Moses who has given you the bread from heaven, but it is my Father who gives you the true bread from heaven. For the bread of God is the bread that comes down from heaven and gives life to the world" (John 6:32–33). Jesus both accepts and rejects the comparison with Moses. Like Moses, he brings bread from heaven, but his is the far superior, "true bread" from heaven. Moreover, unlike both Moses and manna, Jesus claims to be the final fulfillment of God's covenant promises: for "I am the bread of life. Whoever comes to me will never go hungry, and whoever believes in me will never be thirsty" (6:35). Jesus is both manna and greater than manna; feeding upon him now is pledge and foretaste; yet, he will also be the one we will feed upon in the coming age, abiding in him in the final promised land of milk and honey.

In this way, his feeding is both a present possibility for Jesus's hearers by faith—and a future hope. "Everyone who looks to the Son and believes in him shall have eternal life, and I will raise them up at the last day" (6:40). This "eternal life" begins now in trust but ends with resurrection—a face-to-face fellowship with the Lord at the culmination of the kingdom. The appropriate response to an eschatological figure who is, in himself, the fulfillment of God's covenant promises is faith—not merely as intellectual assent but as a deep relational trust.[23]

The surprising claim that Jesus not only brings new manna but *is* the new manna makes his hearers wonder: "Is this not Jesus, the son of Joseph, whose father and mother we know? How can he now say, 'I came down from heaven'?" (6:42). Again, Jesus stresses his superiority to the manna in the wilderness that did not lead to eternal life. Moreover, when asked how this "bread" could be "flesh" to eat, Jesus indicates that this "faith," as a work of God, does indeed

---

22. Brant Pitre, *Jesus and the Jewish Roots of the Eucharist: Unlocking the Secrets of the Last Supper* (New York: Image, 2011), 84–85. While I do not fully agree with Pitre's full account, he nevertheless gives an illuminating account of the eschatological nature of "the new manna" and John 6 in Brant Pitre, *Jesus and the Last Supper* (Grand Rapids: Eerdmans, 2015), 193–244.

23. This is made particularly clear in the context of John 6 by the contrast of those who "believe" with those who "would betray him." The two stand in a distinct relation to Jesus. For more on this point in relation to "faith" in Paul, see C. Kingsley Barrett, *The Gospel according to St. John: An Introduction with Commentary and Notes on the Greek Text*, 2nd ed. (Philadelphia: Westminster John Knox, 1978), 277–78.

require an intimate communion and feeding upon himself, his flesh and blood: "Very truly I tell you, unless you eat the flesh of the Son of Man and drink his blood, you have no life in you. Whoever eats my flesh and drinks my blood has eternal life, and I will raise them up at the last day" (6:53–54).

Note that John's Gospel is not presenting a "fully realized" eschatology in this passage. Jesus *is* the bread of life, and those who trust in and feed upon him have "eternal life," the life that comes from the Son of Man in heaven. And yet, those who taste heavenly life now still must look forward to the coming consummation, when "I will raise them up at the last day." In his own way, the Gospel of John has transitioned from Passover (6:1–14), to the giving of the bread (6:25–40), to the giving of his body and blood (6:43–59). The parallel to the Last Supper accounts in the Synoptic Gospels is not incidental. Moreover, these three stages are not revealing three different things or even asking for three different responses. They reveal Jesus Christ, the true Prophet and King, the new Moses, who brings in the final days through his death and resurrection. He calls his followers to trust in him and feed upon him in a way that involves intimate union with him: "Those who eat my flesh and drink my blood abide in me, and I in them" (6:56 NRSV). In this way, following Jesus means dwelling, abiding, making one's home in Jesus himself. It involves feeding upon his personal presence—his flesh and blood. These actions are central to the Christian life. This is the gospel of union with Christ. In the Christian community, there is a sign and instrument of the Spirit given to help the hungry to feed upon Christ in this way: the Lord's Supper.

In light of John 6, it is clear that both the Lord's Supper and the overall Christian life are Christ-centered, eschatological acts. By faith we feed upon Christ, the new Moses, the Prophet and King of the final age. We abide in Christ and he in us. Yet we are always looking forward. We are nourished with Christ, but we want more of him. Not until the final resurrection on "the last day" will the fullness of this God-given life be experienced.

At the Lord's Supper, *nourishment* is absolutely necessary for those who feed upon and abide in Christ, and if nourishment is central to a congregational practice of the Lord's Supper, then it is very hard to justify an infrequent celebration. The sentiment "If we celebrate weekly, the Supper will no longer be special" *might* be true if the Supper were simply a mental act of remembrance. But what if it is a meal of nourishment? Is a weekly rhythm too frequent for eating a meal of nourishment? The Christian life is one of longing for the age to come but also of feeding upon the personal presence of Christ through Word and sacrament. If we take this exhortation to eat and drink (John 6:53–58) seriously, it's not surprising that Calvin insisted, "It is certain that a Church cannot be said to be well ordered and regulated unless in it the Holy Supper of our Lord is always being celebrated and frequented." In contrast to many in his day who advocated less frequent celebrations, Calvin insisted that "the Lord's Table should have been spread at least once a week for the assembly of Christians, and the promises declared in it should feed us spiritually. . . . All, like hungry men, should flock to such a bounteous repast."[24] Thus, though Calvin did not get his way in Geneva, he insisted that the Supper should be celebrated "at least weekly." Is the congregation hungry for Christ? Let them feed upon Christ by faith at the table.

Yet, if Christ is present with us through Word and sacrament, why do we need to look forward to the final day? If a Christian emphasizes the "real" or "true presence" of Christ at the table, have we not undercut the pivot to long for the age to come? To explore this, we need to turn to the significance of the ascension for the Lord's Supper as a sign of the gospel.

## A King and Priest in Heaven: The Ascended Lord

Christ's ascension and the sending of the Spirit upon the church are deeply connected in New Testament grammar. In Acts 1, the risen Christ promises to come again to "restore the kingdom to Israel," and declares that until that day "you will receive power when the Holy Spirit comes on you; and you will be my witnesses in Jerusalem, and in all Judea and Samaria, and to the ends of the earth." Then "he was taken up before their very eyes, and a cloud hid him from their sight" (Acts 1:6, 8, 9). In the next chapter, the Spirit comes upon the church at Pentecost. In John, Jesus promises the coming of the Spirit, and that this coming can happen only after he has "been glorified" (John 7:38–39).

In a similar way to this, at the Supper, the *ascended Christ* offers himself to his people *by the Spirit*. This is one of the reasons that the prayer of "epiclesis," invoking the Spirit upon the people and the gifts at the table, has long been connected with the liturgy of the Supper. The prayer has ancient Christian origins, and Eastern Orthodox theologian Alexander Schmemann has argued that, properly construed, it culminates the ascent by the Spirit in the overall celebration of the Supper.[25] Likewise, although inhabiting a different theological and liturgical

24. See Calvin's "Articles Concerning the Organization of the Church and of Worship at Geneva (1537)," in *Calvin: Theological Treatises*, ed. J. K. S. Reid (Philadelphia: Westminster, 1954), 48. See also Calvin, *Institutes* 4.17.46.

25. See Alexander Schmemann, *The Eucharist: Sacrament of the Kingdom*, trans. Paul

tradition than Schmemann, Calvin's theology of the Supper evokes the Spirit as the one who lifts believers to their ascended Lord to feed upon Christ.[26]

Why is it so central, both for the Supper and for the gospel, that our access to the ascended Christ is by the Spirit? It points to a fundamental truth about Christian existence: our whole lives are lived between the two advents of Jesus Christ. In the first advent Jesus Christ, the Son of the Father, "was conceived by the Holy Spirit and born of the virgin Mary." In this mighty yet self-giving act, "The Word became flesh and made his dwelling among us" (John 1:14). In the second advent, "he will come to judge the living and the dead."[27] This is the second coming of the Lord—when he comes both as judge and as the one who makes all things new (Rev. 21:5-8). Both the Gospels and the Epistles testify to this coming second advent—and as chapter 6 noted, Paul's expectation of the second advent is key for his discussion of the penultimate judgment at the Lord's Supper.

But what holds together these two advents? The Apostles' Creed wisely connects them in this way: "He [Jesus Christ] ascended to heaven and is seated at the right hand of God the Father almighty." Congregations today often miss the significance of this "interlude" that shows us who we are and who Christ is in our present time. But this interlude comes to us from divine revelation—just as much as the first and second advents. If all our talk of the Lord's Supper is about Christ's *presence*, then we have likely missed the significance of the ascension. The Lord Jesus Christ offers himself at the table, but he does so as the ascended Lord. He does not walk among us as he did among his disciples; we do not yet see him face-to-face. In both the Supper and the Christian life itself, we ache and long and look forward to Christ's second advent: "For whenever you eat this bread and drink this cup, you proclaim the Lord's death until he comes" (1 Cor. 11:26).

But what does the ascension disclose to us as Christian teaching? In the words of Swiss Reformed theologian J.-J. von Allmen, the ascension is "a fundamental element of the faith" because it is "a proof of the universal lordship of Christ."[28] Christ is the true Lord of all creation. In biblical terms, this has some

Kachur (Crestwood, NY: St. Vladimir's Seminary Press, 2003), 214. Schmemann argues that it is a modern mistake to consider the epiclesis to be restricted to the "moment" of consecration.

26. Unfortunately, although the theme of ascent by the Spirit was prominent in Calvin's eucharistic writings, it was more muted in his liturgies, and other written liturgies in the Reformed tradition. J.-J. von Allmen laments this and reflects upon why the epicletic prayer did not feature prominently in early Reformed liturgies. See Allmen, *The Lord's Supper*, 33-35, 80-85.

27. Apostles' Creed, in *Our Faith*, 13.

28. Jean-Jacques von Allmen, "The Ascension," in *Stages of Experience: The Year of the Church* (London: Darton, Longman and Todd, 1965), 71.

quite specific implications. As Thomas Torrance points out, there are "four main verbs" used in the New Testament "to speak of the ascension of Christ: *anabainein*, to go up; *kathizein*, to sit down; *analambanein*, to take up; *hupsoun*, to exalt." These actions connect deeply to Old Testament ways of speaking of royal and priestly actions.[29] They evoke the ascent of Mount Sinai by Moses, the ascent into the holy of holies in the temple, and the ascent of kings to their thrones—ultimately, of YHWH the king's enthronement.[30]

If the God of Israel is to make himself known in Christ the king and priest, it is no wonder that the New Testament speaks of this in terms of his ascent. Christ's kingship—and ascension—is the central "confession" of the book of Hebrews (Heb. 1:1–4), which the author repeatedly admonishes his readers to cling to. The king of this confession is not a "generic" king but a crucified and risen one: "After he had provided purification for sins, he sat down at the right hand of the Majesty in heaven" (Heb. 1:3b). Christ sits down—Christ presides as the exalted king. Even as Christ is "lifted up" to the cross, this is a testimony to his ascending kingship, as the Gospel of John testifies. Likewise, the ascension is a way to speak of Christ the high priest who entered the holy of holies *and* became the perfect sacrifice himself. His sacrifice is lifted to the Father, and he ascends to the Father to reign as king. "When this priest had offered for all time one sacrifice for sins, he sat down at the right hand of God" (Heb. 10:12). Christ is the king and the priest as the crucified and risen Lord.

And yet, in this exalted state, while Christ is king and priest, not all is well with the world. In the words of Hebrews, "since that time [of cross and exaltation] he waits for his enemies to be made his footstool" (Heb. 10:13). Christ waits and we wait until the second advent. Indeed, even those who have died in Christ are *waiting*, even lamenting, until this second advent.[31] Christ is present with his people, yes. His promise is true: "I am with you always, to the very end of the age" (Matt. 28:20). But he is not with us face-to-face—he is with us by the Spirit. Until the second advent, Christ is present in certain ways but absent in others. Unless we hold together this interplay of presence

29. Thomas F. Torrance, *Space, Time, and Resurrection* (Edinburgh: Bloomsbury T. & T. Clark, 2000), 107.

30. Torrance, *Space, Time, and Resurrection*, 109–11.

31. "When he opened the fifth seal, I saw under the altar the souls of those who had been slain because of the word of God and the testimony they had maintained. They called out in a loud voice, 'How long, Sovereign Lord, holy and true, until you judge the inhabitants of the earth and avenge our blood?' Then each of them was given a white robe, and they were told to wait a little longer, until the full number of their fellow servants, their brothers and sisters, were killed just as they had been." Rev. 6:9–11.

and absence, we are left with a disfigured version of both the gospel and the Lord's Supper.[32]

Indeed, the ascension discloses the particular way in which the triune God enables his people to pray, worship, and feed upon Christ in Word and sacrament in the present age. In the ascension, the humanity of Christ—both body and soul—has been exalted. For the book of Hebrews, this leads to confidence in approaching God's throne in worship: "Since we have a great high priest who has ascended into heaven, Jesus the Son of God, let us hold firmly to the faith we profess. For we do not have a high priest who is unable to empathize with our weaknesses, but we have one who has been tempted in every way, just as we are—yet he did not sin" (Heb. 4:14–15). Christ is the priest, the mediator, and he has been exalted. Thus, worship in union with Christ takes place in a dramatic context: forgiveness and new life. Calvin is particularly insightful in unpacking these consequences. We worship in the context of justification—the good news that through Christ the mediator, "we may have in heaven instead of a Judge, a gracious Father."[33] We also may trust that the ascended Lord will bring us new life by the Spirit. For the Spirit is a "guarantee and seal" of our inheritance as God's children (see 2 Cor. 1:22), "because from heaven he so gives life to us." Indeed, the Spirit is the "'spring' [John 4:14] whence all heavenly riches flow forth to us"; reordering our desires, he "enflames our hearts with the love of God and with zealous devotion."[34]

The ascension and exaltation of Christ secure the gifts of justification and sanctification received by the Spirit, undergirding the church's worship. But the ascension also discloses the church's mission in this time between the two advents. The Word of the Father has taken on human flesh, come to us, appeared to us (*parousia*), lived among us. The kingdom has come. Yet, Christ's final appearance (*parousia*) has not yet come. "The ascension of Christ thus introduces, as it were, an *eschatological pause* in the heart of the *parousia* which makes it possible for us to speak of a first advent and a second or final advent of Christ."[35] The church participates in Christ by the Spirit— as adopted children of the Father; she can rest secure in this identity from the first advent. Yet, while it is a rest from the never-ending seduction of self-

32. I am indebted to Michael Horton's insightful account of presence and absence in the economy of grace in Michael S. Horton, *People and Place: A Covenant Ecclesiology* (Louisville: Westminster John Knox, 2008), 1–34.

33. Calvin, *Institutes* 3.11.1.

34. Calvin, *Institutes* 3.1.3.

35. Torrance, *Space, Time, and Resurrection*, 145.

justification, it is also a rest that activates her loves and vocation in grateful service: loving God and neighbor; bearing witness to King Jesus even in the hidden corners of the earth that seem far from his lordship; participating in dying and rising with Christ, in worship and in the world. Stated differently, the first advent is completely sufficient for our salvation—Christ's kingdom is inaugurated. "The Kingdom of Christ was fully inaugurated with his crucifixion in its condition of humiliation, and with his resurrection in triumph over the forces of darkness and evil and his Ascension as Lamb of God to the throne of the Father."[36] However, until that final day in which "at the name of Jesus," every knee bows "in heaven and on earth and under the earth" (Phil. 2:10), the world is not as it should be. Christ's lordship is mocked by violence and injustice, by deceit and oppression, by the terror of death, by the devil. What is the way forward?

To see the church's mission in this-worldly terms of "bringing in the kingdom" here and now, or to simply endure the present until the second coming of Christ? Neither. For "the Church in history exists in an overlap of the two ages, the overlap that is constituted by the ascension to belong to the whole of the Church's world-mission."[37] The Lord's Supper shows how these can come together. Earthy and broken people gather, pray, hear imperfect human words in a sermon, and celebrate a sign-act of the Supper with bread and wine. Yet, because Christ has promised to offer himself by the Spirit to the Father's children, the sacrament is a sign "of the new order which has once and for all broken into our world in Jesus Christ."[38] A divided people—divided by racial tension, by class, by age—comes together to feed upon Christ, to taste the future by the Spirit. Though still sinners and broken, this same people bears witness in loving acts and witness that Jesus Christ is the true Lord, and that the open, gaping wounds of sin and violence and injustice will not have the final word. This Lord Jesus invites all to a banquet—a heavenly banquet, a banquet of the Lamb of God on the throne. He is the true king. And as the one who has brought body and soul to heaven, he is the one who can rightly invite us to this banquet and assure us of our adoption by the Spirit.

---

36. Torrance, *Space, Time, and Resurrection*, 146.
37. Torrance, *Space, Time, and Resurrection*, 148.
38. Torrance, *Space, Time, and Resurrection*, 148.

## Lift Up Your Hearts: Ascension and the Spirit

Celebrant: "Let us lift up our hearts!"
Congregation: "We lift them up to the Lord!"

This acclamation echoes the rich, royal imagery of ascent in the Old Testament psalms. To raise one's *nephesh* in the Psalms involves an ascent of the temple, the hill of the Lord.[39] This same stream of Old Testament thought is incorporated into the theological vocabulary for Christ's ascent in the New Testament. But this is not just a statement about the ascension. Dating back to Hippolytus's *Apostolic Traditions* in the third century, this call and response has a special role in *eucharistic* celebration—that at the Lord's Supper, we lift our eyes to the heavens. At the Supper, we do not look for a gift dropping from heaven as much as an ascent to the heavens—a foretaste of the glorified Christ by the Spirit, joining the angels in singing "Holy, holy, holy, Lord God of Hosts, heaven and earth are full of your glory." Because of the ascension we rise up, we lift up our hearts; because of the ascension we share in Christ's raising up by the Spirit. In the words of Ephesians, "God raised us up with Christ and seated us with him in the heavenly realms in Christ Jesus." We commune with the exalted Lord, and "through him we both have access to the Father" by means of a particular mode: "by one Spirit" (Eph. 2:6, 18).

As scholars like Douglas Farrow have noted, John Calvin's writings were critical for the development of ascension theologies in western, Protestant Christianity.[40] Indeed, Calvin spoke so much of the ascension that in the final Latin edition of the *Institutes* he felt like he had to answer this question of his interlocutors: "But why do we repeat the word 'ascension' so often?"[41] In his theology of ascension, Calvin was not only entering into a conversation about the Lord's Supper but also seeking to change its terms. One of the primary outcomes of this change in terms is that a theology of ascension goes hand in hand with a theology of the Spirit. The Lord's Supper is a "spiritual communion with Christ"—not because it is unreal or a projection, but because until the second advent, all our participation in Christ is always *by the Spirit*. In the

39. See Samuel Terrien, *The Psalms: Strophic Structure and Theological Commentary* (Grand Rapids: Eerdmans, 2003), 254.
40. In Farrow's account, Calvin made a significant contribution on the doctrine of the ascension to address problems in eucharistic theology faced in the divide between early Lutherans and Zwinglians. See Douglas Farrow, *Ascension and Ecclesia: On the Significance of the Doctrine of Ascension* (Grand Rapids: Eerdmans, 1999), 175–80.
41. Calvin, *Institutes* 4.17.27.

words of Calvin, "the Spirit of God is the bond of this participation" at the Supper, "for which reason it is called spiritual."[42] While departing from Calvin in some ways, some of the richest theologies of ascension in the last century, from Thomas Torrance and J.-J. von Allmen, draw deeply upon this strand of the Reformed tradition expressed by Calvin.

The Christian East also emphasizes the ascension and the Spirit—in the Eucharist and in the whole Christian life—even as it disagrees significantly in certain areas with a confessional Reformed account. Alexander Schmemann is a particularly insightful spokesperson for this theme. He gives an exposition of the Orthodox liturgy, reflecting the following conviction: "The early Christians realized that in order to become the temple of the Holy Spirit they must *ascend to heaven* where Christ has ascended."[43] Through the Eucharist "we have followed Christ in His Ascension."[44] This ascension is not a sideline issue for Christian identity, for, as early Christians realized, "this Ascension was the very condition of their mission in the world, of their ministry to the world. For there—in heaven—they were immersed in the new life of the Kingdom; and when, after this 'liturgy of Ascension,' they returned into the world, their faces reflected the light, the 'joy and peace' of that Kingdom and they were truly its witnesses."[45] Schmemann's words are deeply suggestive; they are also a stinging indictment of worship that has been reduced to mere "entertainment" or mere "teaching." To the contrary, in worship, andspecifically in the mystery of the Supper, we ascend the mount to encounter the triune God and return with a glow that we did not generate or produce, like Moses descending Sinai.[46]

Indeed, if we take this biblical imagery of ascent a step further, the ascent of the mount at the Supper is not only like ascending Sinai; it evokes the ascent of Mount Tabor to view the new Moses in his transfigured state. For a moment, the veil falls from the disciples' eyes, and they see the incarnate Son in his proper glory. "There he was transfigured before them. His face shone like the sun, and his clothes became as white as the light" (Matt. 17:2). While

42. Calvin, *Petit Traicté*, translation in Philip Walker Butin, *Revelation, Redemption, and Response: Calvin's Trinitarian Understanding of the Divine-Human Relationship* (New York: Oxford University Press, 1995), 116.

43. Alexander Schmemann, *For the Life of the World: Sacraments and Orthodoxy*, 2nd rev. and enlarged ed. (Crestwood, NY: St. Vladimir's Seminary Press, 1973), 28.

44. Schmemann, *For the Life of the World*, 37.

45. Schmemann, *For the Life of the World*, 28.

46. For an intriguing development of this theology of the sacrament as divine-human encounter in terms of ritual theory, see Martha L. Moore-Keish, *Do This in Remembrance of Me: A Ritual Approach to Reformed Eucharistic Theology* (Grand Rapids: Eerdmans, 2008).

we do not see the radiant face of the exalted Christ face-to-face at the Supper, through the Spirit we can still receive a glow from our encounter with the risen Lord, a taste of the humble glory of the servant and king who feeds us with himself at the table.

Recovering the doctrine of the ascension in the gospel and at the Supper helps us to embrace more deeply the future kingdom that is coming to us by the Spirit. It helps us to pray with Christ, "thy will be done on earth as it is in heaven." And it does so in a particular way: we taste the sweet embrace of Christ now, and we actively anticipate the day in which Christ, the heavenly king, will fully reign on earth. The Lord of the universe is known in our lives, personally and communally. And this same crucified, risen, and exalted Lord has promised to return, saying, "I am making all things new" (Rev. 21:5 NRSV). Recovering the ascension and the work of the Spirit should not make us literally look into the sky, but gaze at the exalted one whom we can only see in part because of his blinding light, for his face shines like the sun (Matt. 17:2). He is exalted, and his kingdom shall fully come to earth.

Yet, there is much that we don't know in this resurrection hope: How will our resurrected bodies look and feel? What exactly will the new heavens and the new earth be like, after the second advent and Christ's judgment and setting things right in the world? While we can't fully answer these questions, what we *do* know is that Christ is the one in heaven, that human flesh is in heaven because of Christ, and that all our hope for the resurrection is centered in the crucified and risen Christ. In the words of Calvin, "Christ, clad in heavenly glory, did not put off the flesh, but that, since we are to have a common resurrection with him, he will make us partners and companions of that same glory in our own flesh."[47]

## A Glorious Adoption: Face-to-Face in the Household of God

As we have noted, the Lord's Supper is a foretaste of the final heaven, not just of paradise, which is the intermediate state. At the Supper, the gathered have fellowship with Christ—but not in a disembodied way. Eyes should not be closed. Noses should smell the wine and bread. Hands should greet, bodies should embrace others in the covenant community, whether young or old; whether black, white, or brown; whether poor or rich; whether talkative or mute; whether mobile or immobile. Through the covenant of grace, the bodies

47. Calvin, *Institutes* 4.17.29.

of the gathered at the table will be fully and finally lifted up to participate in Christ, the eternal Son, sharing in his glory, as embodied sons and daughters of the King.

In its own way, the Lord's Supper thus reminds us that even paradise is not the consummation of God's covenantal promises. Neither Eden nor the paradise that Jesus promises the thief on the cross is exalted and yet earthy enough. Thomas Aquinas held a high view of the intermediate state between death and the general resurrection—where those who have died in Christ enjoy a vision of God as souls who await the general resurrection. But Aquinas rightly recognized that this is not enough. For him, the joy of heavenly worship is not complete without bodies and without the many others who join together in worship:[48] "For man rejoices more with many rejoicing."[49] We need material bodies, and we need other worshipers—both at the Supper and at the final heavenly banquet. The covenantal consummation of God's promises is when God comes to dwell with his people in the new Jerusalem—with bodies, in a community worshiping the Lamb of God upon the throne. Our bodies now connect us to the dust of the earth: we bleed, we defecate, we decay, we die. However, these good yet dusty bodies will be animated by the Spirit in a new way—a "spiritual body," in a rough translation of Paul's *sōma pneumatikon*.[50] "The first man was of the dust of the earth; the second man is of heaven," Paul says (1 Cor. 15:47). We are "of the dust," and we come to the table in that dusty way. But we look forward to the advent of the second Adam, the "the man of heaven." For as children of the Father through Jesus Christ, the second Adam, we are given Spirit-filled bodies. We shall "bear the image of the heavenly man" (1 Cor. 15:49). We shall be adopted sons and daughters of the Father while the eternal Son is the Son of the Father by nature. But we shall all belong to God's household.

Anticipating this now through the Lord's Supper is both an anticipating of the coming kingdom and an act of witness. In the eloquent words of Justo González, in this act of worship we taste the reality that "our lives and our world have a goal, and that this goal is that day when every tribe and people and

---

48. For a detailed account of how Aquinas makes this case, see Morales, "With My Body," 346–51.

49. Quoted in Morales, "With My Body," 349.

50. The common translation of "spiritual body" should not be understood as suggesting that the resurrected body will be ghostly and nonphysical. To the contrary, as N. T. Wright convincingly argues, Paul is referring to a Spirit-animated physical body that "cannot and will not decay or die." See N. T. Wright, *The Resurrection of the Son of God* (Minneapolis: Fortress, 2003), 347–52.

language will worship God and the Lamb." Moreover, in this act of worship, we witness, to "show the unbelieving world its own goal and future."[51]

Thus, our relations with God and one another will reflect deep mysteries of knowing and being known: temple fellowship with God; marital fellowship with God; kin fellowship with others, of all nations and tribes. All these covenantal forms of fellowship are tasted at the table, and they disclose the hope of the embodied, God-centered, worship-focused, communally enacted life of the age to come. The many tongues of Babel spelled confusion. But at Pentecost, many tongues offered diverse praise to the ascended Savior. What sowed confusion now fits into a tapestry of beauty—all to praise the covenant Lord. The dusty people of all tongues and races and tribes gather together around the table now, and an astonishing vision is anticipated for the age to come:

> After this I looked, and there before me was a great multitude that no one could count, from every nation, tribe, people and language, standing before the throne and before the Lamb. They were wearing white robes and were holding palm branches in their hands. And they cried out in a loud voice:
>
> > "Salvation belongs to our God,
> > who sits on the throne,
> > and to the Lamb." (Rev. 7:9–10)

Perhaps there will be a Bach-inspired version of this song of praise, and a hip-hop version, and a bluegrass version. Cacophony may be turned to a complex harmony. We don't know. But we do know this: the same Christ we encounter through the preached and sacramental Word will be praised as the Lord of all. Our celebration of the Supper with persons of various tongues and races gives a foretaste of this multicultural future, centered in the praise of God. "We must be multicultural, not just so that those from other cultures may feel at home among us, but also so that we may feel at home in God's future."[52]

We currently do not see God or one another in fullness, in a face-to-face encounter. But we will see and be seen, face-to-face. In the face-to-face

---

51. Justo L. González, *For the Healing of the Nations: The Book of Revelation in an Age of Cultural Conflict* (Maryknoll, NY: Orbis, 1999), 109. In this section, González is reflecting upon the role of worship in light of the book of Revelation, but his reflections are particularly appropriate to the Lord's Supper.

52. González, *For the Healing of the Nations*, 112.

knowledge of God, all our idolatrous theologies and all our disordered desires are reoriented by the radiance of Christ's face. "For God, who said, 'Let light shine out of darkness,' made his light shine in our hearts to give us the light of the knowledge of God's glory displayed in the face of Christ" (2 Cor. 4:6). This face-to-face knowledge of God will not puff us up, lead to pride, or make us the master of the object of our knowledge (God). To the contrary, it will be knowledge in love of God and neighbor. "Knowledge puffs up while love builds up," Paul says, and "whoever loves God is known by God" (1 Cor. 8:1, 3). The great gospel hope is not just that we will know God but that we will be fully known—and loved—by the Lord of the universe. This is the peculiar form of knowledge that Paul hopes for—to be fully known. And this kind of knowledge bears fruit in love toward one another. "For now we see only a reflection as in a mirror; then we shall see face to face. Now I know in part; then I shall know fully, even as I am fully known. And now these three remain: faith, hope and love. But the greatest of these is love" (1 Cor. 13:12–13).

God is at the center, but the Supper testifies that embodied love is not left behind. The Supper cannot be celebrated alone. It is nothing without Jesus Christ. But it also cannot be a Supper without bodies and people and cultures and song and movement. This messy, ragtag gathering of people—and this broken, groaning creation—will be exalted into the delights of covenantal fellowship. The holy presence of the Lord in his temple will be among all his people. "God's dwelling place is now among the people, and he will dwell with them" (Rev. 21:3). Janet Martin Soskice is right to say that in these covenantal promises for the coming age, we see "a promise of the presence, love, and beauty of a God who desires to be one with humanity."[53] Indeed, it will not be solitary souls gazing upon God, but embodied, social creatures—for "our future is convivial not solitary."[54] The implications of this are profound. We will be embodied, but our flesh will shed no tears (Rev. 21:4).

On that last day, Mount Tabor will be fully ascended by peoples who have been beaten down, misunderstood, and treated with enmity. The radiant light of Christ will not only bring a glow, like the glow of Moses's face on Mount Sinai. It will bring God's holy light to both the social and individual identities that have been corrupted by sin. Face-to-face, we will be known by God, and we will know and be known by one another in a way that heals our broken social identities.

53. Janet Martin Soskice, *The Kindness of God: Metaphor, Gender, and Religious Language* (Oxford: Oxford University Press, 2008), 187.
54. Soskice, *The Kindness of God*, 187.

In this present age we say things to ourselves like this: "They say I'm ugly." "They say I'm stupid." "They hate me because I'm black." "They fear me because I'm a refugee." But when the veil is removed, the one new humanity in Christ will finally show the love, unity, and reconciliation that we seek now at the table, even as its reflection is partial and imperfect. For on that day, "earth and heaven will be renewed so that justice will be at home in them."[55] The homeless, the displaced, the despised will all find a home in the covenant love of the Lord and his people, in the renewed creation in which every nook and cranny gives glory to the Lord. For the Lord of justice will reign; finally, all things in the world shall be set right. The martyrs under the throne will no longer need to lament, crying out for righteous vengeance (Rev. 6:10). The laments of the African American spirituals, sung under the cruel burden of slavery, will roll into the final hallelujah of praise:

> Nobody knows the trouble I've seen,
> Nobody knows but Jesus,
> Nobody knows the trouble I've seen,
> Glory, hallelujah!

Jesus knew, Jesus knows, and the apparently abandoned and the mocked and the scorned will be with this Jesus who knows. The final word will be "glory" and a resounding "hallelujah" in communion with him. Babylon, with its lordless powers of enmity, exploitation, and injustice, will fall. Jesus the Messiah's judgment will be right and true—and a "great multitude in heaven" will shout, "True and just are his judgments" (Rev. 19:1–2).

The bliss of loving knowledge—like the fellowship at the Supper—will be directed toward God and toward others. "Love of God, love of neighbour, and, perhaps most difficult of all, love of self all [are] requisite to final bliss."[56] As a part of this, Christ's own bride will be made beautiful: "I saw the Holy City, the new Jerusalem, coming down out of heaven from God, prepared as a bride beautifully dressed for her husband" (Rev. 21:2). As the song by Puritan writer Samuel Crossan expresses, "My song is love unknown, my Savior's love to me; Love to the loveless shown, that they might lovely be."[57] The Lord loves those who are dust, those who are unlovely, those who betrayed his charms. He

55. Herman Bavinck, *Reformed Dogmatics: Holy Spirit, Church, and New Creation*, ed. John Bolt, trans. John Vriend (Grand Rapids: Baker Academic, 2008), 719.

56. Soskice, *The Kindness of God*, 187.

57. Quoted from Soskice, *The Kindness of God*, 187. I am indebted to her extremely insightful essay "Being Lovely: An Eschatological Anthropology" in these paragraphs.

loves sinners in Christ, and at the second advent they become ex-sinners—so animated by the Spirit in body and life that they sing in delightful communion with God, others, and the whole of creation. For the rejected, for those considered to be "irredeemable," for the lynched, for the ignored, for the disfigured . . . all of these shall be gathered in covenantal fellowship and made to be beautiful and lovely. Violence, rejection, injustice, neglect—these will not have the final word. Jesus Christ will. Because of this, these penultimate acts, forming penultimate identities, will give way to something lovely. "We may acknowledge that we are loved by God, but it is more difficult to accept that we will be made lovely; yet this too is implied by the bridal imagery of Revelation."[58]

We have been created for communion with God and for fellowship with one another. At the table, we gather as hungry, broken communities to eat and drink together, to taste and see the goodness of the Lord, and to experience a foretaste of a dusty yet heavenly banquet. Even now, we may be able to see a sparkle of the loveliness in Christ that will clothe us all in our new, Spirit-animated bodies. For now, embodied worship of the crucified and risen Lord is our highest act of praise in this life. Likewise, embodied worship of the Lamb who was crucified will be our highest act of praise after the second advent. On that day, the Lordship of Jesus Christ will be universally recognized as every knee bows at his throne. Our theology will no longer be theology on pilgrimage, but theology of face-to-face encounter. Covenantal communion will come to its fullness as God's people see the Lord and one another face-to-face in loving knowledge, in light of the joyful, beautiful countenance of Jesus Christ, the bridegroom.

## Congregational Snapshot

It was five minutes before Sunday worship; young and old were swarming like bees around the various rooms in the church building. My daughter, Neti, leapt forward, jetting to Mr. Wolters, who was being pushed in his wheelchair into the sanctuary. She playfully tapped him on one shoulder, hid from him, and grinned as she looked over his other shoulder. Mr. Wolters, one of Neti's favorite church friends, is a ninety-five-year-old white man who lives in a nearby nursing home. When visiting him there, we saw pictures of him as a young man serving in the air force in World War II, and noticed in a letter to his parents that he was a POW. His body was once strong and disciplined; now, to his

---

58. Soskice, *The Kindness of God*, 187.

frustration, it doesn't follow his directions. Neti's story is different. She was born in Ethiopia, is black, and is probably the most energetic second-grader on the planet. These two unlikely friends love seeing each other. Both smiled with recognition, giving a hug as they were drawn with the swarm of people into a sanctuary resounding with an organ prelude.

We made our way up to the balcony with Neti hopping up the steps like a rabbit and laughing at seven-year-old jokes with a friend on the way. My wife, Rachel, came along with our son, Nathaniel, and his book of mazes. The worship leader welcomed the congregation, inviting us to stand and sing "O Worship the King." My daughter stood on the pew; a nearby baby cried; an older couple smiled at my son's drawing. "Frail children of dust, and feeble as frail, in you do we trust, nor find you to fail. Your mercies, how tender, how firm to the end, our Maker, Defender, Redeemer, and Friend!" My daughter spied Mr. Wolters from the balcony, smiled and waved to him in his wheelchair as we moved to the final verse. "O measureless Might, unchanging Love, whom angels delight to worship above! Your ransomed creation, with glory ablaze, in true adoration shall sing to your praise!"

At the front of the sanctuary, the worship leader led us in reciting questions and answers about the Lord's Prayer from the Westminster Standards. Poking Neti in the ribs, I reminded her that she memorized this prayer for Sunday school. We spoke together: "In the second petition (which is, 'Thy kingdom come') we pray, That Satan's kingdom may be destroyed, and that the kingdom of grace may be advanced, ourselves and others brought into it, and kept in it, and that the kingdom of glory may be hastened."[59] After closing together with the Lord's Prayer, we sang another hymn, and the pastor offered a prayer for the Spirit to come and speak the reading and proclamation of God's Word. As the pastor read the Scripture text, I heard familiar yet strange words from 2 Corinthians. They struck me as ones that do not neatly fit with most of our familiar contemporary theologies. Isn't there a danger in speaking of the body this way, and of longing for our heavenly dwelling like this? But Paul's words soon began to break through my theological objections.

> For we know that if the earthly tent we live in is destroyed, we have a building from God, an eternal house in heaven, not built by human hands. Meanwhile we groan, longing to be clothed instead with our heavenly dwelling, because when we are clothed, we will not be found naked. For while we are in this tent, we groan and are bur-

59. Westminster Shorter Catechism, question and answer 102, in *BC*, 239.

dened, because we do not wish to be unclothed but to be clothed instead with our heavenly dwelling, so that what is mortal may be swallowed up by life. Now the one who has fashioned us for this very purpose is God, who has given us the Spirit as a deposit, guaranteeing what is to come. Therefore we are always confident and know that as long as we are at home in the body we are away from the Lord. For we live by faith, not by sight. We are confident, I say, and would prefer to be away from the body and at home with the Lord. So we make it our goal to please him, whether we are at home in the body or away from it. (2 Cor. 5:1–9)

"Is it OK for a Christian to want to die?" The pastor's opening question took my breath away. I looked around and saw others sit up straighter in their seats. "I must confess that I have heard that question more often than I ever wished." He first heard it as a young pastor, having traveled to a house in the country to visit an elderly parishioner with cancer. She told him, "I'm thinking about stopping treatment. Is that right of me? I want to go home." In light of 2 Corinthians 5, the pastor suggested, it's not that we *want* to die as Christians—our bodies are good. But there is something greater awaiting us.

This "earthly tent," the pastor said, evokes the "tabernacle"—a precious dwelling place of God. It is not a cheap tent from a store that we use once and throw away as trash. It is good and precious—a meeting place for Israel and her Lord. However, with Israel in the wilderness, it was a *temporary dwelling*. This earthly body fights decay daily; it is good, but there is something greater that we look forward to. We don't *choose death* as Christians but are "swallowed up by life."

The pastor noted that sometimes as Christians we say, "I want to die and go to heaven." This is right, in certain ways. Paul also longs for "an eternal house in heaven, not built by human hands." We do look forward to a resurrection and to seeing others who have died in an embodied, resurrected state. But here is where we go awry, at times, in saying "I want to die and go to heaven." Jesus is not just a "ticket" to heaven as a place to be reunited to our loved ones, to have no more pain. The *center* of our hope, the reason we groan and long, is not just to be with others but to be with Jesus. For when "we are at home in the body we are away from the Lord" (2 Cor. 5:6). Paul's longing and groaning were for the Lord Jesus.

This leads us to challenging questions: How strongly do we really long to be with Jesus? How much do we groan—to be with Jesus? Do we find our life in his words, in his body and blood? Do we ache to be with him in face-to-face fellowship? Paul gives us a sense of this desire when he says that "whatever were gains to me I now consider loss for the sake of Christ," for "I consider everything a loss because of the surpassing worth of knowing Christ Jesus my Lord." Nothing compares, now or in the age to come, with knowing Jesus and being "at home with the Lord" (2 Cor. 5:8).

We ache, the pastor declared, and yet we are also fed. Christ himself, in giving his promise of self-offering, welcomes us to feed upon him by faith through baptism and the Supper. As C. S. Lewis says, "There are three things that spread the Christ-life to us: baptism, belief, and that mysterious action which different Christians call by different names—Holy Communion, the Mass, the Lord's Supper." These are "the conductors of the new kind of life."[60] We whose bodies ache for relief, we who ache to be with Jesus, we who long for peace and justice—the Father welcomes us. The Father is pleased to feed his children at the banquet, the meal of his covenant family. In this sharing of the bread and cup, our aching bodies are lifted by the Spirit to enjoy communion with the body and blood of Christ, a taste of our heavenly home.

After a prayer of blessing, the pastor proclaimed the words "Beloved in the Lord Jesus Christ, the holy Supper which we are about to celebrate is a feast of remembrance, communion and hope."[61] As he continued, I interrupted Neti's work on her artistic masterpiece with the church's crayons and reminded her that we were going to celebrate the Lord's Supper. "Do you remember what that is?" Neti nodded excitedly as she added a bit of green to the edges of her drawing. Soon we were in the midst of the Communion Prayer, joining "the whole company of heaven" to "worship and adore your glorious name: 'Holy, holy, holy, Lord, God of power and might, heaven and earth are full of your glory. Hosanna in the highest! Blessed is he who comes in the name of the Lord. Hosanna in the highest!'"[62] I tapped Neti again—"There is another part for us!" In unison we said:

> "Christ has died!
> Christ is risen!
> Christ will come again!"

The pastor continued with the petition to "Send your Holy Spirit upon us" in this breaking of the bread, and sharing of the cup.[63] The words of institution followed.

---

60. C. S. Lewis, *Mere Christianity* (San Francisco: HarperSanFrancisco, 2001), 61.
61. *Worship the Lord*, 11.
62. *Worship the Lord*, 12.
63. *Worship the Lord*, 13.

At this point, the kids were bouncing in the pews, so it was with some relief that the assertive organ began "Jesus Shall Reign Where'er the Sun" while the communion elements were being distributed by the elders on silver plates. Nathaniel pointed to the glimmers of light on the sanctuary ceiling while I pulled Neti close, trying to convince her to sing along. "People and realms of ev'ry tongue/Dwell on His love with sweetest song;/And infant voices shall proclaim/Their early blessings on his name. . . . /Let every creature rise and bring/Peculiar honors to our King;/Angels descend with songs again/And earth repeat the loud Amen." The wooden pews shook from the organ's vibrato.

Suddenly, all was quiet. I looked down and saw Mr. Wolters with a chunk of bread in his hand and a little cup on his wheelchair arm. I knew that this was probably the only time all week that he had been out of the nursing home. This was his "meal out," and yet it was a family meal. "And now, let us partake together in this covenant meal. The bread which we break is the communion of the body of Christ."[64] I looked around as young and old—the latter often called the "aunts and uncles" of the kids—raised the bread to their mouths together. I smelled the airy white bread as I put it in my mouth and heard the slightly awkward chewing sound of those in front of me and behind me. And then the cup, together. The person in front of us dropped her empty cup—Nathaniel shot under the pew in an instant to retrieve it and then remained there, hoping to stay there for the rest of the service. But only minutes later the blast of the organ postlude lifted us from our seats. Filled with hope to see Mr. Wolters before he boarded the bus, Neti ran down the balcony steps with her brother trailing behind. On the way, they encountered "Grandpa Norm" with his usual endless supply of mints for the congregation's children, a special treat for the weekly fellowship time that followed worship.

### "Come, Lord Jesus!"

Through the embodied sign-action of eating and drinking with the covenant family at the table, we experience and enact an essential aspect of the gospel itself: the promises of the gospel, like the table, lead us to ache and long for the age to come. The hope is not disembodied or oriented around a solitary individual. Just as the earthy, dusty creatures bathed in the waters of baptism gather to worship Jesus Christ the King, so embodied yet incorruptible creatures who are made new will see God and one another face-to-face, joining

---

64. *Worship the Lord*, 14.

in the chorus singing praise to the Lamb of God who is on the throne. Just as the Father nourishes his covenant children with the new manna of Christ at the table through the Spirit, so will the Father feed his people at the wedding feast of the Lamb in the final heavenly dwelling place. Creation will be made new. Our hope is for something both strange and familiar, beyond comparison and the bounds of our imagination, and yet so close to us as a people of the pulpit and table now: the crucified risen Lord will be worshiped, we shall be known by the Lord as his people, and the hope in what is now unseen will culminate in an embodied reality of face-to-face fellowship with the living God and with others. Until then, we labor to bear witness to Christ, the true Lord, in this good yet corrupted world. We are freed to offer ourselves to God in seeking reconciliation, because we've tasted the end, and it doesn't look like racism or sexism or injustice. We are freed to move toward the abused and the broken, because we've tasted the end, and sin and death don't have the final word. We are freed to befriend the lonely and the forgotten, because we know that alienation doesn't have the final word. Jesus Christ, in his second advent, will have the final word. Until then, we gather at the table and are sent into the world as children of the Father who have tasted heaven by the Spirit, and long for more. Thus we cry, "Come, Lord Jesus!" Together we pray, "Come!"

# Conclusion

So, we return to our wager that a renewed theology and practice of the Lord's Supper can be an instrument for congregations to embrace the gospel message more deeply. When we take an honest look at a congregation's functional theology, we can discern both the goodness of the Spirit's work and the ways in which our own sinful idolatries are at work. We often serve other lords than the Lord Jesus, and we often just skim along the surface of the deep waters of the triune God's work that we encounter in Scripture.

We need a return to the Word—but not as an abstraction. We need to return to the source of our life—Jesus Christ, made known to us through Scripture—to faithful proclamation, and to the sign-actions of baptism and the Lord's Supper. For embodied creatures who often live "in our heads," assuming that our thinking always drives our action, it can be easy to domesticate the good news of Jesus Christ into a set of propositions to be thought, or simply a set of ethical maxims to follow. But the sacraments, and the Lord's Supper in a particular way, can move us from a myopic glimpse to a fulsome encounter, from a one-dimensional "gospel" (such as forgiveness) to a three-dimensional one (justification and new life received in union with Christ). We cannot assume that with rightly ordered doctrine and practice all is well in our Christian life. For the Supper exposes our hunger and draws us by the Spirit to Christ, our food and nourishment. In the Supper, the heart of the Christian life is expressed, enacted, and nourished by the Spirit. It leads us to taste, delight, and dwell in the Lord's presence, longing for his sweetness and the reconciled fellowship of the church.

As such, the Supper is a divinely given instrument for expanding and deepening our embrace of the good news; it is a gift for us in our weakness and in our sin, for we are tempted to reduce the good news to make it more manageable, so rather than losing our lives in following the crucified and risen Lord, we can remain in control of some parts of our lives. We can be tempted to remember the cross but separate it from the resurrection and ascension; the Supper displays the good news that the crucified one has risen and been exalted to the right hand of the Father, and that dying and rising and being lifted up is the story of our own lives by the Spirit. We can be tempted to sentimentalize fellowship with Christ, so that closeness with him means that he simply supports us on our way, while leaving spheres of our lives out of his control. But at the Supper, we taste and see that our communion with Christ is both wonderful and dangerous, for loving communion that anticipates the wedding feast not only brings delight but also calls us to repentance for the ways that we betray our first love. We can be tempted to turn "heaven" into an ethereal place of wish fulfillment, a disembodied place where all of our dreams come true. However, at the Supper, we join the company of heaven to sing praises to the Lamb of God, as we find our true home in God's dwelling place in embodied and communal reality of communion with God and one another. We are tempted to find our identity in countless places, be they social status, or economic security, or our own pious attitudes, or our own charitable actions. But at the Supper we enact our identity as children of the Father, feeding upon Jesus Christ by the Spirit, delighting in Christ and in fellowship with one another. Jesus Christ, who is the good news, is the host and the feast, the temple and the sacrifice, the spouse and the kingdom's King. He is the Lord. We are not the central actors. We are not in charge. Instead, we are drawn in as the covenant people who participate in Christ.

But perhaps this is not enough to convince. Why have I not given a step-by-step formula or a detailed blueprint of how a renewed theology and practice of the Supper lead to a deeper embrace of the gospel? Since both parts of the wager can only be enacted by the triune God, we cannot fit God into the spaces of our own detailed "church renewal" plan, assigning him discrete parts of our plan. Nevertheless, God does not leave us without direction about how to fittingly participate in his drama. We look to preaching, baptism, and the Supper as instruments of the triune God's action because Christ has promised in Scripture to offer himself through the Spirit by these means.

Moreover, I do not offer a "blueprint" because that would not recognize and celebrate the Spirit's gifts and works in particular contexts. My hope for readers is that they would discern, from this proposal, what they need to embrace to move more deeply into a pilgrimage of renewing the celebration of the Lord's Supper and moving more deeply into embracing the good news. While I inhabit the Reformed tradition, I do not present this vision out of a desire to "convert" Christians from other traditions and contexts. Instead, I believe the Reformed confessional tradition can be a way of swimming in catholic waters that leads us to the waterfall of the triune God's love, the source of the many streams and tributaries of the Christian life.

Reformed and Presbyterian churches often miss key aspects of their tradition. For example, many churches in the Reformed tradition follow Zwingli's standard of celebrating the Supper only quarterly (even though their confessions are not simply Zwinglian). Yet, if the Lord's Supper is nourishment, and if it provides a foretaste of the sweetness of our spousal communion with Christ, then celebrating quarterly seems utterly inadequate. Do you want to eat dinner quarterly? Or receive a kiss from your betrothed once every three months? As a Reformed Christian, my friendships with Pentecostal and charismatic Christians have often helped me to rediscover aspects of the Reformed tradition that others had missed, such as the key role of religious affections in the holy fairs. In a different way, my friendships with Lutheran and Anglican Christians have helped me to rediscover the power of Calvin's imperatives for frequent communion. The "retrieval" of the Reformed tradition in this book actually opens doors for deepening ecumenical learning and friendship.

For those who embrace this book's wager, then, there is no set guideline for "what to do next" in a given congregation. Revive the discussion of frequency? Explore how the Supper relates to Christian hope? Take steps to cultivate deeper hunger and thirst for Christ? There are numerous entry points. Congregational change is usually slow; the church is not a business that hires and fires its membership. The church is the covenant community—messy and broken and awkward. Yet it is also the adopted children of the Father, the family of God, sharers in Christ by the Spirit.

In contrast to the trends for church management and marketing, I believe that true congregational renewal occurs through the action of the triune God. He has incorporated us into his drama. He speaks to us through Scripture and provides a three-dimensional icon of the good news in the sign-action of the Supper. Go to the source: find life in Christ, the fountain of the Father's lavish love. For at the table we enact this simple confession: "I am not my own, but belong—body and soul, in life and in death—to my faithful Savior, Jesus Christ." We are not masters of our own destiny, our own church growth, or our own accomplishments. Our true hope, our true identity—in life and in death—is in Jesus Christ. As sharers in Christ, adopted into his household, we are invited to feast together as his people. We find nourishment in the One who is our true life. Let the hungry come and join the feast!

# Bibliography

Abraham, William J. "Analytic Philosophers of Religion." In *The Spiritual Senses: Perceiving God in Western Christianity*, edited by Paul L. Gavrilyuk and Sarah Coakley. Cambridge: Cambridge University Press, 2014.

Allen, Michael, and Scott R. Swain. *Reformed Catholicity: The Promise of Retrieval for Theology and Biblical Interpretation*. Grand Rapids: Baker Academic, 2015.

Allmen, Jean-Jacques von. *The Lord's Supper*. Cambridge: James Clarke, 2003.

Augustine. *Confessions*. Translated by R. S. Pine-Coffin. New Impression ed. London: Penguin Classics, 1961.

Balmer, Randall. *The Making of Evangelicalism: From Revivalism to Politics and Beyond*. Waco: Baylor University Press, 2010.

Barrett, C. Kingsley. *The Gospel according to St. John: An Introduction with Commentary and Notes on the Greek Text*. 2nd ed. Philadelphia: Westminster John Knox, 1978.

Beasley-Murray, George R. *John*. Waco: Word, 1987.

Bebbington, David W. *Evangelicalism in Modern Britain: A History from the 1730s to the 1980s*. Rev. ed. London: Routledge, 2003.

Bell, Catherine. *Ritual: Perspectives and Dimensions*. Rev. ed. Oxford: Oxford University Press, 2009.

Bierma, Lyle D., Charles D. Gunnoe Jr., Karin Maag, and Paul W. Fields. *An Introduction to the Heidelberg Catechism: Sources, History, and Theology*. Grand Rapids: Baker Academic, 2005.

Billings, J. Todd. *Calvin, Participation, and the Gift: The Activity of Believers in Union with Christ*. Oxford: Oxford University Press, 2008.

————. "The Contemporary Reception of Luther and Calvin's Doctrine of Union with Christ: Mapping a Biblical, Catholic, and Reformational Motif." In *Calvin and Luther: The Continuing Relationship*, edited by R. Ward Holder. Göttingen: Vandenhoeck & Ruprecht, 2013.

———. "More Than an Empty Bed," *Regeneration Quarterly*, vol. 8 no. 2 (Winter 2002): 12–13.

———. "The Sacraments." In *Christian Dogmatics: Reformed Theology for the Church Catholic*, edited by Michael Allen and Scott R. Swain. Grand Rapids: Baker Academic, 2016.

———. "Union with Christ and the Double Grace: Calvin's Theology and Its Early Reception." In *Calvin's Theology and Its Reception: Disputes, Developments, and New Possibilities*, edited by J. Todd Billings and I. John Hesselink. Louisville: Westminster John Knox, 2012.

———. *The Word of God for the People of God: An Entryway to the Theological Interpretation of Scripture*. Grand Rapids: Eerdmans, 2010.

Billings, J. Todd, and I. John Hesselink, eds. *Calvin's Theology and Its Reception: Disputes, Developments, and New Possibilities*. Louisville: Westminster John Knox, 2012.

Boersma, Hans. *Heavenly Participation: The Weaving of a Sacramental Tapestry*. Grand Rapids: Eerdmans, 2011.

*Book of Confessions: Study Edition*. Louisville: Geneva Press, 1996.

Boulton, Matthew Myer. *Life in God: John Calvin, Practical Formation, and the Future of Protestant Theology*. Grand Rapids: Eerdmans, 2011.

Brooks, David. *The Social Animal: The Hidden Sources of Love, Character, and Achievement*. New York: Random House, 2012.

Brown, David, and Ann Loades. *Christ: The Sacramental Word—Incarnation, Sacrament, and Poetry*. London: SPCK, 1996.

Brownson, James V. *The Promise of Baptism: An Introduction to Baptism in Scripture and the Reformed Tradition*. Grand Rapids: Eerdmans, 2006.

Bruner, Frederick Dale. *The Gospel of John: A Commentary*. Grand Rapids: Eerdmans, 2012.

Butin, Philip Walker. *Revelation, Redemption, and Response: Calvin's Trinitarian Understanding of the Divine-Human Relationship*. New York: Oxford University Press, 1995.

Calvin, Jean. *Calvin: Theological Treatises*. Edited by J. K. S. Reid. Philadelphia: Westminster, 1954.

Calvin, John. *The Bondage and the Liberation of the Will*. Edited by A. N. S. Lane. Translated by G. I. Davies. Grand Rapids: Baker, 1996.

———. *Calvin's Commentaries*. Edited by D. W. Torrance and T. F. Torrance. 12 vols. Grand Rapids: Eerdmans, 1960–1972.

————. *Calvin's Commentaries.* Translated by Calvin Translation Society. Edited by John King. 22 vols. 1845–1856. Reprint, Grand Rapids: Baker, 1981.

————. *Institutes of the Christian Religion.* Edited by John T. McNeill. Translated by Ford Lewis Battles. Philadelphia: Westminster, 1960.

————. *Institutes of the Christian Religion.* Translated by Henry Beveridge. Digireads.com Publishing, 2014.

————. *Ioannis Calvini opera quae supersunt omnia.* Corpus Reformatorum. Edited by W. Baum et al. 59 vols. Braunschweig, 1863.

Ciampa, Roy E., and Brian S. Rosner. *The First Letter to the Corinthians.* Grand Rapids: Eerdmans, 2010.

Coakley, Sarah. *God, Sexuality, and the Self: An Essay 'On the Trinity.'* Cambridge: Cambridge University Press, 2013.

Cochrane, Arthur C., trans. *Reformed Confessions of the Sixteenth Century.* Louisville: Westminster John Knox, 2003.

Cohen, Will. "The Thing of It: An Orthodox Response to Hunsinger's Not-So-High Sacramental Theology." *Pro Ecclesia* 19, no. 3 (2010): 247–55.

Counihan, Carole, ed. *Food in the USA: A Reader.* New York: Routledge, 2013.

Courtney, William J. "Nominalism and Late Medieval Religion." In *The Pursuit of Holiness in Late Medieval and Renaissance Religion,* edited by Charles Trinkaus with Heiko A. Oberman. Studies in Medieval and Reformation Thought, vol. 10. Leiden: Brill, 1974.

Courvoisier, Jacques. *Zwingli: A Reformed Theologian.* Eugene, OR: Wipf and Stock, 2016.

Cross, Richard. *Duns Scotus.* New York: Oxford University Press, 1999.

Cullmann, Oscar, and Franz J. Leenhardt. *Essays on the Lord's Supper.* Atlanta: John Knox, 1958.

Davis, John Jefferson. *Worship and the Reality of God: An Evangelical Theology of Real Presence.* Downers Grove: IVP Academic, 2010.

deChant, Dell. *The Sacred Santa: Religious Dimensions of Consumer Culture.* Eugene, OR: Wipf and Stock, 2008.

DeHart, Paul J. *Aquinas and Radical Orthodoxy: A Critical Inquiry.* Routledge Studies in Religion 16. New York: Routledge, 2012.

Dorn, Christopher. *The Lord's Supper in the Reformed Church in America: Tradition in Transformation.* New York: Peter Lang, 2007.

Edwards, Jonathan. *Works of Jonathan Edwards.* Vols. 1–26. New Haven: Yale University Press, 1957–2008.

Faith Alive Christian Resources, Christian Reformed Church in North America, and Reformed Church in America. *Our Faith: Ecumenical Creeds, Re-*

*formed Confessions, and Other Resources*. Grand Rapids: Faith Alive Christian Resources, 2013.

Falardeau, Ernest R., and Robert S. Ervin. *ARC Soundings*. Lanham, MD, and Charleston, WV: UPA, 1990.

Farrow, Douglas. *Ascension and Ecclesia: On the Significance of the Doctrine of Ascension*. Grand Rapids: Eerdmans, 1999.

Fawcett, L. *Religion, Ethnicity, and Social Change*. Edited by Jo Campling. Houndmills, UK, and New York: Palgrave Macmillan, 2000.

Fitzmyer, Joseph A. *First Corinthians*. New Haven: Yale University Press, 2008.

———. *The Gospel according to Luke I–IX: Introduction, Translation, and Notes*. Garden City, NY: Doubleday, 1982.

Garland, David E. *1 Corinthians*. Grand Rapids: Baker Academic, 2003.

Gavrilyuk, Paul L., and Sarah Coakley, eds. *The Spiritual Senses: Perceiving God in Western Christianity*. Cambridge: Cambridge University Press, 2014.

George, Timothy. "John Calvin and the Agreement of Zurich (1549)." In *John Calvin and the Church: A Prism of Reform*, edited by Timothy George. Louisville: Westminster John Knox, 1990.

Gerrish, Brian A. *Continuing the Reformation: Essays on Modern Religious Thought*. Chicago: University of Chicago Press, 1994.

———. *Grace and Gratitude: The Eucharistic Theology of John Calvin*. Eugene, OR: Wipf and Stock, 2002.

———. *Old Protestantism and the New*. Edinburgh: T. & T. Clark, 2000.

———. *Thinking with the Church: Essays in Historical Theology*. Grand Rapids: Eerdmans, 2010.

González, Justo L. *For the Healing of the Nations: The Book of Revelation in an Age of Cultural Conflict*. Maryknoll, NY: Orbis, 1999.

Gregory, Brad S. *The Unintended Reformation: How a Religious Revolution Secularized Society*. Cambridge, MA: Belknap Press of Harvard University Press, 2012.

Gregory of Nyssa. *From Glory to Glory: Texts from Gregory of Nyssa's Mystical Writings*. Edited by Jean Danielou and Herbert Musurillo. New York: Charles Scribner's Sons, 1962.

Hays, Richard B. *First Corinthians: A Bible Commentary for Teaching and Preaching*. Interpretation. Louisville: Westminster John Knox, 2011.

Hessel-Robinson, Timothy. "Calvin's Doctrine of the Lord's Supper: Modern Reception and Contemporary Possibilities." In *Calvin's Theology and Its Reception: Disputes, Developments, and New Possibilities*, edited by J. Todd Billings and I. John Hesselink. Louisville: Westminster John Knox, 2012.

Hodge, Charles. *Essays and Reviews: Selected from the Princeton Review*. New York: R. Carter, 1857.

Horton, Michael S. *People and Place: A Covenant Ecclesiology*. Louisville: Westminster John Knox, 2008.

James, Frank A., III. "Roman Commentary: Justification and Sanctification." In *A Companion to Peter Martyr Vermigli*, edited by Torrance Kirby, Emidio Campi, and Frank A. James III. Leiden: Brill Academic, 2009.

Kahneman, Daniel. *Thinking, Fast and Slow*. New York: Farrar, Straus and Giroux, 2013.

Kant, Immanuel. *Religion within the Limits of Reason Alone*. Translated by Theodore M. Greene and Hoyt H. Hudson. Princeton: HarperOne, 2008.

Koester, Anne Y., and Barbara Searle, eds. *Vision: The Scholarly Contributions of Mark Searle to Liturgical Renewal*. Collegeville, MN: Liturgical Press, 2004.

Levenson, Jon D. *Sinai and Zion*. New York: HarperOne, 1987.

Levering, Matthew. *Jesus and the Demise of Death: Resurrection, Afterlife, and the Fate of the Christian*. Waco: Baylor University Press, 2012.

Lewis, C. S. *The Great Divorce*. In *The Complete C. S. Lewis Signature Classics*. San Francisco: HarperOne, 2002.

———. *Mere Christianity*. San Francisco: HarperSanFrancisco, 2001.

Lincoln, Andrew T. *Ephesians*. Word Biblical Commentary, vol. 42. Waco: Nelson, 1990.

Locher, Gottfried W. *Zwingli's Thought: New Perspectives*. Leiden: Brill Academic, 1997.

Long, Kimberly Bracken. *The Eucharistic Theology of the American Holy Fairs*. Louisville: Westminster John Knox, 2011.

Luther, Martin. *Sermons on the Gospel of St. John, Chapters 14–16*. In *Luther's Works*, vol. 24, edited by Jaroslav Jan Pelikan, translated by Martin H. Bertram. Saint Louis: Concordia, 2007.

Manetsch, Scott M. *Calvin's Company of Pastors: Pastoral Care and the Emerging Reformed Church, 1536–1609*. New York: Oxford University Press, 2015.

Marenbon, John. "Aquinas, Radical Orthodoxy and the Importance of Truth." In *Deconstructing Radical Orthodoxy: Postmodern Theology, Rhetoric, and Truth*, edited by Wayne J. Hankey and Douglas Hedley. New ed. Aldershot, UK, and Burlington, VT: Ashgate, 2005.

Marion, Jean-Luc. *In the Self's Place: The Approach of Saint Augustine*. Translated by Jeffrey L. Kosky. Cultural Memory in the Present. Redwood City, CA: Stanford University Press, 2012.

May, Alistair. *The Body for the Lord: Sex and Identity in 1 Corinthians 5–7.* London: Bloomsbury T. & T. Clark, 2004.

McKnight, Scot. *The Heaven Promise: Engaging the Bible's Truth about Life to Come.* New York: WaterBrook, 2016.

Middleton, J. Richard. *A New Heaven and a New Earth: Reclaiming Biblical Eschatology.* Grand Rapids: Baker Academic, 2014.

Milbank, John. "Alternative Protestantism." In *Radical Orthodoxy and the Reformed Tradition: Creation, Covenant, and Participation,* edited by James K. A. Smith and James H. Olthuis. Grand Rapids: Baker Academic, 2005.

———. *Theology and Social Theory: Beyond Secular Reason.* 2nd ed. Oxford: Wiley-Blackwell, 2006.

Milbank, John, Catherine Pickstock, and Graham Ward, eds. *Radical Orthodoxy: A New Theology.* London: Routledge, 1998.

Miles, Sara. *Take This Bread: A Radical Conversion.* New York: Ballantine Books, 2008.

Miller, Vincent J. *Consuming Religion: Christian Faith and Practice in a Consumer Culture.* New York: Bloomsbury Academic, 2005.

Mohler, Albert, Paige Patterson, Mark Dever, Russell D. Moore, and Timothy George. *A Theology for the Church.* Edited by Daniel L. Akin. Rev. ed. Nashville: B & H Academic, 2014.

Mooij, Marieke de. *Consumer Behavior and Culture: Consequences for Global Marketing and Advertising.* 2nd ed. Thousand Oaks, CA: SAGE Publications, 2010.

Moore-Keish, Martha L. *Do This in Remembrance of Me: A Ritual Approach to Reformed Eucharistic Theology.* Grand Rapids: Eerdmans, 2008.

Muller, Richard A. *After Calvin: Studies in the Development of a Theological Tradition.* New York: Oxford University Press, 2003.

———. "Demoting Calvin: The Issue of Calvin and the Reformed Tradition." In *John Calvin, Myth and Reality: Images and Impact of Geneva's Reformer; Papers of the 2009 Calvin Studies Society Colloquium,* edited by Amy Nelson Burnett. Eugene, OR: Wipf and Stock, 2011.

Murphy, Caryle. "Most Americans Believe in Heaven . . . and Hell." Pew Research Center. November 10, 2015. http://www.pewresearch.org/fact-tank/2015/11/10/most-americans-believe-in-heaven-and-hell/.

Musculus, Wolfgang. *Common Places of Christian Religion.* Translated by John Man. London: Reginalde Wolfe, 1578.

Nevin, John Williamson. *The Mystical Presence: A Vindication of the Reformed or Calvinistic Doctrine of the Holy Eucharist.* Edited by J. Philip Horne. N.p.: CreateSpace Independent Publishing Platform, 2012.

Nietzsche, Friedrich. *Thus Spoke Zarathustra.* In *The Portable Nietzsche,* translated by Walter Kaufmann. New York: Penguin Books, 1977.

Old, Hughes Oliphant. *Themes and Variations for a Christian Doxology: Some Thoughts on the Theology of Worship.* Grand Rapids: Eerdmans, 1992.

Olson, Roger E. *Arminian Theology: Myths and Realities.* Downers Grove: IVP Academic, 2009.

Peters, Rebecca Todd. *In Search of the Good Life: The Ethics of Globalization.* New York: Bloomsbury Academic, 2006.

Pickstock, Catherine. *After Writing: On the Liturgical Consummation of Philosophy.* Oxford and Malden, MA: Wiley-Blackwell, 1997.

Pitre, Brant. *Jesus and the Jewish Roots of the Eucharist: Unlocking the Secrets of the Last Supper.* New York: Image, 2011.

———. *Jesus and the Last Supper.* Grand Rapids: Eerdmans, 2015.

*Pro Ecclesia: A Journal of Catholic and Evangelical Theology.* Vol. 25-N3. August 25, 2016. https://journals.rowman.com/issues/1017028-pro-ecclesia-vol -25-n3-a-journal-of-catholic-and-evangelical-theology.

Reuver, Arie de. *Sweet Communion: Trajectories of Spirituality from the Middle Ages through the Further Reformation.* Grand Rapids: Baker Academic, 2007.

Rohls, Jan. *Reformed Confessions: Theology from Zurich to Barmen.* Louisville: Westminster John Knox, 1998.

Rozeboom, Sue A. "Calvin's Doctrine of the Lord's Supper." In *Calvin's Theology and Its Reception: Disputes, Developments, and New Possibilities,* edited by J. Todd Billings and I. John Hesselink. Louisville: Westminster John Knox, 2012.

Schmemann, Alexander. *The Eucharist: Sacrament of the Kingdom.* Translated by Paul Kachur. Crestwood, NY: St. Vladimir's Seminary Press, 2003.

———. *For the Life of the World: Sacraments and Orthodoxy.* 2nd rev. and enlarged ed. Crestwood, NY: St. Vladimir's Seminary Press, 1973.

Schmidt, Leigh Eric. *Holy Fairs: Scotland and the Making of American Revivalism.* 2nd ed. Grand Rapids: Eerdmans, 2001.

Schwanda, Tom. *Soul Recreation: The Contemplative-Mystical Piety of Puritanism.* Eugene, OR: Wipf and Stock, 2012.

Schwarz, Hans. *Theology in a Global Context: The Last Two Hundred Years.* Grand Rapids: Eerdmans, 2005.

Schwobel, Christoph. "Last Things First? The Century of Eschatology in Retrospect." In *Future as God's Gift: Explorations in Christian Eschatology,* edited by David Fergusson and Marcel Sarot. Edinburgh: Bloomsbury T. & T. Clark, 2005.

Smith, Christian, and Patricia Snell. *Souls in Transition: The Religious and Spiritual Lives of Emerging Adults*. Oxford: Oxford University Press, 2009.

Smith, James K. A. *Desiring the Kingdom: Worship, Worldview, and Cultural Formation*. Grand Rapids: Baker Academic, 2009.

———. *Imagining the Kingdom: How Worship Works*. Grand Rapids: Baker Academic, 2013.

Soskice, Janet Martin. *The Kindness of God: Metaphor, Gender, and Religious Language*. Oxford: Oxford University Press, 2008.

Sweeney, Douglas A. "'Falling Away from the General Faith of the Reformation'? The Contest over Calvinism in Nineteenth-Century America." In *John Calvin's American Legacy*, edited by Thomas J. Davis. New York: Oxford University Press, 2010.

Thiselton, Anthony C. *The First Epistle to the Corinthians*. Grand Rapids: Eerdmans, 2013.

———. *Life after Death: A New Approach to the Last Things*. Grand Rapids: Eerdmans, 2011.

Thompson, Marianne Meye. *John: A Commentary*. Louisville: Westminster John Knox, 2015.

Thompson, Nicholas. *Eucharistic Sacrifice and Patristic Tradition in the Theology of Martin Bucer: 1534–1546*. Leiden: Brill, 2005.

Torrance, Thomas F. *Space, Time, and Resurrection*. Edinburgh: Bloomsbury T. & T. Clark, 2000.

Trinkaus, Charles, with Heiko A. Oberman, eds. *The Pursuit of Holiness in Late Medieval and Renaissance Religion*. Papers from the University of Michigan Conference. Leiden: Brill, 1974.

Vander Zee, Leonard J. *Christ, Baptism and the Lord's Supper: Recovering the Sacraments for Evangelical Worship*. Downers Grove: IVP Academic, 2004.

Vonier, Dom Anscar. *A Key to the Doctrine of the Eucharist*. N.p.: Assumption Press, 2013.

Wainwright, Geoffrey. *Eucharist and Eschatology*. London: Epworth Press, 1971.

Wainwright, William J. "Jonathan Edwards and His Puritan Predecessors." In *The Spiritual Senses: Perceiving God in Western Christianity*, edited by Paul L. Gavrilyuk and Sarah Coakley. Cambridge: Cambridge University Press, 2014.

Ward, Graham. "The Church as the Erotic Community." In *Sacramental Presence in a Postmodern Context*, edited by L. Boeve and L. Leijssen. Sterling, VA: Peeters, 2001.

————. *Cities of God*. London: Routledge, 2001.

Webber, Robert E., and Lester Ruth. *Evangelicals on the Canterbury Trail: Why Evangelicals Are Attracted to the Liturgical Church*. Rev. ed. New York: Morehouse, 2013.

Welker, Michael. *What Happens in Holy Communion?* Translated by John F. Hoffmeyer. Grand Rapids: Eerdmans, 2000.

White, James F. *Protestant Worship: Traditions in Transition*. Louisville: Westminster John Knox, 1989.

Willimon, Will. "Too Much Practice." *Christian Century* 127, no. 5 (March 9, 2010): 22–25.

Witvliet, John D. *Worship Seeking Understanding: Windows into Christian Practice*. Grand Rapids: Baker Academic, 2003.

Wolterstorff, Nicholas. "Sacraments as Action, Not Presence." In *Christ: The Sacramental Word—Incarnation, Sacrament, and Poetry*, edited by David Brown and Ann Loades. London: SPCK, 1996.

*Worship the Lord: The Liturgy of the Reformed Church in America*. Grand Rapids: Reformed Church Press, 2005.

Wright, N. T. *How God Became King: The Forgotten Story of the Gospels*. New York: HarperOne, 2012.

————. "Mind, Spirit, Soul and Body: All for One and One for All Reflections on Paul's Anthropology in His Complex Contexts." *NTWrightPage* (blog). March 18, 2011. http://ntwrightpage.com/2016/07/12/mind-spirit-soul-and-body/.

————. *The Resurrection of the Son of God*. Minneapolis: Fortress, 2003.

————. *Simply Jesus: A New Vision of Who He Was, What He Did, and Why He Matters*. New York: HarperOne, 2011.

Yarnold, Edward, SJ. *The Awe-Inspiring Rites of Initiation: The Origins of the RCIA*. 2nd ed. Collegeville, MN: Liturgical Press, 1994.

# Index of Names

Abraham, William, 40
Allen, Michael, 1–2, 157, 177
Allmen, Jean-Jacques von, 170, 184, 189
Aquinas, Thomas, 72, 87–90, 94, 191
Augustine, 22, 25–26, 30–32, 35, 40, 87, 93, 97, 116, 177

Balmer, Randall, 104
Barrett, C. Kingsley, 130, 181
Beasley-Murray, George, 129
Bebbington, David, 124–25
Bell, Catherine, 51
Bierma, Lyle, 60
Billings, J. Todd, 1, 13, 19, 23, 38, 60, 63, 66–67, 73, 81, 93, 95–96, 102, 124, 140, 157
Boersma, Hans, 86–89, 91–93, 95–96, 98, 101
Boulton, Matthew Myer, 37, 38
Brooks, David, 33–35, 39
Brown, David, 72, 205
Brownson, James, 68
Bruner, Frederick, 27
Bullinger, Heinrich, 60–61, 68–70, 126–28
Butin, Philip Walker, 98, 189

Calvin, John, 25, 30, 35, 45–46, 54–55, 58, 64, 66–68, 70–71, 73, 86, 119, 131; and Christian formation, 21, 36–38; and double grace, 18–19, 81, 96, 104, 132; and the ontology of the sacraments, 91–102; seeking Protestant unity on the Lord's Supper, 3, 60–63, 75; theology of the Lord's Supper generally, 5, 26–27, 75, 79, 122–28, 140–41, 147–48, 176, 179, 182–84, 188–90, 203

Ciampa, Roy, 144, 156
Coakley, Sarah, 40–41, 44, 163, 165
Cochrane, Arthur, 69
Cohen, Will, 65
Counihan, Carole, 9
Courtney, William, 89
Courvoisier, Jacques, 119–20
Cross, Richard, 89–90
Cullmann, Oscar, 117–18

Davis, John Jefferson, 61, 63, 84–85, 88, 128
deChant, Dell, 121
DeHart, Paul, 87
de Mooij, Marieke, 9
de Reuver, Arie, 46
Descartes, René, 31
Dorn, Christopher, 2, 110, 126

Edwards, Jonathan, 35, 40–44, 123–25

Farrow, Douglas, 188
Fitzmyer, Joseph, 119, 143, 160, 173

Garland, David, 73, 156
Gavrilyuk, Paul, 40–41, 44
George, Timothy, 60
Gerrish, Brian, 5, 27, 45, 62, 68, 75, 120
González, Justo, 191–92
Gregory, Brad, 90, 94–95
Gregory of Nyssa, 23, 25, 30, 40, 164

Hays, Richard, 142, 144, 146, 156
Hesselink, I. John, 19, 60, 63, 81, 102, 124

# Index of Subjects

Adoption (into God's covenant), 1–7, 13, 25, 28, 44–45, 57, 60, 100, 107, 110–12, 135–37, 140, 151, 155, 159, 175, 186–87, 191, 203

Affections, 2, 10–12, 15–22, 25–37, 41–43, 46–50, 54–59, 67–68, 83, 103, 107, 114, 120–24, 137–41, 144, 160–63, 168, 171, 174–78, 186, 192–93, 202–3

Almsgiving, 67, 140. *See also* Justice

Analogy (theology of), 90, 94, 129, 130–31, 163

Anamnesis, 114. *See also* Remembrance

Anthropology, 31, 41, 44–46, 50, 57–59, 68, 80, 83. *See also* Affections

Ascension, 76–80, 109–10, 117, 128–30, 169–70, 176, 180, 183–93, 202

Assurance, 73–76, 124–25, 174, 187. *See also* Justification

Baptism, 3, 12, 18, 43, 65, 102–3, 146, 149, 160–62, 169–70, 198–202; and faith, 68–73; and invitation to the table, 150–59

Belgic Confession, 67–69, 73–78, 81, 102

Belhar Confession, 154–55

Canons of Dort, 99–100

Church discipline, 139, 142–45, 151–55, 158

Closed communion, 65, 150–51

Conversion, 15, 53–54, 102, 124–28, 131, 142, 151, 166, 203

Covenant, 105, 110, 138, 148–49, 155–59, 169, 181, 191–94; 68–69, 146; covenant community, 1, 18, 55, 69, 115–16, 142–47, 158, 168, 190, 198, 200–203; covenant renewal,

116; Lord's Supper as covenantal meal, 50, 116, 176, 199; and marriage, 152, 160–65; as sign and seal, 69

Cross, 12, 28, 36, 78, 110, 185, 191, 202; forgiveness of sins and remembrance of the, 14–19, 26, 103, 109, 113, 117–19, 128, 136; and labor pains, 130–32; and resurrection, 118, 129–31, 136

Desire. *See* Affections

Double grace, 18–19, 81, 96, 132

Drama. *See* Trinity

Ecumenism, 3, 57–67, 73, 88, 111, 145, 148–50, 153, 194, 203

Evangelicalism, 13, 16–17, 49–52, 55, 63, 66, 84, 104, 113, 124–28

Faith, 24, 30, 40, 61–65, 72–78, 96–98, 116, 124, 127, 131–35, 149–52, 173, 184–86, 193, 197; feeding upon Christ by, 181–83, 198; justification by, 91–92, 95, 104; profession of, 150, 155–56; receiving the Lord's Supper and the gift of, 18, 69–71, 83, 103, 158–59; and union with Christ, 18, 27, 81, 98–102, 179

Feast, 3, 47–50, 80, 109–12, 115, 131, 135–39, 145, 155, 162–63, 169–70, 176, 198–203

Feeding: upon Christ, 26–27, 58, 70–71, 75–77, 101, 108–11, 118, 139–41, 148, 155–58, 162, 167–70, 174, 179–87, 190–202; upon the Word, 12, 20–24, 30, 58

Fencing table. *See* Church discipline

215

# Index of Subjects